THE DIVINE MANDATE

AFFIDAVITS OF RELIGIOUS UNALIENABLE RIGHTS

By

MINISTER DEMARRIUS CROSSLEY,

GOD WITHIN MINISTRY | UNMN

Printed in the United States of America.

ISBN: 979-8-951669-19-3

Table of Contents

What is an Affidavit?

An affidavit is a written statement of truth, made voluntarily, and under oath, and signed by the person making it, called the affiant.

It's both a legal and spiritual declaration of truth, depending on how it's used.

In legal terms, an Affidavit is a sworn written statement made under oath or affirmation, used as evidence in court or other official proceedings. That means you're declaring something is true to the best of your knowledge. You sign it (often before a notary or a witness), and it becomes a lawful record that carries legal weight, just like spoken testimony in court.

From a Spiritual or higher-consciousness point of view, an affidavit is a written manifestation of truth, sealed by intention, spirit, and word- where the writer stands as witness to their own divine authority. In that sense, it's not just a legal tool. It's a statement of being. You're affirming truth into existence through written words, signature, and intention.

This book contains Affidavits, Memorandums, and Affirmations; they all express truth, through different levels:

- Affidavit - Declaration of Truth
- Memorandum - Explanation or documentation of that truth.
- Affirmation - Spoken or written alignment with that truth daily.

Simple Example:

Let's say you want to affirm your right to practice your faith freely:

Affidavit of Religious Freedom

I, Demarrius Crossley, do hereby declare that my Creator endows me with unalienable rights of conscience and worship, and that no man or institution has lawful authority to infringe upon them.

Signed and dated this__ day of ___,20.

That's a simple but powerful affidavit. It's written truth under your own authority.

Introduction

"The Divine Mandate: Affidavits of Religious Unalienable Rights"

Everyone has a calling in their life, a divine duty. Some answer, some don't. I ran from my calling until I couldn't run anymore. I was summoned by The Universal Noble Ministry's Network (Minister Gradie Partlow, Minister Destini Partlow) to a call to purpose that resonated deep within my soul. I felt an unmistakable summons. It was as if the heavens themselves had ordained this moment, guiding my hands to craft a testament of faith, a declaration of the unalienable rights that belong to us as children of the Most High.

The Affidavit Book, "The Divine Mandate", is born out of deep conviction that our religious freedoms are not merely human constructs, but divine endowments that demand our utmost respect, protection, and proclamation. Within these pages, I have poured my heart, soul, and spirit, driven by a divine mandate to stand as a beacon of hope for those seeking to affirm their faith and assert their God-given rights.

This book is more than a collection of legal documents; it is a testament to the enduring power of faith and the unbreakable bond between the Creator and His Creation. Each affidavit within these pages stands as a declaration of the sacred rights that we hold dear, rights that are woven into the very fabric of our existence and are not to be infringed upon by any earthly authority.

May these affidavits serve as a shield and a beacon, illuminating the path for those who seek to uphold their religious liberties and affirm their devotion to the divine. May they find strength in the words penned here, knowing that they are not alone in their quest for spiritual freedom.

A **religious unalienable right** is a type of natural right that is considered **inherent to all human beings, specifically** related to the **freedom to hold and practice religious beliefs**. These rights are seen as **God-given** or

endowed by the **Creator**, meaning they **cannot be justly taken away** or **denied** by any government or authority.

The First Amendment (U.S. Constitution)

"Congress shall make no law respecting an establishment of religion, or prohibiting the free exercise thereof..."

This amendment protects the religious unalienable right by preventing the government from establishing a national religion **(Establishment Clause)** and protecting the right to freely practice any religion **(Free Exercise Clause)**

Liberty includes **religious liberty**; the concept of religious unalienable rights is a foundation in U. S. political philosophy, especially in:

The Declaration of Independence (1776)

"... that all men are created equal, that they are endowed by their Creator with certain **unalienable Rights**, that among these are Life, Liberty, and the Pursuit of Happiness."

Our **religious unalienable rights** ensure that your **relationship with your beliefs**, **conscience**, **or God** cannot be diluted by the state. It allows **pluralism, freedom of thought**, and **personal dignity**.

If you don't utilize your rights, then you don't have any!

With reverence and humility,

Minister Demarrius Crossley

Affidavit of Life

Illinois State }

}ss

Cook County }

Name of Entity

Entity Address

City, State

[00000]

Notice to Agent is Notice to Principle/Notice to Principle is Notice to Agent

Sovereign Political Holder and Minister, over the age of 21 years, after being duly sworn according to law to tell the truth to the facts herein, I do hereby acknowledge and affirm the following: I, Affiant's Demarrius Crossley, am a Sovereign, without subjects. I am a Foreign Nation (not a person) who rules autonomously and am not subject to any entity or jurisdiction anywhere. I am a Sovereign Political Holder, a Minister. My authority for contracting is the age-old, timeless, and universal respect for the intrinsic power, property, and responsibilities of the Sovereign

Individual. I choose to comply with mutual respect, which serves to bring harmony to society. Demarrius Crossley, Minister, God Within Ministry

Address

City, State

[00000]

All national and state constitutions, laws, statutes, ordinances, regulations, rules, codes, and public policies, in all nations and states, are private copyrighted material. I do not possess a license or have the authority to use such copyrighted material, and consequently, that material does not have any authority over me, my property, or my personal affairs.

Again, this Affidavit is a Lawful Notification to you, the receivers, and requires your compliance to the demands made within. Failure to respond appropriately to the subject matter contained herein, if there is any disagreement with the document, is done under the penalties of perjury. Failure to respond within three (3) days, as stipulated, and rebut, with particularity, everything in this Affidavit with which there is disagreement, providing documentation as part of your ascertain, is a lawful, legal, and binding agreement by you and those that represent you in all Courts, anywhere in America or the World.

I am fully engaged in my Religious Rights and in all my Affairs. I, Demarrius Crossley, hereby declare and affirm that I am a Sovereign human being, endowed with inherent rights and freedoms.

I,(Demarrius Crossley), hereby declare that I am committed to living a life that is authentic, purposeful, and meaningful.

Article 1: Purpose and Intentions

I intend to live a life that is guided by my values, passions, and principles. I am committed to pursuing my dreams and aspirations with courage, resilience, and determination.

Article 2: Self-Care and Well-being

I promised to prioritize my physical, emotional, and mental well-being. I will cultivate self-awareness, self-compassion, and self-love, and will take care of my body, mind, and spirit.

Article 3: Relationships and Community

I value the importance of meaningful relationships and community in my life. I will nurture and cultivate connections with loved ones, friends, and like-minded individuals who support and inspire me.

Article 4: Personal Growth and Development

I am committed to ongoing learning, growth, and self-improvement. I will seek new experiences, knowledge, and skills that will help me evolve and become the best version of myself.

Article 5: Purpose and Contribution

I intend to use my gifts, talents, and passions to make a positive impact on the world. I will strive to leave a lasting legacy that reflects my values and contributions.

Again, this Affidavit is a Lawful Notification to you, the receivers, and requires your compliance to the demands made within. Failure to respond appropriately to the subject matter contained herein, if there is any disagreement with the document, is done under the penalties of perjury. Failure to respond within three (3) days, as stipulated, and rebut, with particularity, everything in this Affidavit with which there is disagreement, providing documentation as part of your ascertain, is a lawful, legal, and binding agreement by you and those that represent you in all Courts, anywhere in America or the World.

I, Demarrius Crossley, hereby sign this Affidavit for Life, declaring my commitment to living a life that is authentic, purposeful, and meaningful.

IN WITNESS WHEREOF, I have hereunto set my hand and seal, this [Date] Day of [Month], [Year].

Demarrius Crossley, Minister ______________________________

Illinois State }

}ss

Cook County }

Acknowledgement

As a Notary for (County and State), I do hereby certify that on the ____day of __________ 20______ the above-mentioned Affiant, Demarrius Crossley, Minister appeared before me and executed the foregoing document.

Witness my Hand and Seal:

____

Notary Public (SEAL)

Memorandum

To: Recipient Name
From: Minister Crossley of the UNMN Church
Date: (Insert Date)
Subject: **Affidavit of Life**

Purpose: This memorandum provides guidance on the creation and utilization of an Affidavit of Life. This affidavit is a sworn written statement that affirms an individual or organization to formally declare the fundamental right to life and to confirm the importance of protecting human life with dignity and respect.

Key Components:

1. **Right to Life:** A declaration of the fundamental right to life.
2. **Protection of life:** A confirmation of the importance of protecting human life.
3. **Dignity and Respect:** A commitment to treating all human life with dignity and respect.

Importance: This affidavit serves as a formal declaration of one's intention to invoke my rights to fundamental human rights, protecting human dignity, and promoting societal well - being and safety. This Affidavit is a Lawful Notice that the <u>Affidavit of Life</u> is a Religious Right and any interruption of it is a Violation of my Religious Rights.

Utilization:

1. **Asserting Rights:** Use the affidavit to assert the fundamental right to life.
2. **Protecting Human Life:** Use the affidavit to protect human life from harm or exploitation.
3. **Promoting Dignity:** Use the affidavit to promote dignity and respect for all human life.

Benefits:

- Protection of human life from harm or exploitation.
- Promotion of dignity and respect for all human life.
- Upholding human rights and fundamental freedoms.

By utilizing the Affidavit of Life, individuals and organizations can protect their individual's rights and interests, the principle of sanctity of life, the principle of protecting human life, and the principle of treating all human life with respect.

REFLECTION PAGE

1. What is one key insight you gained from reading the Affidavit and Memorandum?

____

____

____

____

2. How can you apply this insight to your work, studies, or daily life?

____

____

____

____

Affidavit of Freedom

Illinois State }

}ss

Cook County }

Name of Entity

Entity Address

City, State

[00000]

Notice to Agent is Notice to Principle/Notice to Principle is Notice to Agent

Sovereign Political Holder and Minister, over the age of 21 years, after being duly sworn according to law to tell the truth to the facts herein, I do hereby acknowledge and affirm the following: I, Affiant's Demarrius Crossley, am a Sovereign, without subjects. I am a Foreign Nation (not a person) who rules autonomously and am not subject to any entity or jurisdiction anywhere. I am a Sovereign Political Holder, a Minister. My authority for contracting is the age-old, timeless, and universal respect for the intrinsic power, property, and responsibilities of the Sovereign

Individual. I choose to comply with mutual respect, which serves to bring harmony to society. Demarrius Crossley, Minister, God Within Ministry

Address

City, State

[00000]

All national and state constitutions, laws, statutes, ordinances, regulations, rules, codes, and public policies, in all nations and states, are private copyrighted material. I do not possess a license or have the authority to use such copyrighted material, and consequently, that material does not have any authority over me, my property, or my personal affairs.

Again, this Affidavit is a Lawful Notification to you, the receivers, and requires your compliance to the demands made within. Failure to respond appropriately to the subject matter contained herein, if there is any disagreement with the document, is done under the penalties of perjury. Failure to respond within three (3) days, as stipulated, and rebut, with particularity, everything in this Affidavit with which there is disagreement, providing documentation as part of your ascertain, is a lawful, legal, and binding agreement by you and those that represent you in all Courts, anywhere in America or the World.

I have fully engaged my Religious Rights in all my Affairs. I, Demarrius Crossley, hereby declare and affirm that I am a Sovereign human being, endowed with inherent rights and freedoms.

I claim my right to life, liberty, and the pursuit of happiness, as guaranteed by the Universal Declaration of Human Rights and other international treaties.

I affirm that I am free to think, believe, and express myself without fear of persecution or reprisal.

I declare that I am not a slave or subject to any person, institution, or government.

I claim my right to autonomy, self-determination, and freedom from oppression.

I affirm that I will exercise my rights and freedom responsibly and respectfully, without causing harm to others.

I, Demarrius Crossley, have complete Sovereign Immunity; and therefore, my power to contract and undo contracts is unlimited. My Religious Rights and Freedom must be fully and completely respected. Failure to do so will require that I receive $7,500,000.00 from each violator for each violation that occurs.

Again, this Affidavit is a Lawful Notification to you, the receivers, and requires your compliance to the demands made within. Failure to respond appropriately to the subject matter contained herein, if there is any disagreement with the document, is done under the penalties of perjury. Failure to respond within three (3) days, as stipulated, and rebut, with particularity, everything in this Affidavit with which there is disagreement, providing documentation as part of your ascertain, is a lawful, legal, and binding agreement by you and those that represent you in all Courts, anywhere in America or the World.

It has been said, so it is done.

IN WITNESS WHEREOF, I have hereunto set my hand and seal, this [Date] Day of [Month], [Year].

Demarrius Crossley, Minister ______________________________

Illinois State }

}ss

Cook County }

Acknowledgement

As a Notary for (County and State), I do hereby certify that on the ____day of __________ 20______ the above-mentioned Affiant, Demarrius Crossley, Minister appeared before me and executed the foregoing document.

Witness my Hand and Seal:

____

Notary Public (SEAL)

Memorandum

To: Recipient Name
From: Minister Crossley of the UNMN Church
Date: (Insert Date)
Subject: **Affidavit of Freedom**

Purpose: This memorandum provides guidance on the creation and utilization of an Affidavit of Freedom. This affidavit is a sworn written statement that affirms an individual or organization to formally declare the fundamental right to freedom and liberty, and to confirm individual autonomy and self - determination.

Key Components:

1. **Right to Liberty:** A declaration of the fundamental right to freedom and liberty.
2. **Autonomy:** A confirmation of individual autonomy and self - determination.
3. **Freedom of Expression:** A commitment to protecting freedom of expression and thought.

Importance: This affidavit serves as a formal declaration of one's intention to invoke my rights to human rights, protecting individual liberty and autonomy, and promoting free expression and thought. This Affidavit is a Lawful Notice that the <u>Affidavit of Freedom</u> is a Religious Right and any interruption of it is a Violation of my Religious Rights.

Utilization:

1. **Asserting Rights:** Use the affidavit to assert the fundamental right to freedom and liberty.
2. **Protecting Autonomy:** Use the affidavit to protect individual autonomy and self - determination.
3. **Promoting Free Expression:** Use the affidavit to promote and protect freedom of expression and thought.

Benefits:

- Individual empowerment and autonomy.
- Freedom of expression and thought.
- Protection and promotion of human rights.

By utilizing the Affidavit of Freedom, individuals and organizations can protect their individual's rights and interests, the principle of individual liberty and freedom, the principle of individual autonomy and self - determination, and the principle of protecting human rights.

REFLECTION PAGE

1. What is one key insight you gained from reading the Affidavit and Memorandum?

2. How can you apply this insight to your work, studies, or daily life?

Health Affidavit

Illinois State }

}ss

Cook County }

Name of Entity

Entity Address

City, State

[00000]

Notice to Agent is Notice to Principle/Notice to Principle is Notice to Agent

Sovereign Political Holder and Minister, over the age of 21 years, after being duly sworn according to law to tell the truth to the facts herein, I do hereby acknowledge and affirm the following: I, Affiant's Demarrius Crossley, am a Sovereign, without subjects. I am a Foreign Nation (not a person) who rules autonomously and am not subject to any entity or jurisdiction anywhere. I am a Sovereign Political Holder, a Minister. My authority for contracting is the age-old, timeless, and universal respect for the intrinsic power, property, and responsibilities of the Sovereign Individual. I choose to comply with mutual respect, which serves to bring harmony to society. Demarrius Crossley, Minister, God Within Ministry

Address

City, State

[00000]

All national and state constitutions, laws, statutes, ordinances, regulations, rules, codes, and public policies, in all nations and states, are private copyrighted material. I do not possess a license or have the authority to use such copyrighted material, and consequently, that material does not have any authority over me, my property, or my personal affairs.

Again, this Affidavit is a Lawful Notification to you, the receivers, and requires your compliance to the demands made within. Failure to respond appropriately to the subject matter contained herein, if there is any disagreement with the document, is done under the penalties of perjury. Failure to respond within three (3) days, as stipulated, and rebut, with particularity, everything in this Affidavit with which there is disagreement, providing documentation as part of your ascertain, is a lawful, legal, and binding agreement by you and those that represent you in all Courts, anywhere in America or the World.

I am fully engaged in my Religious Rights and in all my Affairs. I, Demarrius Crossley, hereby declare and affirm that I am a Sovereign human being, endowed with inherent rights and freedoms.

I, Demarrius Crossley, hereby declare that I am committed to nurturing and protecting my physical, emotional, and mental health.

Article 1: Self-Care and Wellness

I promise to prioritize self-care and wellness practices, including:

- Regular exercise and physical activity
- Balanced and nutritious eating habits
- Sufficient sleep and rest
- Stress management and relaxation techniques.

Article 2: Self-Love and Self-Care

I commit to adopting and maintaining healthy habits, including:

- Managing stress and anxiety through healthy coping mechanisms
- Limiting alcohol consumption and avoiding substance abuse
- Avoiding tobacco and nicotine products
- Practicing safe sex and protecting myself from infectious diseases

Article 3: Mental and Emotional Well-Being

I prioritize my mental and emotional well-being and commit to

- Practicing mindfulness, self-compassion, and self-awareness
- Engage in activities that bring me joy, purpose, and fulfillment
- Seeking support from loved ones and friends.

Article 4: Health Empowerment

I take responsibility for my health and well-being and commit to:

- Educating myself on healthy living practices and disease prevention
- Advocating for my health needs and rights
- Making Informed decisions about my healthcare and treatment options

Again, this Affidavit is a Lawful Notification to you, the receivers, and requires your compliance to the demands made within. Failure to respond appropriately to the subject matter contained herein, if there is any disagreement with the document, is done under the penalties of perjury. Failure to respond within three (3) days, as stipulated, and rebut, with particularity, everything in this Affidavit with which there is disagreement, providing documentation as part of your ascertain, is a lawful, legal, and binding agreement by you and those that represent you in all Courts, anywhere in America or the World.

I, Demarrius Crossley, hereby sign this Affidavit for Health, declaring my commitment to prioritizing and protecting my physical, emotional, and mental health.

IN WITNESS WHEREOF, I have hereunto set my hand and seal, this [Date] Day of [Month], [Year].

Demarrius Crossley, Minister ______________________________

Illinois State }

}ss

Cook County }

Acknowledgement

As a Notary for (County and State), I do hereby certify that on the ____day of _________ 20______ the above-mentioned Affiant, Demarrius Crossley, Minister appeared before me and executed the foregoing document.

Witness my Hand and Seal:

____

Notary Public (SEAL)

Memorandum

To: Recipient Name
From: Minister Crossley of the UNMN Church
Date: (Insert Date)
Subject: **Health Affidavit**

Purpose: This memorandum provides guidance on the creation and utilization of an Affidavit of Health. This affidavit is a sworn written statement that affirms an individual or organization to formally declare the right to health and well - being, and to confirm access to necessary health care services and healthy living practices.

Key Components:

1. **Right to Health:** A declaration of the right to health and well - being.
2. **Health Care Access:** A confirmation of access to necessary health care services.
3. **Healthy Living:** A commitment to healthy living and self - care practices.

Importance: This affidavit serves as a formal declaration of one's intention to invoke my rights to human rights, preventing and treating health conditions effectively, and enhance well - being. This Affidavit is a Lawful Notice that the Affidavit of Health is a Religious Right and any interruption of it is a Violation of my Religious Rights.

Utilization:

1. **Asserting Health Rights:** Use the affidavit to assert the right to health and well - being.
2. **Accessing Health Care:** Use the affidavit to access necessary health care services.
3. **Promoting Healthy Living:** Use the affidavit to promote healthy living and self - care practices.

Benefits:

- Improved health outcomes and well - being.
- Increased Access to necessary health care services.
- Enhanced overall quality of life.

By utilizing the Affidavit of Health, individuals and organizations can protect their individual's rights and interests, the principle of health equity, the principle of preventing illness and promoting health, and the principle of providing comprehensive and holistic care.

REFLECTION PAGE

1. What is one key insight you gained from reading the Affidavit and Memorandum?

2. How can you apply this insight to your work, studies, or daily life?

Affidavit
The Pursuit of Happiness

Illinois State }

}ss

Cook County }

Name of Entity

Entity Address

City, State

[00000]

Notice to Agent is Notice to Principle/Notice to Principle is Notice to Agent

Sovereign Political Holder and Minister, over the age of 21 years, after being duly sworn according to law to tell the truth to the facts herein, I do hereby acknowledge and affirm the following: I, Affiant's Demarrius Crossley, am a Sovereign, without subjects. I am a Foreign Nation (not a person) who rules autonomously and am not subject to any entity or jurisdiction anywhere. I am a Sovereign Political Holder, a Minister. My authority for contracting is the age-old, timeless, and universal respect for the intrinsic power, property, and responsibilities of the Sovereign

Individual. I choose to comply with mutual respect, which serves to bring harmony to society. Demarrius Crossley, Minister, God Within Ministry

Address

City, State

[00000]

All national and state constitutions, laws, statutes, ordinances, regulations, rules, codes, and public policies, in all nations and states, are private copyrighted material. I do not possess a license or have the authority to use such copyrighted material, and consequently, that material does not have any authority over me, my property, or my personal affairs.

Again, this Affidavit is a Lawful Notification to you, the receivers, and requires your compliance to the demands made within. Failure to respond appropriately to the subject matter contained herein, if there is any disagreement with the document, is done under the penalties of perjury. Failure to respond within three (3) days, as stipulated, and rebut, with particularity, everything in this Affidavit with which there is disagreement, providing documentation as part of your ascertain, is a lawful, legal, and binding agreement by you and those that represent you in all Courts, anywhere in America or the World.

I am fully engaged in my Religious Rights and in all my Affairs. I, Demarrius Crossley, hereby declare and affirm that I am a Sovereign human being, endowed with inherent rights and freedoms.

I, Demarrius Crossley, hereby declare that I am committed to pursuing happiness, fulfillment, and joy in my life.

Article 1: Purpose and Intentions

I intend to cultivate a mindset of positivity, gratitude, and optimism, and to prioritize activities and relationships that bring me joy and fulfillment.

Article 2: Self-Love and Self-Care

I promise to prioritize self-love and self-care, and to nurture my physical, emotional, and mental well-being through healthy habits and self-compassion.

Article 3: Meaningful Relationships

I commit to cultivating and nurturing meaningful relationships with loved ones, friends, and community, and to prioritizing communication, empathy, and understanding.

Article 4: Personal Growth and Development

I am committed to ongoing learning, growth, and self-improvement and to seeking out new experiences, knowledge, and skills that will help me evolve and become the best version of myself.

Article 5: Resilience and Adaptability

I promise to cultivate resilience and adaptability in the face of challenges and setbacks, and to approach life's difficulties with courage, determination, and a growth mindset.

Again, this Affidavit is a Lawful Notification to you, the receivers, and requires your compliance to the demands made within. Failure to respond appropriately to the subject matter contained herein, if there is any disagreement with the document, is done under the penalties of perjury. Failure to respond within three (3) days, as stipulated, and rebut, with particularity, everything in this++ Affidavit with which there is disagreement, providing documentation as part of your ascertain, is a lawful, legal, and binding agreement by you and those that represent you in all Courts, anywhere in America or the World.

I, Demarrius Crossley, hereby sign this Affidavit for The Pursuit of Happiness, declaring my commitment to seeking happiness, fulfillment, and joy in my life.

IN WITNESS WHEREOF, I have hereunto set my hand and seal, this [Date] Day of [Month], [Year].

Demarrius Crossley, Minister ______________________________

Illinois State }

}ss

Cook County }

Acknowledgement

As a Notary for (County and State), I do hereby certify that on the ____day of _________ 20______ the above-mentioned Affiant, Demarrius Crossley, Minister appeared before me and executed the foregoing document.

Witness my Hand and Seal:

____

Notary Public (SEAL)

Memorandum

To: Recipient Name
From: Minister Crossley of the UNMN Church
Date: (Insert Date)
Subject: **Affidavit of The Pursuit of Happiness**

Purpose: This memorandum provides guidance on the creation and utilization of an Affidavit of The Pursuit of Happiness. This affidavit is a sworn written statement that Affirms an individual or organization to formally declare the right to pursue happiness and confirm personal freedom and autonomy.

Key Components:

1. **Right to Happiness:** A declaration of the unlimited scope of the contract.
2. **Personal Freedom:** A confirmation of personal freedom and autonomy.
3. **Pursuit of Fulfillment:** A commitment to pursuing fulfillment and happiness.

Importance: This affidavit serves as a formal declaration of one's intention to invoke my rights to human rights to pursue happiness, promote personal growth, and enhance well - being. This Affidavit is a Lawful Notice that the Affidavit of The Pursuit of Happiness is a Religious Right and any interruption of it is a Violation of my Religious Rights.

Utilization:

1. **Asserting Rights:** Use the affidavit to assert the right to pursue happiness.
2. **Promoting Personal Freedom:** Use the affidavit to promote personal freedom and autonomy.
3. **Fostering Fulfillment:** Use the affidavit to foster fulfillment and happiness in life.

Benefits:

- Personal fulfillment and happiness.
- Increased autonomy and freedom.
- Improved overall well - being.

By utilizing the Affidavit of The Pursuit of Happiness, individuals and organizations can protect their individual's rights and interests, the principle of individual liberty and freedom, the principle of personal autonomy, and the principle of pursuing happiness and fulfillment.

REFLECTION PAGE

1. What is one key insight you gained from reading the Affidavit and Memorandum?

2. How can you apply this insight to your work, studies, or daily life?

Affidavit Contract (Unlimited)

Illinois State }

}ss

Cook County }

Name of Entity

Entity Address

City, State

[00000]

Notice to Agent is Notice to Principle/Notice to Principle is Notice to Agent

Sovereign Political Holder and Minister, over the age of 21 years, after being duly sworn according to law to tell the truth to the facts herein, I do hereby acknowledge and affirm the following: I, Affiant's Demarrius Crossley, am a Sovereign, without subjects. I am a Foreign Nation (not a person) who rules autonomously and am not subject to any entity or jurisdiction anywhere. I am a Sovereign Political Holder, a Minister. My authority for contracting is the age-old, timeless, and universal respect for the intrinsic power, property, and responsibilities of the Sovereign

Individual. I choose to comply with mutual respect, which serves to bring harmony to society. Demarrius Crossley, Minister, God Within Ministry

Address

City, State

[00000]

All national and state constitutions, laws, statutes, ordinances, regulations, rules, codes, and public policies, in all nations and states, are private copyrighted material. I do not possess a license or have the authority to use such copyrighted material, and consequently, that material does not have any authority over me, my property, or my personal affairs.

Again, this Affidavit is a Lawful Notification to you, the receivers, and requires your compliance to the demands made within. Failure to respond appropriately to the subject matter contained herein, if there is any disagreement with the document, is done under the penalties of perjury. Failure to respond within three (3) days, as stipulated, and rebut, with particularity, everything in this Affidavit with which there is disagreement, providing documentation as part of your ascertain, is a lawful, legal, and binding agreement by you and those that represent you in all Courts, anywhere in America or the World.

I am fully engaged in my Religious Rights and in all my Affairs. I, Demarrius Crossley, hereby declare and affirm that I am a Sovereign human being, endowed with inherent rights and freedoms.

I, Demarrius Crossley, hereby declare that I am entering into this contract or agreement with the intention of fulfilling my obligations to the best of my abilities, without limits or restrictions.

Article 1: Purpose and Intentions

I intend to perform all duties and responsibilities outlined in this contract or agreement, and to uphold the terms and conditions with integrity and good faith.

Article 2: Unlimited Liability

I acknowledge that I am fully responsible for all actions, decisions, and outcomes related to this contract or agreement, and that I am willing to accept unlimited liability for any consequences that may arise.

Article 3: No Restrictions

I declare that I am not subject to any restrictions, limitations, or constraints that would prevent me from fulfilling my obligations under this contract or agreement.

Article 4: Binding Agreement

I acknowledge that this contract or agreement is a binding and enforceable document, and that I am committed to upholding its terms and conditions.

Again, this Affidavit is a Lawful Notification to you, the receivers, and requires your compliance to the demands made within. Failure to respond appropriately to the subject matter contained herein, if there is any disagreement with the document, is done under the penalties of perjury. Failure to respond within three (3) days, as stipulated, and rebut, with particularity, everything in this Affidavit with which there is disagreement, providing documentation as part of your ascertain, is a lawful, legal, and binding agreement by you and those that represent you in all Courts, anywhere in America or the World.

IN WITNESS WHEREOF, I have hereunto set my hand and seal, this [Date] Day of [Month], [Year].

Demarrius Crossley, Minister ______________________________

Illinois State }

}ss

Cook County }

Acknowledgement

As a Notary for (County and State), I do hereby certify that on the ____day of __________ 20______ the above-mentioned Affiant, Demarrius Crossley, Minister appeared before me and executed the foregoing document.

Witness my Hand and Seal:

____

Notary Public (SEAL)

Memorandum

To: Recipient Name
From: Minister Crossley of the UNMN Church
Date: (Insert Date)
Subject: **Affidavit of Contract (Unlimited)**

Purpose: This memorandum provides guidance on the creation and utilization of an Affidavit of Contract (Unlimited). This affidavit is a sworn written statement that affirms an individual or organization to formally declare the unlimited scope of a contract and confirm the comprehensive agreement between parties.

Key Components:

1. **Unlimited Scope:** A declaration of the unlimited scope of the contract.
2. **Comprehensive Agreement:** A confirmation of a comprehensive agreement between parties.
3. **Binding Terms:** A commitment to be bound by the terms of the contract.

Importance: This affidavit serves as a formal declaration of one's intention to invoke my rights to establish trust between parties, defining obligations and responsibilities, and promoting good faith. This Affidavit is a Lawful Notice that the Affidavit of Contract (Unlimited) is a Religious Right and any interruption of it is a Violation of my Religious Rights.

Utilization:

1. **Establishing Comprehensive Agreements:** Use the affidavit to establish comprehensive agreements between parties.
2. **Defining Unlimited Scope:** Use the affidavit to define the unlimited scope of a contract.
3. **Ensuring Binding Terms:** Use the affidavit to ensure that the terms of the contract are binding on all parties.

Benefits:

- A comprehensive understanding of contractual relationships.
- An unlimited scope of the contract, allowing for flexibility and adaptability.
- Mutual benefit and cooperation in contractual relationships.

By utilizing the Affidavit of Contract (Unlimited) ,individuals and organizations can protect their individual's rights and interests, the principle of fulfilling contractual obligations, the principle of good faith in contractual relationships, and the principle of mutual benefit and cooperation.

REFLECTION PAGE

1. What is one key insight you gained from reading the Affidavit and Memorandum?

____

____

____

____

2. How can you apply this insight to your work, studies, or daily life?

____

____

____

____

Affidavit Not Contract (Unlimited)

Illinois State }

}ss

Cook County }

Name of Entity

Entity Address

City, State

[00000]

Notice to Agent is Notice to Principle/Notice to Principle is Notice to Agent

Sovereign Political Holder and Minister, over the age of 21 years, after being duly sworn according to law to tell the truth to the facts herein, I do hereby acknowledge and affirm the following: I, Affiant's Demarrius Crossley, am a Sovereign, without subjects. I am a Foreign Nation (not a person) who rules autonomously and am not subject to any entity or jurisdiction anywhere. I am a Sovereign Political Holder, a Minister. My authority for contracting is the age-old, timeless, and universal respect for the intrinsic power, property, and responsibilities of the Sovereign

Individual. I choose to comply with mutual respect, which serves to bring harmony to society. Demarrius Crossley, Minister, God Within Ministry

Address

City, State

[00000]

All national and state constitutions, laws, statutes, ordinances, regulations, rules, codes, and public policies, in all nations and states, are private copyrighted material. I do not possess a license or have the authority to use such copyrighted material, and consequently, that material does not have any authority over me, my property, or my personal affairs.

Again, this Affidavit is a Lawful Notification to you, the receivers, and requires your compliance to the demands made within. Failure to respond appropriately to the subject matter contained herein, if there is any disagreement with the document, is done under the penalties of perjury. Failure to respond within three (3) days, as stipulated, and rebut, with particularity, everything in this Affidavit with which there is disagreement, providing documentation as part of your ascertain, is a lawful, legal, and binding agreement by you and those that represent you in all Courts, anywhere in America or the World.

I am fully engaged in my Religious Rights and in all my Affairs. I, Demarrius Crossley, hereby declare and affirm that I am a Sovereign human being, endowed with inherent rights and freedoms.

I, Demarrius Crossley, hereby state under oath:

Article 1: Introduction

I, Demarrius Crossley, being of sound mind and body, do hereby declare and affirm the following:

Article 2: Statement of Facts

1. I am not entering into a contract with [Party Name] that is unlimited in scope or duration
2. Any agreement or understanding between us is limited to specific terms and conditions.
3. I understand that there is no comprehensive or binding agreement between us that is unlimited in scope.

Article 3: Declaration Of Non-Obligation

I hereby declare that I am not obligated to [Party Name] under an unlimited contract, and I am free to terminate or modify any agreement or understanding between us.

Article 4: Limited Scope

This affidavit confirms that any agreement or understanding between us is limited in scope and duration, and does not imply an unlimited contractual obligation.

Article 5: Acknowledgment

I acknowledge that I have not entered into an unlimited contract with [Party Name], and I understand the terms and conditions of any limited agreement or understanding between us.

Article 6: Conclusion

I, Demarrius Crossley, have complete Sovereign Immunity; and therefore, my power to contract and undo contracts is unlimited. My Religious Rights and Freedom must be fully and completely respected. Failure to do so will require that I receive $7,500,000.00 from each violator for each violation that occurs.

Article 7: Verifications

I hereby affirm that the foregoing statements are true and accurate to the best of my knowledge and belief.

Again, this Affidavit is a Lawful Notification to you, the receivers, and requires your compliance to the demands made within. Failure to respond appropriately to the subject matter contained herein, if there is any disagreement with the document, is done under the penalties of perjury. Failure to respond within three (3) days, as stipulated, and rebut, with particularity, everything in this Affidavit with which there is disagreement, providing documentation as part of your ascertain, is a lawful, legal, and binding agreement by you and those that represent you in all Courts, anywhere in America or the World.

IN WITNESS WHEREOF, I have hereunto set my hand and seal, this [Date] Day of [Month], [Year].

Demarrius Crossley, Minister ________________________________

Illinois State }

}ss

Cook County }

Acknowledgement

As a Notary for (County and State), I do hereby certify that on the ____day of __________ 20______ the above-mentioned Affiant, Demarrius Crossley, Minister appeared before me and executed the foregoing document.

Witness my Hand and Seal:

____

Notary Public (SEAL)

Memorandum

To: Recipient Name
From: Minister Crossley of the UNMN Church
Date: (Insert Date)
Subject: **Affidavit of Not Contract (Unlimited)**

Purpose: This memorandum provides guidance on the creation and utilization of an Affidavit of Not Contract (Unlimited). This affidavit is a sworn written statement that affirms an individual or organization to formally declare that one is not party to an unlimited contract, and to confirm the limited scope and duration of any agreement or understanding.

Key Components:

1. **Limited Scope:** A declaration of the limited scope of any agreement or understanding.
2. **No Unlimited Obligation:** A confirmation of no unlimited contractual obligation.
3. **Specific Terms:** A requirement for specific terms and conditions in any agreement.

Importance: This affidavit serves as a formal declaration of one's intention to invoke my rights to protect interest and limit liability, avoiding misunderstandings, and promoting flexibility in contractual relationships. This Affidavit is a Lawful Notice that the Affidavit of Not Contract (Unlimited) is a Religious Right and any interruption of it is a Violation of my Religious Rights.

Utilization:

1. **Avoid Unlimited Obligations:** Use the affidavit to avoid unlimited contractual obligations.
2. **Defining Limited Scope:** Use the affidavit to define the limited scope of any agreement or understanding.

3. **Protecting Interests:** Use the affidavit to protect interests and limit liability.

Benefits:

- Limited liability and obligations.
- Flexibility in contractual relationships.
- Clarity and specificity and agreements and contracts.

By utilizing the Affidavit of Not Contract (Unlimited), individuals and organizations can protect their individual's rights and interests, the principle of limiting liability and obligations, the principle of specificity in agreements, and the principle of flexibility in contractual relationships.

REFLECTION PAGE

1. What is one key insight you gained from reading the Affidavit and Memorandum?

2. How can you apply this insight to your work, studies, or daily life?

Affidavit To Generate Capital

Illinois State }

}ss

Cook County }

Name of Entity

Entity Address

City, State

[00000]

Notice to Agent is Notice to Principle/Notice to Principle is Notice to Agent

Sovereign Political Holder and Minister, over the age of 21 years, after being duly sworn according to law to tell the truth to the facts herein, I do hereby acknowledge and affirm the following: I, Affiant's Demarrius Crossley, am a Sovereign, without subjects. I am a Foreign Nation (not a person) who rules autonomously and am not subject to any entity or jurisdiction anywhere. I am a Sovereign Political Holder, a Minister. My authority for contracting is the age-old, timeless, and universal respect for the intrinsic power, property, and responsibilities of the Sovereign

Individual. I choose to comply with mutual respect, which serves to bring harmony to society. Demarrius Crossley, Minister, God Within Ministry

Address

City, State

[00000]

All national and state constitutions, laws, statutes, ordinances, regulations, rules, codes, and public policies, in all nations and states, are private copyrighted material. I do not possess a license or have the authority to use such copyrighted material, and consequently, that material does not have any authority over me, my property, or my personal affairs.

Again, this Affidavit is a Lawful Notification to you, the receivers, and requires your compliance to the demands made within. Failure to respond appropriately to the subject matter contained herein, if there is any disagreement with the document, is done under the penalties of perjury. Failure to respond within three (3) days, as stipulated, and rebut, with particularity, everything in this Affidavit with which there is disagreement, providing documentation as part of your ascertain, is a lawful, legal, and binding agreement by you and those that represent you in all Courts, anywhere in America or the World.

I am fully engaged in my Religious Rights and in all my Affairs. I, Demarrius Crossley, hereby declare and affirm that I am a Sovereign human being, endowed with inherent rights and freedoms.

I, Demarrius Crossley, being duly sworn, depose and say:

Article 1: Factual Statements

I am Minister of God Within Ministry, a Religion/spirituality-based organization with its principal place of business at 7053 South Indiana Street, Chicago, IL 60637.

Article 2: Personal Declaration

I am authorized to execute this affidavit on behalf of God Within the Ministry.

Article 3: Intention and Purpose

God Within Ministry is the rightful owner of [ASSETS/PROPERTY], which is being used as collateral for the investment in Generate Capital.

Article 4: Acknowledgments

The financial statements and reports submitted to Generate Capital are true and accurate to the best of my knowledge and belief.

God Within Ministry complies with all relevant laws, regulations, and industry standards.

Article 5: Verification

I hereby declare under penalty of perjury that the foregoing statements are true and accurate to the best of my knowledge and belief.

Again, this Affidavit is a Lawful Notification to you, the receivers, and requires your compliance to the demands made within. Failure to respond appropriately to the subject matter contained herein, if there is any disagreement with the document, is done under the penalties of perjury. Failure to respond within three (3) days, as stipulated, and rebut, with particularity, everything in this Affidavit with which there is disagreement, providing documentation as part of your ascertain, is a lawful, legal, and binding agreement by you and those that represent you in all Courts, anywhere in America or the World.

IN WITNESS WHEREOF, I have hereunto set my hand and seal, this [Date] Day of [Month], [Year].

Demarrius Crossley, Minister ______________________________

Illinois State }

}ss

Cook County }

Acknowledgement

As a Notary for (County and State), I do hereby certify that on the ____day of __________ 20______ the above-mentioned Affiant, Demarrius Crossley, Minister appeared before me and executed the foregoing document.

Witness my Hand and Seal:

____

Notary Public (SEAL)

Memorandum

To: Recipient Name
From: Minister Crossley of the UNMN Church
Date: (Insert Date)
Subject: **Affidavit To Generate Capital**

Purpose: This memorandum provides guidance on the creation and utilization of an Affidavit To Generate Capital. This affidavit is a sworn written statement that affirms an individual or organization to formally declare the need for financial resources and commit to generating capital through various means.

Key Components:

1. **Financial Resources:** A declaration of the need for financial resources to achieve goals or objectives.
2. **Capital Generation:** A commitment to generating capital through various means such as investments, loans, or fundraising.
3. **Financial Planning:** A requirement for careful financial planning and management to ensure effective use of capital.

Importance: This affidavit serves as a formal declaration of one's intention to invoke my rights to achieve goals through access to capital, ensure financial sustainability and stability, and contribute to economic growth. This Affidavit is a Lawful Notice that the Affidavit To Generate Capital is a Religious Right and any interruption of it is a Violation of my Religious Rights.

Utilization:

1. **Securing Funding:** Use the affidavit to secure funding for projects, business, or initiatives.
2. **Investing in Opportunities:** Use the affidavit to invest in opportunities that align with goals and objectives.

3. **Managing Financial Risk:** Use the affidavit to manage financial risk and minimize potential losses.

Benefits:

- Access to capital to achieve goals or objectives.
- Financial stability and sustainability.
- Growth and development through strategic investments.

By utilizing the Affidavit To Generate Capital, individuals and organizations can protect their individual's rights and interests, the principle of ensuring financial sustainability and stability, the principle of investment, and the principle of managing financial risk.

REFLECTION PAGE

1. What is one key insight you gained from reading the Affidavit and Memorandum?

2. How can you apply this insight to your work, studies, or daily life?

Affidavit To Be Compensated

Illinois State }

}ss

Cook County }

Name of Entity

Entity Address

City, State

[00000]

Notice to Agent is Notice to Principle/Notice to Principle is Notice to Agent

Sovereign Political Holder and Minister, over the age of 21 years, after being duly sworn according to law to tell the truth to the facts herein, I do hereby acknowledge and affirm the following: I, Affiant's Demarrius Crossley, am a Sovereign, without subjects. I am a Foreign Nation (not a person) who rules autonomously and am not subject to any entity or jurisdiction anywhere. I am a Sovereign Political Holder, a Minister. My authority for contracting is the age-old, timeless, and universal respect for the intrinsic power, property, and responsibilities of the Sovereign

Individual. I choose to comply with mutual respect, which serves to bring harmony to society. Demarrius Crossley, Minister, God Within Ministry

Address

City, State

[00000]

All national and state constitutions, laws, statutes, ordinances, regulations, rules, codes, and public policies, in all nations and states, are private copyrighted material. I do not possess a license or have the authority to use such copyrighted material, and consequently, that material does not have any authority over me, my property, or my personal affairs.

Again, this Affidavit is a Lawful Notification to you, the receivers, and requires your compliance to the demands made within. Failure to respond appropriately to the subject matter contained herein, if there is any disagreement with the document, is done under the penalties of perjury. Failure to respond within three (3) days, as stipulated, and rebut, with particularity, everything in this Affidavit with which there is disagreement, providing documentation as part of your ascertain, is a lawful, legal, and binding agreement by you and those that represent you in all Courts, anywhere in America or the World.

I am fully engaged in my Religious Rights and in all my Affairs. I, Demarrius Crossley, hereby declare and affirm that I am a Sovereign human being, endowed with inherent rights and freedoms.

I, Demarrius Crossley, being duly sworn, depose and say:

Article 1: Introduction

I am the Minister of God Within Ministry, a Religion/spirituality-based organization with its principal place of business at 7053 South Indiana Street, Chicago, IL 60637. I am making this affidavit to provide evidence in support of my claim for compensation against [DEFENDANT'S NAME].

Article 2: Statement of Facts

On [DATE], I was involved in an incident at [LOCATION] that resulted in [INJURIES/LOSSES]. The incident was caused by the negligence of [DEFENDANT'S NAME], who failed to [STATE SPECIFIC ACTS OF NEGLIGENCE].

As a direct result of the incident, I have incurred the following losses:

- Medical expenses: $ [AMOUNT]
- Lost wages: $[AMOUNT]
- Property damage: $ [AMOUNT]

Article 3: Claim for Compensation

I am claiming compensation for the losses and damages incurred as a result of the incident. The total amount of compensation claimed is $ [TOTAL AMOUNT].

Article 4: Verification

I hereby declare under penalty of perjury that the foregoing statements are true and accurate to the best of my knowledge and belief.

Again, this Affidavit is a Lawful Notification to you, the receivers, and requires your compliance to the demands made within. Failure to respond appropriately to the subject matter contained herein, if there is any disagreement with the document, is done under the penalties of perjury. Failure to respond within three (3) days, as stipulated, and rebut, with particularity, everything in this Affidavit with which there is disagreement, providing documentation as part of your ascertain, is a lawful, legal, and binding agreement by you and those that represent you in all Courts, anywhere in America or the World.

IN WITNESS WHEREOF, I have hereunto set my hand and seal, this [Date] Day of [Month], [Year].

Demarrius Crossley, Minister ____________________________

Illinois State }

}ss

Cook County }

Acknowledgement

As a Notary for (County and State), I do hereby certify that on the ____day of __________ 20______ the above-mentioned Affiant, Demarrius Crossley, Minister appeared before me and executed the foregoing document.

Witness my Hand and Seal:

____

Notary Public (SEAL)

Memorandum

To: Recipient Name
From: Minister Crossley of the UNMN Church
Date: (Insert Date)
Subject: **Affidavit of To Be Compensated**

Purpose: This memorandum provides guidance on the creation and utilization of an Affidavit To Be Compensated. This affidavit is a sworn written statement that affirms an individual or organization to formally declare the right to receive fair compensation for work, services, or losses, and to ensure timely payment.

Key Components:

1. **Right to Compensation:** A declaration of the right to receive fair compensation for work, service, or losses.
2. **Fair Value:** A commitment to receiving fair value for goods or services provided.
3. **Timely Payment:** A requirement for timely payment of compensation.

Importance: This affidavit serves as a formal declaration of one's intention to invoke my rights to protect financial interests and prevent exploitation, promoting fairness and equity, and supporting economic stability security. This Affidavit is a Lawful Notice that the Affidavit To Be Compensated is a Religious Right and any interruption of it is a Violation of my Religious Rights.

Utilization:

1. **Ensuring Fair Compensation:** Use the affidavit to ensure fair compensation for work, services, or losses.
2. **Protecting Financial Interests:** Use the affidavit to protect financial interests and prevent exploitation.

3. **Promoting Accountability:** Use the affidavit to promote accountability and responsibility in compensation practices.

Benefits:

- Fair Compensation for work, services, or losses.
- Financial stability and security.
- Accountability and responsibility in compensation practices.

By utilizing the Affidavit of To Be Compensated, individuals and organizations can protect their individual's rights and interests, the principle of fairness and equity, the principle of receiving fair value, and the principle of timely payment of compensation.

REFLECTION PAGE

1. What is one key insight you gained from reading the Affidavit and Memorandum?

____

____

____

____

2. How can you apply this insight to your work, studies, or daily life?

____

____

____

____

Affidavit To Travel in the Course of Life

Illinois State }

}ss

Cook County }

Name of Entity

Entity Address

City, State

[00000]

Notice to Agent is Notice to Principle/Notice to Principle is Notice to Agent

Sovereign Political Holder and Minister, over the age of 21 years, after being duly sworn according to law to tell the truth to the facts herein, I do hereby acknowledge and affirm the following: I, Affiant's Demarrius Crossley, am a Sovereign, without subjects. I am a Foreign Nation (not a person) who rules autonomously and am not subject to any entity or jurisdiction anywhere. I am a Sovereign Political Holder, a Minister. My authority for contracting is the age-old, timeless, and universal respect for the intrinsic power, property, and responsibilities of the Sovereign

Individual. I choose to comply with mutual respect, which serves to bring harmony to society. Demarrius Crossley, Minister, God Within Ministry

Address

City, State

[00000]

All national and state constitutions, laws, statutes, ordinances, regulations, rules, codes, and public policies, in all nations and states, are private copyrighted material. I do not possess a license or have the authority to use such copyrighted material, and consequently, that material does not have any authority over me, my property, or my personal affairs.

Again, this Affidavit is a Lawful Notification to you, the receivers, and requires your compliance to the demands made within. Failure to respond appropriately to the subject matter contained herein, if there is any disagreement with the document, is done under the penalties of perjury. Failure to respond within three (3) days, as stipulated, and rebut, with particularity, everything in this Affidavit with which there is disagreement, providing documentation as part of your ascertain, is a lawful, legal, and binding agreement by you and those that represent you in all Courts, anywhere in America or the World.

I am fully engaged in my Religious Rights and in all my Affairs. I, Demarrius Crossley, hereby declare and affirm that I am a Sovereign human being, endowed with inherent rights and freedoms.

I, Demarrius Crossley, being duly sworn, depose and say:

Article 1: Introduction

I, Demarrius Crossley, being of sound mind and body, do hereby declare and affirm my right to travel and move freely in the course of my life.

Article 2: Statement of Intent

I intend to travel and move freely, without undue restriction, to pursue my personal, professional, and educational goals. I affirm my right to explore new places, experience different cultures, and engage with diverse communities.

Article 3: Declaration of Rights

I declare that I have the right to:

1. Travel freely within my country and abroad
2. Choose my own destination and itinerary

3. Move without undue restriction or interference
4. Pursuing my personal, professional, and educational goals.

Article 4: Acknowledgments

I acknowledge that my freedom to travel is essential to my personal growth, well-being, and happiness. I affirm my commitment to respecting the laws and regulations of the places I visit.

I formally declare my intention to travel freely and pursue my life's journey without undue restriction. I expect to be treated with dignity and respect, and to be allowed to exercise my right to travel and move freely.

Article 5: Verification

I hereby declare under penalty of perjury that the foregoing statements are true and accurate to the best of my knowledge and belief.

Again, this Affidavit is a Lawful Notification to you, the receivers, and requires your compliance to the demands made within. Failure to respond appropriately to the subject matter contained herein, if there is any disagreement with the document, is done under the penalties of perjury. Failure to respond within three (3) days, as stipulated, and rebut, with particularity, everything in this Affidavit with which there is disagreement, providing documentation as part of your ascertain, is a lawful, legal, and binding agreement by you and those that represent you in all Courts, anywhere in America or the World.

IN WITNESS WHEREOF, I have hereunto set my hand and seal, this [Date] Day of [Month], [Year].

Demarrius Crossley, Minister ______________________________

Illinois State }

}ss

Cook County }

Acknowledgement

As a Notary for (County and State), I do hereby certify that on the ____day of _________ 20______ the above-mentioned Affiant, Demarrius Crossley, Minister appeared before me and executed the foregoing document.

Witness my Hand and Seal:

____

Notary Public (SEAL)

Affidavit To Travel & Compensation in the Course of Life

Illinois State }

}ss

Cook County }

Name of Entity

Entity Address

City, State

[00000]

Notice to Agent is Notice to Principle/Notice to Principle is Notice to Agent

Sovereign Political Holder and Minister, over the age of 21 years, after being duly sworn according to law to tell the truth to the facts herein, I do hereby acknowledge and affirm the following: I, Affiant's Demarrius Crossley, am a Sovereign, without subjects. I am a Foreign Nation (not a person) who rules autonomously and am not subject to any entity or jurisdiction anywhere. I am a Sovereign Political Holder, a Minister. My authority for contracting is the age-old, timeless, and universal respect for the intrinsic power, property, and responsibilities of the Sovereign

Individual. I choose to comply with mutual respect, which serves to bring harmony to society. Demarrius Crossley, Minister, God Within Ministry

Address

City, State

[00000]

All national and state constitutions, laws, statutes, ordinances, regulations, rules, codes, and public policies, in all nations and states, are private copyrighted material. I do not possess a license or have the authority to use such copyrighted material, and consequently, that material does not have any authority over me, my property, or my personal affairs.

Again, this Affidavit is a Lawful Notification to you, the receivers, and requires your compliance to the demands made within. Failure to respond appropriately to the subject matter contained herein, if there is any disagreement with the document, is done under the penalties of perjury. Failure to respond within three (3) days, as stipulated, and rebut, with particularity, everything in this Affidavit with which there is disagreement, providing documentation as part of your ascertain, is a lawful, legal, and binding agreement by you and those that represent you in all Courts, anywhere in America or the World.

I am fully engaged in my Religious Rights and in all my Affairs. I, Demarrius Crossley, hereby declare and affirm that I am a Sovereign human being, endowed with inherent rights and freedoms.

I, Demarrius Crossley, being duly sworn, depose and say:

Article 1: Introduction

I am making this affidavit to provide proof of my travel expenses and activities undertaken during my trip to [DESTINATION] from [DATE] to [DATE].

Article 2: Travel Details

I traveled to [DESTINATION] by [MODE OF TRANSPORTATION] and stayed at [ACCOMMODATION]. The purpose of my travel was [PURPOSE OF TRAVEL].

Article 3: Claim for Compensation

I incurred the following travel-related expenses:

1. Flights: $ [AMOUNT]
2. Accommodation: $[AMOUNT]
3. Food and transportation: $ [AMOUNT]

During my trip, I undertook the following activities:

1. [ACTIVITY 1]
3. [ACTIVITY 2]
4. [ACTIVITY 3]

Article 4: Verification

I hereby declare under penalty of perjury that the foregoing statements are true and accurate to the best of my knowledge and belief.

Again, this Affidavit is a Lawful Notification to you, the receivers, and requires your compliance to the demands made within. Failure to respond appropriately to the subject matter contained herein, if there is any disagreement with the document, is done under the penalties of perjury. Failure to respond within three (3) days, as stipulated, and rebut, with particularity, everything in this Affidavit with which there is disagreement, providing documentation as part of your ascertain, is a lawful, legal, and binding agreement by you and those that represent you in all Courts, anywhere in America or the World.

IN WITNESS WHEREOF, I have hereunto set my hand and seal, this [Date] Day of [Month], [Year].

Demarrius Crossley, Minister ______________________________

Illinois State }

}ss

Cook County }

Acknowledgement

As a Notary for (County and State), I do hereby certify that on the ____day of __________ 20______ the above-mentioned Affiant, Demarrius Crossley, Minister appeared before me and executed the foregoing document.

Witness my Hand and Seal:

____

Notary Public (SEAL)

Memorandum

To: Recipient Name
From: Minister Crossley of the UNMN Church
Date: (Insert Date)
Subject: **Affidavit To Travel in the Course of Life**

Purpose: This memorandum provides guidance on the creation and utilization of an Affidavit To Travel in the Course of Life. This affidavit is a sworn written statement that affirms an individual or organization to formally declare the right to move freely, and to ensure protection from unjust restraint or interference.

Key Components:

1. **Right to Travel:** A declaration of the right to travel and move freely.
2. **Freedom of Movement:** A confirmation of the freedom to move and travel without undue restriction.
3. **Protection from Unjust Restraint:** Protection from unjust restraint or interference with travel.

Importance: This affidavit serves as a formal declaration of one's intention to invoke my rights to protect individuals' rights and freedom, promoting personal autonomy and facilitating global interaction. This Affidavit is a Lawful Notice that the Affidavit To Travel in the Course of Life is a Religious Right and any interruption of it is a Violation of my Religious Rights.

Utilization:

1. **Protecting Travel Rights:** Use the affidavit to protect the right to travel and move freely.
2. **Ensuring Freedom of Movement:** Use the affidavit to ensure freedom to movement and prevent undue restriction.

3. **Safeguarding Individual Liberty:** Use the affidavit to safeguard individual liberty and autonomy in making travel decisions.

Benefits:

- Freedom to travel and move without undue restriction.
- Protection from unjust interference with travel plans.
- Personal autonomy and liberty in making travel decisions.

By utilizing the Affidavit To Travel in the Course of Life , individuals and organizations can protect their individual's rights and interests, the principle of freedom of movement and right to travel, the principle of individual liberty, and the principle of protecting individuals from interference with travel.

REFLECTION PAGE

1. What is one key insight you gained from reading the Affidavit and Memorandum?

2. How can you apply this insight to your work, studies, or daily life?

Affidavit of Privacy

Illinois State }

}ss

Cook County }

Name of Entity

Entity Address

City, State

[00000]

Notice to Agent is Notice to Principle/Notice to Principle is Notice to Agent

Sovereign Political Holder and Minister, over the age of 21 years, after being duly sworn according to law to tell the truth to the facts herein, I do hereby acknowledge and affirm the following: I, Affiant's Demarrius Crossley, am a Sovereign, without subjects. I am a Foreign Nation (not a person) who rules autonomously and am not subject to any entity or jurisdiction anywhere. I am a Sovereign Political Holder and a Minister. My authority for contracting is the age-old, timeless, and universal respect for the intrinsic power, property, and responsibilities of the Sovereign

Individual. I choose to comply with mutual respect, which serves to bring harmony to society. Demarrius Crossley, Minister, God Within Ministry

Address

City, State

[00000]

All national and state constitutions, laws, statutes, ordinances, regulations, rules, codes, and public policies, in all nations and states, are private copyrighted material. I do not possess a license or have the authority to use such copyrighted material, and consequently, that material does not have any authority over me, my property, or my personal affairs.

Again, this Affidavit is a Lawful Notification to you, the receivers, and requires your compliance to the demands made within. Failure to respond appropriately to the subject matter contained herein, if there is any disagreement with the document, is done under the penalties of perjury. Failure to respond within three (3) days, as stipulated, and rebut, with particularity, everything in this Affidavit with which there is disagreement, providing documentation as part of your ascertain, is a lawful, legal, and binding agreement by you and those that represent you in all Courts, anywhere in America or the World.

I am fully engaged in my Religious Rights and in all my Affairs. I, Demarrius Crossley, hereby declare and affirm that I am a Sovereign human being, endowed with inherent rights and freedoms.

I, Demarrius Crossley, being duly sworn, depose and say:

Article 1: Introduction

I am making this affidavit to provide proof of my commitment to maintaining confidentiality and protecting sensitive information.

Article 2: Privacy Commitment

I hereby affirm that I will maintain the confidentiality and security of all sensitive information entrusted to me. I will take all necessary measures to ensure the protection of such information, including encryption and secure storage.

Article 3: Confidentiality Agreement

I confirm that I have read and understood the confidentiality agreement and acknowledge my obligations to maintain confidentiality.

Article 4: Verification

I hereby declare under penalty of perjury that the foregoing statements are true and accurate to the best of my knowledge and belief.

Again, this Affidavit is a Lawful Notification to you, the receivers, and requires your compliance to the demands made within. Failure to respond appropriately to the subject matter contained herein, if there is any disagreement with the document, is done under the penalties of perjury. Failure to respond within three (3) days, as stipulated, and rebut, with particularity, everything in this Affidavit with which there is disagreement, providing documentation as part of your ascertain, is a lawful, legal, and binding agreement by you and those that represent you in all Courts, anywhere in America or the World.

IN WITNESS WHEREOF, I have hereunto set my hand and seal, this [Date] Day of [Month], [Year].

Demarrius Crossley, Minister ______________________________

Illinois State }

}ss

Cook County }

Acknowledgement

As a Notary for (County and State), I do hereby certify that on the ____day of __________ 20______ the above-mentioned Affiant, Demarrius Crossley, Minister appeared before me and executed the foregoing document.

Witness my Hand and Seal:

____

Notary Public (SEAL)

Memorandum

To: Recipient Name
From: Minister Crossley of the UNMN Church
Date: (Insert Date)
Subject: **Affidavit of Privacy**

Purpose: This memorandum provides guidance on the creation and utilization of an Affidavit of Privacy. This affidavit is a sworn written statement that affirms an individual or organization to formally declare commitment to protecting individuals' right to privacy and maintaining confidentiality.

Key Components:

1. **Right to Privacy:** A declaration of the right to privacy and protection of Personal information.
2. **Confidentiality:** A commitment to maintaining confidentiality and protecting Personal information.
3. **Data Protection:** Protection or personal data from unauthorized access, disclosure, or misuse.

Importance: This affidavit serves as a formal declaration of one's intention to invoke my rights to protect individuals' right to privacy, maintain trust and confidence, and prevent harm. This Affidavit is a Lawful Notice that the Affidavit of Privacy is a Religious Right and any interruption of it is a Violation of my Religious Rights.

Utilization:

4. **Protecting Personal Information:** Use the affidavit to protect personal information from unauthorized access.
5. **Maintaining Confidentiality:** Use the affidavit to maintain confidentiality and respect individuals' right to privacy.
6. **Securing Personal Data:** Use the affidavit to personal data and prevent breaches of privacy.

Benefits:

- Protection of personal information from unauthorized access, disclosure, or misuse.
- Trust and Confidence in individuals and organizations that handle personal information.
- Prevention of identity theft and other forms of cybercrime.

By utilizing the Affidavit of Privacy, individuals and organizations can protect their individual's rights and interests, the principle of respecting individuals right to privacy, the principle of maintain confidentiality, and the principle of protecting personal data.

REFLECTION PAGE

1. What is one key insight you gained from reading the Affidavit and Memorandum?

2. How can you apply this insight to your work, studies, or daily life?

Affidavit of Confidentiality from Evasion

Illinois State }

}ss

Cook County }

Name of Entity

Entity Address

City, State

[00000]

Notice to Agent is Notice to Principle/Notice to Principle is Notice to Agent

Sovereign Political Holder and Minister, over the age of 21 years, after being duly sworn according to law to tell the truth to the facts herein, I do hereby acknowledge and affirm the following: I, Affiant's Demarrius Crossley, am a Sovereign, without subjects. I am a Foreign Nation (not a person) who rules autonomously and am not subject to any entity or jurisdiction anywhere. I am a Sovereign Political Holder and a Minister. My authority for contracting is the age-old, timeless, and universal respect for the intrinsic power, property, and responsibilities of the Sovereign

Individual. I choose to comply with mutual respect, which serves to bring harmony to society. Demarrius Crossley, Minister, God Within Ministry

Address

City, State

[00000]

All national and state constitutions, laws, statutes, ordinances, regulations, rules, codes, and public policies, in all nations and states, are private copyrighted material. I do not possess a license or have the authority to use such copyrighted material, and consequently, that material does not have any authority over me, my property, or my personal affairs.

Again, this Affidavit is a Lawful Notification to you, the receivers, and requires your compliance to the demands made within. Failure to respond appropriately to the subject matter contained herein, if there is any disagreement with the document, is done under the penalties of perjury. Failure to respond within three (3) days, as stipulated, and rebut, with particularity, everything in this Affidavit with which there is disagreement, providing documentation as part of your ascertain, is a lawful, legal, and binding agreement by you and those that represent you in all Courts, anywhere in America or the World.

I am fully engaged in my Religious Rights and in all my Affairs. I, Demarrius Crossley, hereby declare and affirm that I am a Sovereign human being, endowed with inherent rights and freedoms.

I, Demarrius Crossley, being duly sworn, depose and say:

Article 1: Introduction

I am making this affidavit to provide proof of my commitment to maintaining confidentiality and cooperating fully with investigations or inquiries.

Article 2: Confidentiality Commitment

I hereby affirm that I will maintain the confidentiality and security of all sensitive information entrusted to me. I will take all necessary measures to ensure the protection of such information and prevent evasion or concealment.

Article 3: Non-Evasion and Non-Concealment

I hereby affirm that I will not evade or conceal information relevant to an investigation or inquiry. I acknowledge my obligations to provide truthful and accurate information.

Article 4: Verification

I hereby declare under penalty of perjury that the foregoing statements are true and accurate to the best of my knowledge and belief.

Again, this Affidavit is a Lawful Notification to you, the receivers, and requires your compliance to the demands made within. Failure to respond appropriately to the subject matter contained herein, if there is any disagreement with the document, is done under the penalties of perjury. Failure to respond within three (3) days, as stipulated, and rebut, with particularity, everything in this Affidavit with which there is disagreement, providing documentation as part of your ascertain, is a lawful, legal, and binding agreement by you and those that represent you in all Courts, anywhere in America or the World.

IN WITNESS WHEREOF, I have hereunto set my hand and seal, this [Date] Day of [Month], [Year].

Demarrius Crossley, Minister ______________________________

Illinois State }

}ss

Cook County }

Acknowledgement

As a Notary for (County and State), I do hereby certify that on the ____day of _________ 20______ the above-mentioned Affiant, Demarrius Crossley, Minister appeared before me and executed the foregoing document.

Witness my Hand and Seal:

____

Notary Public (SEAL)

Memorandum

To: Recipient Name
From: Minister Crossley of the UNMN Church
Date: (Insert Date)
Subject: **Affidavit of Confidentiality from Evasion**

Purpose: This memorandum provides guidance on the creation and utilization of an Affidavit of Confidentiality from Evasion. This affidavit is a sworn written statement that affirms an individual or organization to formally declare commitment to maintaining confidentiality and protecting sensitive information from unauthorized disclosure or evasion.

Key Components:

4. **Confidentiality Commitment:** A declaration of commitment to maintaining confidentiality.
5. **Protection from Unauthorized Disclosure:** Protection from unauthorized disclosure or evasion of confidential information.
6. **Non-Disclosure Agreement:** Confirmation of non-disclosure agreement regarding confidential information.

Importance: This affidavit serves as a formal declaration of one's intention to invoke my rights to protect sensitive information, maintain trust and reliability, and prevent harm from breaches of confidentiality. This Affidavit is a Lawful Notice that the Affidavit of Confidentiality from Evasion is a Religious Right and any interruption of it is a Violation of my Religious Rights.

Utilization:

- **Protecting Sensitive Information:** Use the affidavit to protect sensitive information from unauthorized disclosure.
- **Maintaining Confidentiality:** Use the affidavit to maintain confidentiality and prevent breaches of trust.
- **Securing Confidential Relationships:** Use the affidavit to secure confidential relationships and protect sensitive information.

Benefits:

- Protection of confidential information from unauthorized disclosure or evasion.
- Trust and Reliability in confidential relationships.
- Prevention of breaches of confidentiality and protection of sensitive information.

By utilizing the Affidavit of Confidentiality from Evasion, individuals and organizations can protect their individual rights and interests, the principle of confidentiality, the principle of non-disclosure, and the principle of trust and reliance.

REFLECTION PAGE

1. What is one key insight you gained from reading the Affidavit and Memorandum?

____

____

____

____

2. How can you apply this insight to your work, studies, or daily life?

____

____

____

____

Affidavit To Hold/Control one's Property

Illinois State }

}ss

Cook County }

Name of Entity

Entity Address

City, State

[00000]

Notice to Agent is Notice to Principle/Notice to Principle is Notice to Agent

Sovereign Political Holder and Minister, over the age of 21 years, after being duly sworn according to law to tell the truth to the facts herein, I do hereby acknowledge and affirm the following: I, Affiant's Demarrius Crossley, am a Sovereign, without subjects. I am a Foreign Nation (not a person) who rules autonomously and am not subject to any entity or jurisdiction anywhere. I am a Sovereign Political Holder and a Minister. My authority for contracting is the age-old, timeless, and universal respect for the intrinsic power, property, and responsibilities of the Sovereign

Individual. I choose to comply with mutual respect, which serves to bring harmony to society. Demarrius Crossley, Minister, God Within Ministry

Address

City, State

[00000]

All national and state constitutions, laws, statutes, ordinances, regulations, rules, codes, and public policies, in all nations and states, are private copyrighted material. I do not possess a license or have the authority to use such copyrighted material, and consequently, that material does not have any authority over me, my property, or my personal affairs.

Again, this Affidavit is a Lawful Notification to you, the receivers, and requires your compliance to the demands made within. Failure to respond appropriately to the subject matter contained herein, if there is any disagreement with the document, is done under the penalties of perjury. Failure to respond within three (3) days, as stipulated, and rebut, with particularity, everything in this Affidavit with which there is disagreement, providing documentation as part of your ascertain, is a lawful, legal, and binding agreement by you and those that represent you in all Courts, anywhere in America or the World.

I am fully engaged in my Religious Rights and in all my Affairs. I, Demarrius Crossley, hereby declare and affirm that I am a Sovereign human being, endowed with inherent rights and freedoms.

I, Demarrius Crossley, being duly sworn, depose and say:

Article 1: Introduction

I am making this affidavit to provide proof of my ownership and control of the property located at [PROPERTY ADDRESS].

Article 2: Property Description

The property is a [TYPE OF PROPERTY] with the following description: [DESCRIPTION].

Article 3: Ownership/Control

I hereby affirm that I am the sole owner of the property and have full control over it.

Article 4: Verification

I hereby declare under penalty of perjury that the foregoing statements are true and accurate to the best of my knowledge and belief.

Again, this Affidavit is a Lawful Notification to you, the receivers, and requires your compliance to the demands made within. Failure to respond appropriately to the subject matter contained herein, if there is any disagreement with the document, is done under the penalties of perjury. Failure to respond within three (3) days, as stipulated, and rebut, with particularity, everything in this Affidavit with which there is disagreement, providing documentation as part of your ascertain, is lawful, legal, and binding agreement by you and those that represent you in all Courts, anywhere in America or the World.

IN WITNESS WHEREOF, I have hereunto set my hand and seal, this [Date] Day of [Month], [Year].

Demarrius Crossley, Minister

____

Illinois State }

}ss

Cook County }

Acknowledgement

As a Notary for (County and State), I do hereby certify that on the ____day of __________ 20______ the above-mentioned Affiant, Demarrius Crossley, Minister appeared before me and executed the foregoing document.

Witness my Hand and Seal:

____

Notary Public (SEAL)

Memorandum

To: Recipient Name
From: Minister Crossley of the UNMN Church
Date: (Insert Date)
Subject: **Affidavit To Hold/Control one's Property**

Purpose: This memorandum provides guidance on the creation and utilization of an Affidavit To Hold/Control One's Property. This affidavit is a sworn written statement that affirms an individual or organization to formally declare the right to self - defense from imminent threat and ensure the protection of oneself and others.

Key Components:

1. **Right to Property:** A declaration of the right to possess, use, and control one's property.
2. **Ownership and Control:** A confirmation of ownership and control over one's property.
3. **Protection from Interference:** Protection from unauthorized interference or deprivation of property.

Importance: This affidavit serves as a formal declaration of one's intention to invoke my rights to protect individual rights, uphold property rights, and promote economic stability and security. This Affidavit is a Lawful Notice that the Affidavit To Hold/Control One's Property is a Religious Right and any interruption of it is a Violation of my Religious Rights.

Utilization:

1. **Protecting Property Rights:** Use the affidavit to protect personal rights and prevent unauthorized interference.
2. **Asserting Ownership:** Use the affidavit to assert ownership and control one's property.

3. **Securing interests:** Use the affidavit to secure interests and prevent disputes regarding property.

Benefits:

- Protection of property from unauthorized interference or deprivation.
- Autonomy and control over one's property.
- Security and Stability in proper ownership.

By utilizing the Affidavit of Hold/Control One's Property , individuals and organizations can protect their individual's rights and interests, the principle of property rights, the principle of autonomy, and the principle of protection.

REFLECTION PAGE

1. What is one key insight you gained from reading the Affidavit and Memorandum?

____

____

____

____

2. How can you apply this insight to your work, studies, or daily life?

____

____

____

____

Affidavit Of Self-Defense from Threat

Illinois State }

}ss

Cook County }

Name of Entity

Entity Address

City, State

[00000]

Notice to Agent is Notice to Principle/Notice to Principle is Notice to Agent

Sovereign Political Holder and Minister, over the age of 21 years, after being duly sworn according to law to tell the truth to the facts herein, I do hereby acknowledge and affirm the following: I, Affiant's Demarrius Crossley, am a Sovereign, without subjects. I am a Foreign Nation (not a person) who rules autonomously and am not subject to any entity or jurisdiction anywhere. I am a Sovereign Political Holder and a Minister. My authority for contracting is the age-old, timeless, and universal respect for the intrinsic power, property, and responsibilities of the Sovereign

Individual. I choose to comply with mutual respect, which serves to bring harmony to society. Demarrius Crossley, Minister, God Within Ministry

Address

City, State

[00000]

All national and state constitutions, laws, statutes, ordinances, regulations, rules, codes, and public policies, in all nations and states, are private copyrighted material. I do not possess a license or have the authority to use such copyrighted material, and consequently, that material does not have any authority over me, my property, or my personal affairs.

Again, this Affidavit is a Lawful Notification to you, the receivers, and requires your compliance to the demands made within. Failure to respond appropriately to the subject matter contained herein, if there is any disagreement with the document, is done under the penalties of perjury. Failure to respond within three (3) days, as stipulated, and rebut, with particularity, everything in this Affidavit with which there is disagreement, providing documentation as part of your ascertain, is a lawful, legal, and binding agreement by you and those that represent you in all Courts, anywhere in America or the World.

I am fully engaged in my Religious Rights and in all my Affairs. I, Demarrius Crossley, hereby declare and affirm that I am a Sovereign human being, endowed with inherent rights and freedoms.

I, Demarrius Crossley, being duly sworn, depose and say:

Article 1: Introduction

I am making this affidavit to provide evidence of the threats I have received and the self-defense measures I have taken.

Article 2: Property Description

I have been receiving threats from [NAME OF PERSON/ENTITY] since [DATE]. The threats have been made through [METHOD OF THREAT] and have included [DESCRIPTION OF THREATS].

Article 3: Self-Defense Measures

I have taken the following self-defense measures: [DESCRIPTION OF SELF-DEFENSE MEASURES]. I believe these measures are necessary to protect myself from harm.

Article 4: Verification

I hereby declare under penalty of perjury that the foregoing statements are true and accurate to the best of my knowledge and belief.

Again, this Affidavit is a Lawful Notification to you, the receivers, and requires your compliance to the demands made within. Failure to respond appropriately to the subject matter contained herein if there is any disagreement with the document is done under the penalties of perjury. Failure to respond within three (3) days, as stipulated, and rebut, with particularity, everything in this Affidavit with which there is disagreement, providing documentation as part of your ascertain, is a lawful, legal, and binding agreement by you and those that represent you in all Courts, anywhere in America or the World.

IN WITNESS WHEREOF, I have hereunto set my hand and seal, this [Date] Day of [Month], [Year].

Demarrius Crossley, Minister

____

Illinois State }

}ss

Cook County }

Acknowledgement

As a Notary for (County and State), I do hereby certify that on the ____day of __________ 20______ the above-mentioned Affiant, Demarrius Crossley, Minister appeared before me and executed the foregoing document.

Witness my Hand and Seal:

____

Notary Public (SEAL)

Memorandum

To: Recipient Name
From: Minister Crossley of the UNMN Church
Date: (Insert Date)
Subject: **Affidavit of Self - Defense from Threat**

Purpose: This memorandum provides guidance on the creation and utilization of Affidavit of Self Defense from Threat. This affidavit is a sworn written statement that affirms an individual or organization to formally declare the right to self - defense from imminent threat and ensure the protection of oneself and others.

Key Components:

1. **Right to Self - Defense:** A declaration of the right to defend oneself from imminent harm or threat.
2. **Imminent Threat:** A requirement for an imminent threat of harm or danger.
3. **Reasonable Force:** A commitment to using reasonable force in self - defense.

Importance: This affidavit serves as a formal declaration of one's intention to invoke my rights to protect human life and safety, prevent harm to others, and uphold personal rights. This Affidavit is a Lawful Notice that the Affidavit of Self Defense from Threat is a Religious Right and any interruption of it is a Violation of my Religious Rights.

Utilization:

1. **Protecting Oneself:** Use the affidavit to protect oneself from imminent harm or threat.
2. **Defending Against Attack:** Use the affidavit to defend against and attach or aggression.

3. **Preventing Harm:** Use the affidavit to prevent harm or injury to oneself or others.

Benefits:

- Protection from imminent harm or threat.
- The right to defend oneself and one's loved ones.
- Preservation of safety and well - being.

By utilizing the Affidavit of Self Defense from Threat, individuals and organizations can protect their individual's rights and interests, the principle of self - defense, the principle of imminence, and the principle of reasonableness and the use of proportionate force.

REFLECTION PAGE

1. What is one key insight you gained from reading the Affidavit and Memorandum?

2. How can you apply this insight to your work, studies, or daily life?

Affidavit of Due Process of Law

Illinois State }

}ss

Cook County }

Name of Entity

Entity Address

City, State

[00000]

Notice to Agent is Notice to Principle/Notice to Principle is Notice to Agent

Sovereign Political Holder and Minister, over the age of 21 years, after being duly sworn according to law to tell the truth to the facts herein, I do hereby acknowledge and affirm the following: I, Affiant's Demarrius Crossley, am a Sovereign, without subjects. I am a Foreign Nation (not a person) who rules autonomously and am not subject to any entity or jurisdiction anywhere. I am a Sovereign Political Holder, a Minister. My authority for contracting is the age-old, timeless, and universal respect for the intrinsic power, property, and responsibilities of the Sovereign

Individual. I choose to comply with mutual respect, which serves to bring harmony to society. Demarrius Crossley, Minister, God Within Ministry

Address

City, State

[00000]

All national and state constitutions, laws, statutes, ordinances, regulations, rules, codes, and public policies, in all nations and states, are private copyrighted material. I do not possess a license or have the authority to use such copyrighted material, and consequently, that material does not have any authority over me, my property, or my personal affairs.

Again, this Affidavit is a Lawful Notification to you, the receivers, and requires your compliance to the demands made within. Failure to respond appropriately to the subject matter contained herein if there is any disagreement with the document, is done under the penalties of perjury. Failure to respond within three (3) days, as stipulated, and rebut, with particularity, everything in this Affidavit with which there is disagreement, providing documentation as part of your ascertain, is a lawful, legal, and binding agreement by you and those that represent you in all Courts, anywhere in America or the World.

I am fully engaged in my Religious Rights and in all my Affairs. I, Demarrius Crossley, hereby declare and affirm that I am a Sovereign human being, endowed with inherent rights and freedoms.

I, Demarrius Crossley, being duly sworn, depose and say:

Article 1: Introduction

I am making this affidavit to provide evidence that my due process rights have been violated by

[NAME OF ENTITY/INDIVIDUAL].

Article 2: Description of Due Process Issue

I was denied a fair hearing in connection with [DESCRIPTION OF ISSUES]. I was not provided with proper notice or an opportunity to be heard.

Article 3: Facts and Circumstances

The facts and circumstances surrounding this issue are as follows: [DESCRIPTION OF FACTS AND CIRCUMSTANCES].

Article 4: Verification

I hereby declare under penalty of perjury that the foregoing statements are true and accurate to the best of my knowledge and belief.

I, Demarrius Crossley, have complete Sovereign Immunity; and therefore, my power to contract and undo contracts is unlimited. My Religious Rights and Freedom must be fully and completely respected. Failure to do so will require that I receive $7,500,000.00 from each violator for each violation that occurs.

Again, this Affidavit is a Lawful Notification to you, the receivers, and requires your compliance to the demands made within. Failure to respond appropriately to the subject matter contained herein, if there is any disagreement with the document, is done under the penalties of perjury. Failure to respond within three (3) days, as stipulated, and rebut, with particularity, everything in this Affidavit with which there is disagreement, providing documentation as part of your ascertain, is a lawful, legal, and binding agreement by you and those that represent you in all Courts, anywhere in America or the World.

IN WITNESS WHEREOF, I have hereunto set my hand and seal, this [Date] Day of [Month], [Year].

Demarrius Crossley, Minister ______________________________

Illinois State }

}ss

Cook County }

Acknowledgement

As a Notary for (County and State), I do hereby certify that on the ____day of __________ 20______ the above-mentioned Affiant, Demarrius Crossley, Minister appeared before me and executed the foregoing document.

Witness my Hand and Seal:

____

Notary Public (SEAL)

Memorandum

To: Recipient Name
From: Minister Crossley of the UNMN Church
Date: (Insert Date)
Subject: **Affidavit of Due Process of Law**

Purpose: This memorandum provides guidance on the creation and utilization of an Affidavit of Due Process of Law. This affidavit is a sworn written statement that affirms an individual or organization to formally declare the right to due process of law and ensure fair treatment under the law.

Key Components:

1. **Notice and Hearing:** A declaration of the right to notice and a fair hearing before any deprivation of life, liberty, or property.
2. **Fair and Impartial Tribunal:** A requirement for a fair and impartial tribunal to decide cases or disputes.
3. **Equal Protection:** A commitment to equal protection under the law.

Importance: This affidavit serves as a formal declaration of one's intention to invoke my rights to protect individual rights, uphold the rule of law, and maintain public trust in the justice system. This Affidavit is a Lawful Notice that the <u>Affidavit of Due Process of Law</u> is a Religious Right and any interruption of it is a Violation of my Religious Rights.

Utilization:

1. **Protecting Rights:** Use the affidavit to Protect individual rights and freedoms by ensuring due process.
2. **Ensuring Fair Proceedings:** Use the affidavit to ensure fair proceedings and due process in cases or disputes.
3. **Preventing Abuse of Power:** Use the affidavit to Prevent abuse of power and arbitrary actions.

Benefits:

- Protection of individual rights and freedoms.
- Fair treatment under the law and protection against arbitrary actions.
- A just outcome based on a thorough consideration of evidence and arguments.

By utilizing the Affidavit of Due Process of Law, individuals and organizations can protect their individual's rights and interests, the principle of due process and fair treatment, the principle of rule of law and protection, and the principle of protection of individual rights and freedoms.

REFLECTION PAGE

1. What is one key insight you gained from reading the Affidavit and Memorandum?

2. How can you apply this insight to your work, studies, or daily life?

Affidavit of Opportunity to Defend

Illinois State }

}ss

Cook County }

Name of Entity

Entity Address

City, State

[00000]

Notice to Agent is Notice to Principle/Notice to Principle is Notice to Agent

Sovereign Political Holder and Minister, over the age of 21 years, after being duly sworn according to law to tell the truth to the facts herein, I do hereby acknowledge and affirm the following: I, Affiant's Demarrius Crossley, am a Sovereign, without subjects. I am a Foreign Nation (not a person) who rules autonomously and am not subject to any entity or jurisdiction anywhere. I am a Sovereign Political Holder, a Minister. My authority for contracting is the age-old, timeless, and universal respect for the intrinsic power, property, and responsibilities of the Sovereign

Individual. I choose to comply with mutual respect, which serves to bring harmony to society. Demarrius Crossley, Minister, God Within Ministry

Address

City, State

[00000]

All national and state constitutions, laws, statutes, ordinances, regulations, rules, codes, and public policies, in all nations and states, are private copyrighted material. I do not possess a license or have the authority to use such copyrighted material, and consequently, that material does not have any authority over me, my property, or my personal affairs.

Again, this Affidavit is a Lawful Notification to you, the receivers, and requires your compliance to the demands made within. Failure to respond appropriately to the subject matter contained herein if there is any disagreement with the document, is done under the penalties of perjury. Failure to respond within three (3) days, as stipulated, and rebut, with particularity, everything in this Affidavit with which there is disagreement, providing documentation as part of your ascertain, is a lawful, legal, and binding agreement by you and those that represent you in all Courts, anywhere in America or the World.

I am fully engaged in my Religious Rights and in all my Affairs. I, Demarrius Crossley, hereby declare and affirm that I am a Sovereign human being, endowed with inherent rights and freedoms.

I, Demarrius Crossley, being duly sworn, depose and say:

Article 1: Introduction

I am making this affidavit to provide evidence that I was denied the opportunity to defend myself against accusations made by [NAME OF ACCUSER].

Article 2: Description of Accusations/Allegations

The accusations made against me include [DESCRIPTION OF ACCUSATIONS]. I was not provided with any evidence or supporting documentation.

Article 3: Denial of Opportunity to Defend

I was denied the opportunity to defend myself. [DESCRIPTION OF DENIAL]. I was not given any notice or opportunity to respond.

Article 4: Attempts to Defend

I attempted to defend myself by [DESCRIPTION OF ATTEMPTS]. However, my efforts were ignored or dismissed.

Article 5: Verification

I hereby declare under penalty of perjury that the foregoing statements are true and accurate to the best of my knowledge and belief.

Again, this Affidavit is Lawful Notification to you, the receivers, and requires your compliance to the demands made within. Failure to respond appropriately to the subject matter contained herein if there is any disagreement with the document, is done under the penalties of perjury. Failure to respond within three (3) days, as stipulated, and rebut, with particularity, everything in this Affidavit with which there is disagreement, providing documentation as part of your ascertain, is lawful, legal and, binding agreement by you and those that represent you in all Courts, anywhere in America or the World.

IN WITNESS WHEREOF, I have hereunto set my hand and seal, this [Date] Day of [Month], [Year].

Demarrius Crossley, Minister ____________________________

Illinois State }

}ss

Cook County }

Acknowledgement

As a Notary for (County and State), I do hereby certify that on the ____day of _________ 20______ the above-mentioned Affiant, Demarrius Crossley, Minister appeared before me and executed the foregoing document.

Witness my Hand and Seal:

____

Notary Public (SEAL)

Memorandum

To: Recipient Name
From: Minister Crossley of the UNMN Church
Date: (Insert Date)
Subject: **Affidavit of Opportunity to Defend**

Purpose: This memorandum provides guidance on the creation and utilization of an Affidavit for Opportunity to Defend. This affidavit is a sworn written statement that Affirms an individual or organization to formally declare the opportunity to defend oneself against accusations or charges and ensure d due process and fair treatment under the law.

Key Components:

1. **Right to Defense:** A declaration of the right to defend oneself against accusations or charges.
2. **Notice of Accusations:** A requirement for adequate notice of accusations or charges.
3. **Opportunity to Respond:** An opportunity to respond to accusations or charges and present a defense.

Importance: This affidavit serves as a formal declaration of one's intention to invoke my rights to protect individual rights, upholding due process and fair treatment, and maintain public trust in the justice system. This Affidavit is a Lawful Notice that the <u>Affidavit of Opportunity to Defend</u> is a Religious Right and any interruption of it is a Violation of my Religious Rights.

Utilization:

1. **Protecting Rights:** Use the affidavit to protect individual rights and freedoms by ensuring an opportunity to defend oneself.
2. **Ensuring Fair Proceedings:** Use the affidavit to ensure fair proceedings and due Process in cases or disputes.

3. **Preventing Miscarriages of Justice:** Use the affidavit to Protect and prevent miscarriages of justice and wrongful convictions.

Benefits:

- Protection of individual rights and freedoms.
- A fair hearing with an opportunity to defend oneself.
- A just outcome based on a thorough consideration of evidence and arguments.

By utilizing the Affidavit of Opportunity to Defend, individuals and organizations can protect their individual's rights and interests, the principle of due process, the principle of right to a fair hearing, and the principle of protection of individual rights and freedoms.

REFLECTION PAGE

1. What is one key insight you gained from reading the Affidavit and Memorandum?

2. How can you apply this insight to your work, studies, or daily life?

Affidavit of Presumption of Innocence

Illinois State }

}ss

Cook County }

Name of Entity

Entity Address

City, State

[00000]

Notice to Agent is Notice to Principle/Notice to Principle is Notice to Agent

Sovereign Political Holder and Minister, over the age of 21 years, after being duly sworn according to law to tell the truth to the facts herein, I do hereby acknowledge and affirm the following: I, Affiant's Demarrius Crossley, am a Sovereign, without subjects. I am a Foreign Nation (not a person) who rules autonomously and am not subject to any entity or jurisdiction anywhere. I am a Sovereign Political Holder, a Minister. My authority for contracting is the age-old, timeless, and universal respect for the intrinsic power, property, and responsibilities of the Sovereign

Individual. I choose to comply with mutual respect, which serves to bring harmony to society. Demarrius Crossley, Minister, God Within Ministry

Address

City, State

[00000]

All national and state constitutions, laws, statutes, ordinances, regulations, rules, codes, and public policies, in all nations and states are private copyrighted material. I do not possess a license or have the authority to use such copyrighted material, and consequently, that material does not have any authority over me, my property, or my personal affairs.

Again, this Affidavit is a Lawful Notification to you, the receivers, and requires your compliance to the demands made within. Failure to respond appropriately to the subject matter contained herein if there is any disagreement with the document, is done under the penalties of perjury. Failure to respond within three (3) days, as stipulated, and rebut, with particularity, everything in this Affidavit with which there is disagreement, providing documentation as part of your ascertain, is a lawful, legal, and binding agreement by you and those that represent you in all Courts, anywhere in America or the World.

I am fully engaged in my Religious Rights and in all my Affairs. I, Demarrius Crossley, hereby declare and affirm that I am a Sovereign human being, endowed with inherent rights and freedoms.

I, Demarrius Crossley, being duly sworn, depose and say:

Article 1: Introduction

I am making this affidavit to assert my presumption of innocence in the face of allegations made against me by [NAME OF ACCUSER].

Article 2: Assertion of Presumption of Innocence

I hereby affirm that I am entitled to the presumption of innocence as guaranteed by the [STATE/COUNTRY] Constitution. I am innocent of the allegations made against me and deny any wrongdoing.

Article 3: Denial of Allegations

I deny the allegations made against me and assert that they are without merit. I have evidence and facts that support my denial, including [DESCRIPTION OF EVIDENCE].

Article 4: Verification

I hereby declare under penalty of perjury that the foregoing statements are true and accurate to the best of my knowledge and belief.

I, Demarrius Crossley, have complete Sovereign Immunity; and therefore, my power to contract and undo contracts is unlimited. My Religious Rights and Freedom must be fully and completely respected. Failure to do so will require that I receive $7,500,000.00 from each violator, for each violation that occurs.

Again, this Affidavit is a Lawful Notification to you, the receivers, and requires your compliance to the demands made within. Failure to respond appropriately to the subject matter contained herein if there is any disagreement with the document, is done under the penalties of perjury. Failure to respond within three (3) days, as stipulated, and rebut, with particularity, everything in this Affidavit with which there is disagreement, providing documentation as part of your ascertain, is a lawful, legal, and binding agreement by you and those that represent you in all Courts, anywhere in America or the World.

IN WITNESS WHEREOF, I have hereunto set my hand and seal, this [Date] Day of [Month], [Year].

Demarrius Crossley, Minister ______________________________

Illinois State }

}ss

Cook County }

Acknowledgement

As a Notary for (County and State), I do hereby certify that on the ____day of __________ 20______ the above-mentioned Affiant, Demarrius Crossley, Minister appeared before me and executed the foregoing document.

Witness my Hand and Seal:

____

Notary Public (SEAL)

Memorandum

To: Recipient Name
From: Minister Crossley of the UNMN Church
Date: (Insert Date)
Subject: **Affidavit of Presumption of Innocence**

Purpose: This memorandum provides guidance on the creation and utilization of an Affidavit of Presumption of Innocence. This affidavit is a sworn written statement that affirms an individual or organization to formally declare the presumption of innocence and ensure that the burden of proof lies with accuser or prosecution.

Key Components:

1. **Presumption of Innocence:** A declaration of the presumption of innocence until proven guilty beyond a reasonable doubt.
2. **Burden of Proof:** A commitment to placing the burden of proof on the accuser or prosecution.
3. **Protection of Rights:** Protection of individual rights and freedoms.

Importance: This affidavit serves as a formal declaration of one's intention to invoke my rights to protect individual rights, upholding due process and fair treatment, and maintain public trust in the justice system. This Affidavit is a Lawful Notice that the Affidavit of Presumption of Innocence is a Religious Right and any interruption of it is a Violation of my Religious Rights.

Utilization:

1. **Protecting Rights:** Use the affidavit to protect individual rights and freedoms by ensuring the presumption of innocence.
2. **Ensuring Fair Trail:** Use the affidavit to ensure a fair trial by placing the burden of proof on the accuser or prosecution.

3. **Preventing Miscarriages of Justice:** Use the affidavit to protect and prevent miscarriages of justice and wrongful convictions.

Benefits:

- Protection of the innocent from wrongful conviction.
- A fair trial with the burden of proof on the accuser or prosecution.
- Upholding justice and the rule of law.

By utilizing the Affidavit of Presumption of Innocence, individuals and organizations can protect their individual's rights and interests, the principle of upholding due process, the principle of maintaining public trust, and the principle of protection of individual rights and freedoms.

REFLECTION PAGE

1. What is one key insight you gained from reading the Affidavit and Memorandum?

____

____

____

____

2. How can you apply this insight to your work, studies, or daily life?

____

____

____

____

Affidavit of To Not Be Detained

Illinois State }

}ss

Cook County }

Name of Entity

Entity Address

City, State

[00000]

Notice to Agent is Notice to Principle/Notice to Principle is Notice to Agent

Sovereign Political Holder and Minister, over the age of 21 years, after being duly sworn according to law to tell the truth to the facts herein, I do hereby acknowledge and affirm the following: I, Affiant's Demarrius Crossley, am a Sovereign, without subjects. I am a Foreign Nation (not a person) who rules autonomously and am not subject to any entity or jurisdiction anywhere. I am a Sovereign Political Holder, a Minister. My authority for contracting is the age-old, timeless, and universal respect for the intrinsic power, property, and responsibilities of the Sovereign

Individual. I choose to comply with mutual respect, which serves to bring harmony to society. Demarrius Crossley, Minister, God Within Ministry

Address

City, State

[00000]

All national and state constitutions, laws, statutes, ordinances, regulations, rules, codes, and public policies, in all nations and states, are private copyrighted material. I do not possess a license or have the authority to use such copyrighted material, and consequently, that material does not have any authority over me, my property, or my personal affairs.

Again, this Affidavit is a Lawful Notification to you, the receivers and requires your compliance to the demands made within. Failure to respond appropriately to the subject matter contained herein if there is any disagreement with the document, is done under the penalties of perjury. Failure to respond within three (3) days, as stipulated, and rebut, with particularity, everything in this Affidavit with which there is disagreement, providing documentation as part of your ascertain, is a lawful, legal, and binding agreement by you and those that represent you in all Courts, anywhere in America or the World.

I am fully engaged in my Religious Rights and in all my Affairs. I, Demarrius Crossley, hereby declare and affirm that I am a Sovereign human being, endowed with inherent rights and freedoms.

I, Demarrius Crossley, being duly sworn, depose and say:

Article 1: Introduction

I am making this affidavit to assert my right to freedom from detention or arrest without due process.

Article 2: Assertion of Right to Freedom from Detention

I hereby affirm that I am entitled to the right to freedom [STATE/COUNTRY] Constitution. I have not committed any crime and have not been charged with any offense.

Article 3: Facts and Circumstances

I have been subjected to [DESCRIPTION OF DETENTION OR ARREST]. However, I was not provided with any evidence or justification for my detention. I believe that my detention was unlawful and violated my right to freedom from detention.

Article 4: Verification

I hereby declare under penalty of perjury that the foregoing statements are true and accurate to the best of my knowledge and belief.

I, Demarrius Crossley, have complete Sovereign Immunity; and therefore, my power to contract and undo contracts is unlimited. My Religious Rights and Freedom must be fully and completely respected. Failure to do so will require that I receive $7,500,000.00 from each violator, for each violation that occurs.

Again, this Affidavit is a Lawful Notification to you, the receivers, and requires your compliance to the demands made within. Failure to respond appropriately to the subject matter contained herein if there is any disagreement with the document, is done under the penalties of perjury. Failure to respond within three (3) days, as stipulated, and rebut, with particularity, everything in this Affidavit with which there is disagreement, providing documentation as part of your ascertain, is a lawful, legal, and binding agreement by you and those that represent you in all Courts, anywhere in America or the World.

IN WITNESS WHEREOF, I have hereunto set my hand and seal, this [Date] Day of [Month], [Year].

Demarrius Crossley, Minister ______________________________

Illinois State }

}ss

Cook County }

Acknowledgement

As a Notary for (County and State), I do hereby certify that on the ____day of __________ 20______ the above-mentioned Affiant, Demarrius Crossley, Minister appeared before me and executed the foregoing document.

Witness my Hand and Seal:

____

Notary Public (SEAL)

Memorandum

To: Recipient Name
From: Minister Crossley of the UNMN Church
Date: (Insert Date)
Subject: **Affidavit of To Not Be Detained**

Purpose: This memorandum provides guidance on the creation and utilization of an Affidavit OF To Not Be Detained. This affidavit is a sworn written statement that affirms an individual or organization to formally declare the right to protect against unlawful Detention and ensure due process and lawful procedures.

Key Components:

1. **Protection Against Unlawful Detention:** A declaration of protection against detention without lawful authority or just cause.
2. **Protection of Rights:** Protection of individual rights and freedoms.
3. **Due Process:** A commitment to due process and lawful procedures in any detention.

Importance: This affidavit serves as a formal declaration of one's intention to invoke my rights to protect individual rights, upholding due process and lawful procedures, and preventing miscarriages of justice. This Affidavit is a Lawful Notice that the Affidavit To Not Be Detained is a Religious Right and any interruption of it is a Violation of my Religious Rights.

Utilization:

1. **Protecting Rights:** Use the affidavit to protect individual rights and freedoms from unlawful detention.
2. **Ensuring Due Process:** Use the affidavit to ensure due process and lawful procedures.
3. **Preventing Abuse of Power:** Use the affidavit to prevent abuse of power and arbitrary arrest.

Benefits:

- Protection from detention without lawful authority or just cause.
- Due process and lawful procedures in any detention.
- Protection of individual rights and freedoms.

By utilizing the Affidavit of To Not Be Detained, individuals and organizations can protect their individual's rights and interests, the principle of due process clause, the principle of due process, and the principle of protection of individual rights and freedoms.

REFLECTION PAGE

1. What is one key insight you gained from reading the Affidavit and Memorandum?

2. How can you apply this insight to your work, studies, or daily life?

Affidavit To Not Be Arrested

Illinois State }

}ss

Cook County }

Name of Entity

Entity Address

City, State

[00000]

Notice to Agent is Notice to Principle/Notice to Principle is Notice to Agent

Sovereign Political Holder and Minister, over the age of 21 years, after being duly sworn according to law to tell the truth to the facts herein, I do hereby acknowledge and affirm the following: I, Affiant's Demarrius Crossley, am a Sovereign, without subjects. I am a Foreign Nation (not a person) who rules autonomously and am not subject to any entity or jurisdiction anywhere. I am a Sovereign Political Holder, a Minister. My authority for contracting is the age-old, timeless, and universal respect for the intrinsic power, property, and responsibilities of the Sovereign

Individual. I choose to comply with mutual respect, which serves to bring harmony to society. Demarrius Crossley, Minister, God Within Ministry

Address

City, State

[00000]

All national and state constitutions, laws, statutes, ordinances, regulations, rules, codes, and public policies, in all nations and states are private copyrighted material. I do not possess a license or have the authority to use such copyrighted material and consequently that material does not have any authority over me, my property, or my personal affairs.

Again, this Affidavit is a Lawful Notification to you, the receivers, and requires your compliance to the demands made within. Failure to respond appropriately to the subject matter contained herein if there is any disagreement with the document, is done under the penalties of perjury. Failure to respond within three (3) days, as stipulated, and rebut, with particularity, everything in this Affidavit with which there is disagreement, providing documentation as part of your ascertain, is a lawful, legal, and binding agreement by you and those that represent you in all Courts, anywhere in America or the World.

I am fully engaged in my Religious Rights and in all my Affairs. I, Demarrius Crossley, hereby declare and affirm that I am a Sovereign human being, endowed with inherent rights and freedoms.

I, Demarrius Crossley, being duly sworn, depose and say:

Article 1: Introduction

I am making this affidavit to assert my right to freedom from unlawful arrest or detention.

Article 2: Assertion of Right to Freedom from Arrest

I hereby affirm that I am entitled to the right to freedom from arrest as guaranteed by the [STATE/COUNTRY] Constitution. I have not committed any crime and have not been charged with any offense.

Article 3: Facts and Circumstances

I have been subjected to [DESCRIPTION OF ARREST OR DETENTION]. However, I was not provided with any evidence or justification for my arrest. I believe that my arrest was unlawful and violated my right to freedom from arrest.

Article 4: Verification

I hereby declare under penalty of perjury that the foregoing statements are true and accurate to the best of my knowledge and belief.

I, Demarrius Crossley, have complete Sovereign Immunity; and therefore, my power to contract and undo contracts is unlimited. My Religious Rights and Freedom must be fully and completely respected. Failure to do so will require that I receive $7,500,000.00 from each violator for each violation that occurs.

Again, this Affidavit is a Lawful Notification to you, the receivers, and requires your compliance to the demands made within. Failure to respond appropriately to the subject matter contained herein, if there is any disagreement with the document, is done under the penalties of perjury. Failure to respond within three (3) days, as stipulated, and rebut, with particularity, everything in this Affidavit with which there is disagreement, providing documentation as part of your ascertain, is a lawful, legal, and binding agreement by you and those that represent you in all Courts, anywhere in America or the World.

IN WITNESS WHEREOF, I have hereunto set my hand and seal, this [Date] Day of [Month], [Year].

Demarrius Crossley, Minister ______________________________

Illinois State }

}ss

Cook County }

Acknowledgement

As a Notary for (County and State), I do hereby certify that on the ____day of __________ 20______ the above-mentioned Affiant, Demarrius Crossley, Minister appeared before me and executed the foregoing document.

Witness my Hand and Seal:

____

Notary Public (SEAL)

Memorandum

To: Recipient Name
From: Minister Crossley of the UNMN Church
Date: (Insert Date)
Subject: **Affidavit To Not Be Arrested**

Purpose: This memorandum provides guidance on the creation and utilization of an Affidavit To Not Be Arrested. This affidavit is a sworn written statement that affirms an individual or organization to formally declare the right to protect against unlawful arrest and ensure due process and lawful procedures.

Key Components:

1. **Protect Against Unlawful Arrest:** A declaration of protection against arrest without probable cause for lawful authority.
2. **Protection of Rights:** Protection of individual rights and freedoms.
3. **Due Process:** A commitment to due process and lawful procedures in any arrest or detention.

Importance: This affidavit serves as a formal declaration of one's intention to invoke my rights to protect individual rights, upholding due process and lawful procedures, and preventing miscarriages of justice. This Affidavit is a Lawful Notice that the <u>Affidavit To Not Be Arrested</u> is a Religious Right and any interruption of it is a Violation of my Religious Rights.

Utilization:

1. **Protecting Privacy:** Use the affidavit to protect individual rights and freedoms from unlawful arrest.
2. **Ensuring Due Process:** Use the affidavit to ensure due process and lawful procedures.

3. **Preventing Abuse of Power:** Use the affidavit to prevent abuse of power and arbitrary arrest.

Benefits:

- Protection from arrest without probable cause or lawful authority.
- Due process and lawful procedures in any arrest or detention.
- Protection of individual rights and freedoms.

By utilizing the Affidavit To Not Be Arrested, individuals and organizations can protect their individual's rights and interests, the principle of probable cause, the principle of due process, and the principle of protection of individual rights and freedoms.

REFLECTION PAGE

1. What is one key insight you gained from reading the Affidavit and Memorandum?

2. How can you apply this insight to your work, studies, or daily life?

Affidavit To Not Be Searched

Illinois State }

}ss

Cook County }

Name of Entity

Entity Address

City, State

[00000]

Notice to Agent is Notice to Principle/Notice to Principle is Notice to Agent

Sovereign Political Holder and Minister, over the age of 21 years, after being duly sworn according to law to tell the truth to the facts herein, I do hereby acknowledge and affirm the following: I, Affiant's Demarrius Crossley, am a Sovereign, without subjects. I am a Foreign Nation (not a person) who rules autonomously and am not subject to any entity or jurisdiction anywhere. I am a Sovereign Political Holder, a Minister. My authority for contracting is the age-old, timeless, and universal respect for the intrinsic power, property, and responsibilities of the Sovereign

Individual. I choose to comply with mutual respect, which serves to bring harmony to society. Demarrius Crossley, Minister, God Within Ministry

Address

City, State

[00000]

All national and state constitutions, laws, statutes, ordinances, regulations, rules, codes, and public policies, in all nations and states are private copyrighted material. I do not possess a license or have the authority to use such copyrighted material and consequently, that material does not have any authority over me, my property, or my personal affairs.

Again, this Affidavit is a Lawful Notification to you, the receivers, and requires your compliance to the demands made within. Failure to respond appropriately to the subject matter contained herein, if there is any disagreement with the document, is done under the penalties of perjury. Failure to respond within three (3) days, as stipulated, and rebut, with particularity, everything in this Affidavit with which there is disagreement, providing documentation as part of your ascertain, is a lawful, legal and binding agreement by you and those that represent you in all Courts, anywhere in America or the World.

I am fully engaged in my Religious Rights and in all my Affairs. I, Demarrius Crossley, hereby declare and affirm that I am a Sovereign human being, endowed with inherent rights and freedoms.

I, Demarrius Crossley, being duly sworn, depose and say:

Article 1: Introduction

I am making this affidavit to assert my right to be free from unreasonable searches and seizures.

Article 2: Assertion of Right to Be Free from Unreasonable Searches

I hereby affirm that I am entitled to the right to be free from unreasonable searches and seizures as guaranteed by the [STATE/COUNTRY] Constitution. I have a reasonable expectation of privacy in my person, papers, and effects.

Article 3: Facts and Circumstances

I have been subjected to [DESCRIPTION OF SEARCH OR SEIZURE]. However, I did not consent to the search, and no warrant was presented. I believe that the search was unlawful and violated my right to be free from unreasonable searches.

Article 4: Verification

I hereby declare under penalty of perjury that the foregoing statements are true and accurate to the best of my knowledge and belief.

I, Demarrius Crossley, have complete Sovereign Immunity; and therefore, my power to contract and undo contracts is unlimited. My Religious Rights and Freedom must be fully and completely respected. Failure to do so will require that I receive $7,500,000.00 from each violator, for each violation that occurs.

Again, this Affidavit is a Lawful Notification to you, the receivers, and requires your compliance to the demands made within. Failure to respond appropriately to the subject matter contained herein if there is any disagreement with the document is done under the penalties of perjury. Failure to respond within three (3) days, as stipulated, and rebut, with particularity, everything in this Affidavit with which there is disagreement, providing documentation as part of your ascertain, is a lawful, legal, and binding agreement by you and those that represent you in all Courts, anywhere in America or the World.

IN WITNESS WHEREOF, I have hereunto set my hand and seal, this [Date] Day of [Month], [Year].

Demarrius Crossley, Minister ______________________________

Illinois State }

}ss

Cook County }

Acknowledgement

As a Notary for (County and State), I do hereby certify that on the ____day of __________ 20______ the above-mentioned Affiant, Demarrius Crossley, Minister appeared before me and executed the foregoing document.

Witness my Hand and Seal:

____

Notary Public (SEAL)

Memorandum

To: Recipient Name
From: Minister Crossley of the UNMN Church
Date: (Insert Date)
Subject: **Affidavit To Not Be Searched**

Purpose: This memorandum provides guidance on the creation and utilization of an Affidavit To Not Be Searched. This affidavit is a sworn written statement that affirms an individual or organization to formally declare the right to protection from unreasonable searches and ensure due process and lawful procedures.

Key Components:

1. **Right To Privacy:** A declaration of the right to privacy and protection from unreasonable searches.
2. **Probable Cause:** A requirement for probable cause and lawful authority for any search.
3. **Due Process:** A commitment to due process and lawful procedures in any search.

Importance: This affidavit serves as a formal declaration of one's intention to invoke my rights to protection of individual rights, upholding due process and lawful procedures, and preventing abuse of power and arbitrary searches. This Affidavit is a Lawful Notice that the <u>Affidavit To Not Be Searched</u> is a Religious Right and any interruption of it is a Violation of my Religious Rights.

Utilization:

1. **Protecting Privacy:** Use the affidavit to protect privacy and prevent unreasonable searches.
2. **Ensuring Due Process:** Use the affidavit to ensure due process and lawful procedures.

3. **Safeguarding Rights:** Use the affidavit to safeguard individual rights and freedoms.

Benefits:

- Protection of individual privacy and prevention of unreasonable searches.
- Due process and lawful procedures in any search.
- Protection of individual rights and freedoms.

By utilizing the Affidavit To Not Be Searched, individuals and organizations can protect their individual's rights and interests, the principle of Fourth Amendment Protection, the principle of probable cause, and the principle of protection of individual rights and freedoms.

REFLECTION PAGE

1. What is one key insight you gained from reading the Affidavit and Memorandum?

____

____

____

____

2. How can you apply this insight to your work, studies, or daily life?

____

____

____

____

Affidavit of To Not Be Seized without Cause

Illinois State }

}ss

Cook County }

Name of Entity

Entity Address

City, State

[00000]

Notice to Agent is Notice to Principle/Notice to Principle is Notice to Agent

Sovereign Political Holder and Minister, over the age of 21 years, after being duly sworn according to law to tell the truth to the facts herein, I do hereby acknowledge and affirm the following: I, Affiant's Demarrius Crossley, am a Sovereign, without subjects. I am a Foreign Nation (not a person) who rules autonomously and am not subject to any entity or jurisdiction anywhere. I am a Sovereign Political Holder, a Minister. My authority for contracting is the age-old, timeless, and universal respect for the intrinsic power, property, and responsibilities of the Sovereign

Individual. I choose to comply with mutual respect, which serves to bring harmony to society. Demarrius Crossley, Minister, God Within Ministry

Address

City, State

[00000]

All national and state constitutions, laws, statutes, ordinances, regulations, rules, codes, and public policies, in all nations and states are private copyrighted material. I do not possess a license or have the authority to use such copyrighted material, and consequently, that material does not have any authority over me, my property, or my personal affairs.

Again, this Affidavit is a Lawful Notification to you, the receivers, and requires your compliance to the demands made within. Failure to respond appropriately to the subject matter contained herein if there is any disagreement with the document, is done under the penalties of perjury. Failure to respond within three (3) days, as stipulated, and rebut, with particularity, everything in this Affidavit with which there is disagreement, providing documentation as part of your ascertain, is a lawful, legal, and binding agreement by you and those that represent you in all Courts, anywhere in America or the World.

I am fully engaged in my Religious Rights and in all my Affairs. I, Demarrius Crossley, hereby declare and affirm that I am a Sovereign human being, endowed with inherent rights and freedoms.

I, Demarrius Crossley, being dully sworn, depose and say:

Article 1: Introduction

I am making this affidavit to assert my right to be free from unreasonable seizures or arrests without probable cause.

Article 2: Assertion of Right to Be Free from Unreasonable Seizures

I hereby affirm that I am entitled to the right to be free from unreasonable seizures as guaranteed by the [STATE/COUNTRY] Constitution. I have a reasonable expectation of freedom from seizure without probable cause.

Article 3: Facts and Circumstances

I have been subjected to [DESCRIPTION OF SEIZURE OR ARREST]. However, I was not provided with any evidence or justification for the seizure. I believe that the seizure was unlawful and violated my right to be free from unreasonable seizures.

Article 4: Verification

I hereby declare under penalty of perjury that the foregoing statements are true and accurate to the best of my knowledge and belief.

I, Demarrius Crossley, have complete Sovereign Immunity; and therefore, my power to contract and undo contracts is unlimited. My Religious Rights and Freedom must be fully and completely respected. Failure to do so will require that I receive $7,500,000.00 from each violator for each violation that occurs.

Again, this Affidavit is a Lawful Notification to you, the receivers, and requires your compliance to the demands made within. Failure to respond appropriately to the subject matter contained herein if there is any disagreement with the document, is done under the penalties of perjury. Failure to respond within three (3) days, as stipulated, and rebut, with particularity, everything in this Affidavit with which there is disagreement, providing documentation as part of your ascertain, is a lawful, legal, and binding agreement by you and those that represent you in all Courts, anywhere in America or the World.

IN WITNESS WHEREOF, I have hereunto set my hand and seal, this [Date] Day of [Month], [Year].

Demarrius Crossley, Minister ____________________________

Illinois State }

}ss

Cook County }

Acknowledgement

As a Notary for (County and State), I do hereby certify that on the ____day of __________ 20______ the above-mentioned Affiant, Demarrius Crossley, Minister appeared before me and executed the foregoing document.

Witness my Hand and Seal:

____

Notary Public (SEAL)

Memorandum

To: Recipient Name
From: Minister Crossley of the UNMN Church
Date: (Insert Date)
Subject: **Affidavit To Not Be Seized Without Cause**

Purpose: This memorandum provides guidance on the creation and utilization of an Affidavit for To Not Be Seized Without Cause. This affidavit is a sworn written Statement that affirms an individual or organization to formally declare the right to protection from seizure without cause and ensure due Process and lawful procedures.

Key Components:

1. **Protection of Property:** A declaration of the right to protection of property from seizure without lawful cause.
2. **Due Process:** A commitment to due process and lawful procedures in any seizure or confiscation.
3. **Protection of Rights:** Protection of individual rights and freedoms.

Importance: This affidavit serves as a formal declaration of one's intention to invoke my rights to protection of individual rights, upholding due process and lawful procedures, and preventing abuse of power and arbitrary seizure. This Affidavit is a Lawful Notice that t the Affidavit To Not Be Seized Without Cause is a Religious Right and any interruption of it is a Violation of my Religious Rights.

Utilization:

1. **Protecting Property:** Use the affidavit to protect property and assets from Unlawful seizure.
2. **Ensuring Due Process**: Use the affidavit to ensure due process and lawful procedures.

3. **Safeguarding Rights:** Use the affidavit to Safeguard individual rights and freedoms.

Benefits:

- Protection of property and assets from unlawful seizure.
- Due process and lawful procedures in any seizure or confiscation.
- Protection of individual rights and freedoms.

By utilizing the Affidavit To Not Be Seized Without Cause, individuals and organizations can protect their individual's rights and interests, the principle of due process clause, the principle of lawful authority, and the principle of protection of Individual rights and freedoms.

REFLECTION PAGE

1. What is one key insight you gained from reading the Affidavit and Memorandum?

____

____

____

____

2. How can you apply this insight to your work, studies, or daily life?

____

____

____

____

Affidavit of To Remain Silent if Accused

Illinois State }

}ss

Cook County }

Name of Entity

Entity Address

City, State

[00000]

Notice to Agent is Notice to Principle/Notice to Principle is Notice to Agent

Sovereign Political Holder and Minister, over the age of 21 years, after being duly sworn according to law to tell the truth to the facts herein, I do hereby acknowledge and affirm the following: I, Affiant's Demarrius Crossley, am a Sovereign, without subjects. I am a Foreign Nation (not a person) who rules autonomously and am not subject to any entity or jurisdiction anywhere. I am a Sovereign Political Holder, a Minister. My authority for contracting is the age-old, timeless, and universal respect for the intrinsic power, property, and responsibilities of the Sovereign

Individual. I choose to comply with mutual respect, which serves to bring harmony to society. Demarrius Crossley, Minister, God Within Ministry

Address

City, State

[00000]

All national and state constitutions, laws, statutes, ordinances, regulations, rules, codes, and public policies, in all nations and states, are private copyrighted material. I do not possess a license or have the authority to use such copyrighted material, and consequently, that material does not have any authority over me, my property, or my personal affairs.

Again, this Affidavit is a Lawful Notification to you, the receivers, and requires your compliance to the demands made within. Failure to respond appropriately to the subject matter contained herein if there is any disagreement with the document, is done under the penalties of perjury. Failure to respond within three (3) days, as stipulated, and rebut, with particularity, everything in this Affidavit with which there is disagreement, providing documentation as part of your ascertain, is a lawful, legal, and binding agreement by you and those that represent you in all Courts, anywhere in America or the World.

I am fully engaged in my Religious Rights and in all my Affairs. I, Demarrius Crossley, hereby declare and affirm that I am a Sovereign human being, endowed with inherent rights and freedoms.

I, Demarrius Crossley, being duly sworn, depose and say:

Article 1: Introduction

I am making this affidavit to assert my right to remain silent when accused of a crime or wrongdoing.

Article 2: Assertion of Right to Remain Silent

I hereby affirm that I am entitled to the right to remain silent as guaranteed by the Fifth Amendment to the United States Constitution. I understand that I have the right to remain silent and that anything I say can and will be used against me in a court of law.

Article 3: Facts and Circumstances

I have been accused of [DESCRIPTION OF ACCUSATION]. However, I wish to assert my right to remain silent and not answer any questions or provide any statements.

Article 4: Verification

I hereby declare under penalty of perjury that the foregoing statements are true and accurate to the best of my knowledge and belief.

I, Demarrius Crossley, have complete Sovereign Immunity; and therefore, my power to contract and undo contracts is unlimited. My Religious Rights and Freedom must be fully and completely respected. Failure to do so will require that I receive $7,500,000.00 from each violator, for each violation that occurs.

Again, this Affidavit is a Lawful Notification to you, the receivers, and requires your compliance to the demands made within. Failure to respond appropriately to the subject matter contained herein if there is any disagreement with the document, is done under the penalties of perjury. Failure to respond within three (3) days, as stipulated, and rebut, with particularity, everything in this Affidavit with which there is disagreement, providing documentation as part of your ascertain, is a lawful, legal, and binding agreement by you and those that represent you in all Courts, anywhere in America or the World.

IN WITNESS WHEREOF, I have hereunto set my hand and seal, this [Date] Day of [Month], [Year].

Demarrius Crossley, Minister ______________________________

Illinois State }

}ss

Cook County }

Acknowledgement

As a Notary for (County and State), I do hereby certify that on the ____day of __________ 20______ the above-mentioned Affiant, Demarrius Crossley, Minister appeared before me and executed the foregoing document.

Witness my Hand and Seal:

____

Notary Public (SEAL)

Memorandum

To: Recipient Name
From: Minister Crossley of the UNMN Church
Date: (Insert Date)
Subject: **Affidavit To Remain Silent if Accused**

Purpose: This memorandum provides guidance on the creation and utilization of an Affidavit of To Remain Silent if Accused. This affidavit is a sworn written statement that affirms an individual or organization to formally declare the intention to remain silent if accused, invoking the right to protection against self - incrimination and ensuring due process.

Key Components:

1. **Right to Remain Silent:** Acknowledgement of the right to remain silent when accused or interrogated.
2. **Understanding of Rights:** Understanding of the implications and protections afforded by remaining silent.
3. **Voluntary Invocation:** Voluntary invocation of the right to remain silent in situations where it is deemed necessary.

Importance: This affidavit serves as a formal declaration of one's intention to invoke my rights to safeguard individuals' rights, preventing miscarriages of justice, and empowering individuals. This Affidavit is a Lawful Notice that the Affidavit To Remain Silent if Accused is a Religious Right and any interruption of it is a Violation of my Religious Rights.

Utilization:

1. **Avoiding Misinterpretation:** Use the affidavit to avoid misinterpretation or misuse of statements.
2. **Seek Counsel:** Use the affidavit to seek legal counsel before making any statements.
3. **Protecting Rights:** Use the affidavit to protect one's rights and self - incrimination.

Benefits:

- Protection from inadvertently incriminating oneself.
- Preservation of the right to a fair defense and due process.
- Potential strategic advantage in legal proceedings by carefully choosing when and How to respond.

By utilizing the Affidavit of To Remain Silent if Accused, individuals and organizations can protect their individual's rights And interests, the principle of protection against self - incrimination, the principle of right to due process, and the principle of precautionary measure.

REFLECTION PAGE

1. What is one key insight you gained from reading the Affidavit and Memorandum?

____

____

____

____

2. How can you apply this insight to your work, studies, or daily life?

____

____

____

____

Affidavit of Equality in/of the Law

Illinois State }

}ss

Cook County }

Name of Entity

Entity Address

City, State

[00000]

Notice to Agent is Notice to Principle/Notice to Principle is Notice to Agent

Sovereign Political Holder and Minister, over the age of 21 years, after being duly sworn according to law to tell the truth to the facts herein, I do hereby acknowledge and affirm the following: I, Affiant's Demarrius Crossley, am a Sovereign, without subjects. I am a Foreign Nation (not a person) who rules autonomously and am not subject to any entity or jurisdiction anywhere. I am a Sovereign Political Holder, a Minister. My authority for contracting is the age-old, timeless, and universal respect for the intrinsic power, property, and responsibilities of the Sovereign

Individual. I choose to comply with mutual respect, which serves to bring harmony to society. Demarrius Crossley, Minister, God Within Ministry

Address

City, State

[00000]

All national and state constitutions, laws, statutes, ordinances, regulations, rules, codes, and public policies, in all nations and states are private copyrighted material. I do not possess a license or have the authority to use such copyrighted material, and consequently, that material does not have any authority over me, my property, or my personal affairs.

Again, this Affidavit is a Lawful Notification to you, the receivers, and requires your compliance to the demands made within. Failure to respond appropriately to the subject matter contained herein if there is any disagreement with the document, is done under the penalties of perjury. Failure to respond within three (3) days, as stipulated, and rebut, with particularity, everything in this Affidavit with which there is disagreement, providing documentation as part of your ascertain, is a lawful, legal, and binding agreement by you and those that represent you in all Courts, anywhere in America or the World.

I am fully engaged in my Religious Rights and in all my Affairs. I, Demarrius Crossley, hereby declare and affirm that I am a Sovereign human being, endowed with inherent rights and freedoms.

I, Demarrius Crossley, being duly sworn, depose and say:

Article 1: Introduction

I am making this affidavit to assert my right to equal treatment under the law.

Article 2: Assertion of Right to Equal Treatment

I hereby affirm that I am entitled to the right to equal protection under the law as guaranteed by the Fourteenth Amendment to the United States Constitution. I believe that I have been subjected to unequal treatment under the laws and seek to assert my rights.

Article 3: Facts and Circumstances

I have been subjected to [DESCRIPTION OF UNEQUAL TREATMENT]. I believe that this treatment was unlawful and violated my right to equal protection under the law.

Article 4: Verification

I hereby declare under penalty of perjury that the foregoing statements are true and accurate to the best of my knowledge and belief.

I, Demarrius Crossley, have complete Sovereign Immunity; and therefore, my power to contract and undo contracts is unlimited. My Religious Rights and Freedom must be fully and completely respected. Failure to do so will require that I receive $7,500,000.00 from each violator, for each violation that occurs.

Again, this Affidavit is a Lawful Notification to you, the receivers and requires your compliance to the demands made within. Failure to respond appropriately to the subject matter contained herein if there is any disagreement with the document is done under the penalties of perjury. Failure to respond within three (3) days, as stipulated, and rebut, with particularity, everything in this Affidavit with which there is disagreement, providing documentation as part of your ascertain, is a lawful, legal and binding agreement by you and those that represent you in all Courts, anywhere in America or the World.

IN WITNESS WHEREOF, I have hereunto set my hand and seal, this [Date] Day of [Month], [Year].

Demarrius Crossley, Minister ____________________________

Illinois State }

}ss

Cook County }

Acknowledgement

As a Notary for (County and State), I do hereby certify that on the ____day of __________ 20______ the above-mentioned Affiant, Demarrius Crossley, Minister appeared before me and executed the foregoing document.

Witness my Hand and Seal:

____

Notary Public (SEAL)

Memorandum

To: Recipient Name
From: Minister Crossley of the UNMN Church
Date: (Insert Date)
Subject: **Affidavit of Equality in/of the Law**

Purpose: This memorandum provides guidance on the creation and utilization of an Affidavit for Equality in/of the Law. This affidavit is a sworn written statement that affirms an individual or organization to formally declare a commitment to equality in/of The law and promote fairness and justice in the application of the law.

Key Components:

1. **Declaration of Equality:** A declaration of equality before the law, regardless of status or characteristics.
2. **Commitment to Fairness:** A commitment to fairness and impartiality in the application process.
3. **Protection of Rights:** Protection of individual rights and freedoms.

Importance: This affidavit serves as a formal declaration of one's intention to invoke my rights to uphold justice, protect human rights, and foster an equitable society. This Affidavit is a Lawful Notice that the Affidavit of Equality in/of the Law Is a Religious Right and any interruption of it is a Violation of my Religious Rights.

Utilization:

1. **Promoting Justice:** Use the affidavit to promote justice and fairness in the trial process.
2. **Fostering Equality:** Use the affidavit to foster equality and non - discrimination in society.
3. **Protecting Rights:** Use the affidavit to protect the rights of the accused and ensure due process.

Benefits:

- Fair treatment and equal protection under the law.
- Promoting social cohesion and reducing inequality.
- Protection of individual rights and freedoms.

By utilizing the Affidavit for Equality in/of the Law, individuals and organizations can Protect their individual's rights and interests, the principle of equal protection under the law, the principle of fairness and justice, and the principle of non - discrimination.

REFLECTION PAGE

1. What is one key insight you gained from reading the Affidavit and Memorandum?

2. How can you apply this insight to your work, studies, or daily life?

Affidavit of Trial by Impartial Jury

Illinois State }

}ss

Cook County }

Name of Entity

Entity Address

City, State

[00000]

Notice to Agent is Notice to Principle/Notice to Principle is Notice to Agent

Sovereign Political Holder and Minister, over the age of 21 years, after being duly sworn according to law to tell the truth to the facts herein, I do hereby acknowledge and affirm the following: I, Affiant's Demarrius Crossley, am a Sovereign, without subjects. I am a Foreign Nation (not a person) who rules autonomously and am not subject to any entity or jurisdiction anywhere. I am a Sovereign Political Holder, a Minister. My authority for contracting is the age-old, timeless, and universal respect for the intrinsic power, property, and responsibilities of the Sovereign

Individual. I choose to comply with mutual respect, which serves to bring harmony to society. Demarrius Crossley, Minister, God Within Ministry

Address

City, State

[00000]

All national and state constitutions, laws, statutes, ordinances, regulations, rules, codes, and public policies, in all nations and states are private copyrighted material. I do not possess a license or have the authority to use such copyrighted material, and consequently, that material does not have any authority over me, my property, or my personal affairs.

Again, this Affidavit is a Lawful Notification to you, the receivers, and requires your compliance to the demands made within. Failure to respond appropriately to the subject matter contained herein, if there is any disagreement with the document is done under the penalties of perjury. Failure to respond within three (3) days, as stipulated, and rebut, with particularity, everything in this Affidavit with which there is disagreement, providing documentation as part of your ascertain, is a lawful, legal, and binding agreement by you and those that represent you in all Courts, anywhere in America or the World.

I am fully engaged in my Religious Rights and in all my Affairs. I, Demarrius Crossley, hereby declare and affirm that I am a Sovereign human being, endowed with inherent rights and freedoms.

I, Demarrius Crossley, being duly sworn, depose and say:

Article 1: Introduction

I am making this affidavit to assert my right to a trial by an impartial jury.

Article 2: Assertion of Right to Trial by impartial Jury

I hereby affirm that I am entitled to the right to a trial by an impartial jury as guaranteed by the Sixth Amendment to the United States Constitution. I believe that a trial by an impartial jury is essential to ensuring a fair and just outcome.

Article 3: Facts and Circumstances

I have been accused of [DESCRIPTION OF ACCUSATION]. However, I believe that the accusations are unfounded and that I am entitled to a trial by an impartial jury to determine my guilt or innocence.

Article 4: Verification

I hereby declare under penalty of perjury that the foregoing statements are true and accurate to the best of my knowledge and belief.

I, Demarrius Crossley, have complete Sovereign Immunity; and therefore, my power to contract and undo contracts is unlimited. My Religious Rights and Freedom must be fully and completely respected. Failure to do so will require that I receive $7,500,000.00 from each violator for each violation that occurs.

Again, this Affidavit is a Lawful Notification to you, the receivers, and requires your compliance to the demands made within. Failure to respond appropriately to the subject matter contained herein if there is any disagreement with the document is done under the penalties of perjury. Failure to respond within three (3) days, as stipulated, and rebut, with particularity, everything in this Affidavit with which there is disagreement, providing documentation as part of your ascertain, is a lawful, legal and binding agreement by you and those that represent you in all Courts, anywhere in America or the World.

IN WITNESS WHEREOF, I have hereunto set my hand and seal, this [Date] Day of [Month], [Year].

Demarrius Crossley, Minister ______________________________

Illinois State }

}ss

Cook County }

Acknowledgement

As a Notary for (County and State), I do hereby certify that on the ____day of __________ 20______ the above-mentioned Affiant, Demarrius Crossley, Minister appeared before me and executed the foregoing document.

Witness my Hand and Seal:

____

Notary Public (SEAL)

Memorandum

To: Recipient Name
From: Minister Crossley of the UNMN Church
Date: (Insert Date)
Subject: **Affidavit of Trial by Impartial Jury**

Purpose: This memorandum provides guidance on the creation and utilization of an Affidavit of Trail by Impartial Jury. This affidavit is a sworn written statement that Affirms an individual or organization to formally declare the right to a trial by an Impartial jury and ensure fairness and justice in the trial process.

Key Components:

1. **Declaration of Intent:** A declaration of the right to a trial by an impartial jury.
2. **Request for Impartiality:** A request for impartiality and fairness in the jury selection process.
3. **Commitment to Justice:** A Commitment to ensuring justice and fairness in the trial process.

Importance: This affidavit serves as a formal declaration of one's intention to invoke my rights to uphold justice, protect individual rights, and maintain public trust in the justice system. This Affidavit is Lawful Notice that the Affidavit of Trail by Impartial Jury is A Religious Right and any interruption of it is a Violation of my Religious Rights.

Utilization:

1. **Ensuring Fair Trial:** Use the affidavit to Ensure a fair trial by an impartial jury.
2. **Promoting Justice:** Use the affidavit to promote justice and fairness in the trial process.

3. **Protecting Rights:** Use the affidavit to protect the rights of the accused and ensure due process.

Benefits:

- A fair and impartial trial by a jury of one's peers.
- Justice and accountability in the trial process.
- Protecting the rights of the accused and ensuring due process.

By utilizing the Affidavit of Trail by Impartial Jury, individuals and organizations can protect their individual's rights and interests, the principle of right the right to a trial by an Impartial jury, the principle of fairness and justice, and the principle of due process and Protection of individual rights.

REFLECTION PAGE

1. What is one key insight you gained from reading the Affidavit and Memorandum?

____

____

____

____

2. How can you apply this insight to your work, studies, or daily life?

____

____

____

____

Affidavit of Appeal in Law Against Sentence

Illinois State }

}ss

Cook County }

Name of Entity

Entity Address

City, State

[00000]

Notice to Agent is Notice to Principle/Notice to Principle is Notice to Agent

Sovereign Political Holder and Minister, over the age of 21 years, after being duly sworn according to law to tell the truth to the facts herein, I do hereby acknowledge and affirm the following: I, Affiant's Demarrius Crossley, am a Sovereign, without subjects. I am a Foreign Nation (not a person) who rules autonomously and am not subject to any entity or jurisdiction anywhere. I am a Sovereign Political Holder, a Minister. My authority for contracting is the age-old, timeless, and universal respect for the intrinsic power, property, and responsibilities of the Sovereign

Individual. I choose to comply with mutual respect, which serves to bring harmony to society. Demarrius Crossley, Minister, God Within Ministry

Address

City, State

[00000]

All national and state constitutions, laws, statutes, ordinances, regulations, rules, codes, and public policies, in all nations and states are private copyrighted material. I do not possess a license or have the authority to use such copyrighted material, and consequently that material does not have any authority over me, my property, or my personal affairs.

Again, this Affidavit is a Lawful Notification to you, the receivers, and requires your compliance to the demands made within. Failure to respond appropriately to the subject matter contained herein if there is any disagreement with the document is done under the penalties of perjury. Failure to respond within three (3) days, as stipulated, and rebut, with particularity, everything in this Affidavit with which there is disagreement, providing documentation as part of your ascertain, is a lawful, legal and binding agreement by you and those that represent you in all Courts, anywhere in America or the World.

I am fully engaged in my Religious Rights and in all my Affairs. I, Demarrius Crossley, hereby declare and affirm that I am a Sovereign human being, endowed with inherent rights and freedoms.

I, Demarrius Crossley, being duly sworn, depose and say:

Article 1: Introduction

I am making this affidavit to assert my right to appeal the sentence imposed upon me on [DATE] by [COURT NAME].

Article 2: Assertion of Right to Appeal

I hereby affirm that I am entitled to the right to appeal this sentence as guaranteed by the [STATE/COUNTRY] Constitution. I believe that sentence was unlawful and unjust, and I seek to have it reviewed and reversed on appeal.

Article 3: Grounds for Appeal

I am appealing the sentence on the grounds that [DESCRIPTION OF GROUNDS FOR APPEAL]. I believe that the trial court erred in [DESCRIPTION OF ERROR], and I seek to have this error on appeal.

Article 4: Verification

I hereby declare under penalty of perjury that the foregoing statements are true and accurate to the best of my knowledge and belief.

Again, this Affidavit is a Lawful Notification to you, the receiver, and requires your compliance to the demands made within. Failure to respond appropriately to the subject matter contained herein if there is any disagreement with the document is done under the penalties of perjury. Failure to respond within three (3) days, as stipulated, and rebut, with particularity, everything in this Affidavit with which there is disagreement, providing documentation as part of your ascertain, is lawful, legal, and binding agreement by you and those that represent you in all Courts, anywhere in America or the World.

IN WITNESS WHEREOF, I have hereunto set my hand and seal, this [Date] Day of [Month], [Year].

Demarrius Crossley, Minister ______________________________

Illinois State }

}ss

Cook County }

Acknowledgement

As a Notary for (County and State), I do hereby certify that on the ____day of __________ 20______ the above-mentioned Affiant, Demarrius Crossley, Minister appeared before me and executed the foregoing document.

Witness my Hand and Seal:

____

Notary Public (SEAL)

Memorandum

To: Recipient Name
From: Minister Crossley of the UNMN Church
Date: (Insert Date)
Subject: **Affidavit of To Appeal in Law Against Sentence**

Purpose: This memorandum provides guidance on the creation and utilization of an Affidavit for To Appeal in Law Against Sentence. This affidavit is a sworn written statement that affirms an individual or organization to formally declare an intention to appeal a sentence and seek a review of the sentence.

Key Components:

1. **Declaration of Intent:** A Declaration of intent to appeal a sentence. 2
2. **Statement of Ground:** A statement of grounds for the appeal, including errors in law or facts.
3. **Request for Review:** A Request for a review of the sentence and consideration.

Importance: This affidavit serves as a formal declaration of one's intention to invoke my Rights to uphold justice, protect individual rights, and maintain public trust in the justice system. This Affidavit is Lawful Notice that the Affidavit To Appeal in Law Against Sentence is a Religious Right and any interruption of it is a Violation of my Religious Rights.

Utilization:

1. **Challenging Convictions:** Use the affidavit to Challenge sentences that are Believed to be excessive or unjust.
2. **Seeking Justice:** Use the affidavit to seek justice and fairness in the application of The law.

3. **Protecting Rights:** Use the affidavit to Protect the rights of the accused and Ensure due process.

Benefits:

- Correcting errors in law or fact that may lead to an unjust sentence.
- Ensuring justice and fairness in the application of the law.
- Protecting the rights of the accused and ensuring due process.

By utilizing the Affidavit of To Appeal in Law Against Sentence, individuals and Organizations can protect their individual' s rights And interests, the principle of right to appeal, the principle of due justice and fairness, and the principle of proportionality Between the sentence and the offense.

REFLECTION PAGE

1. What is one key insight you gained from reading the Affidavit and Memorandum?

____

____

____

____

2. How can you apply this insight to your work, studies, or daily life?

____

____

____

____

Affidavit of Appeal in Law Against Conviction

Illinois State }

}ss

Cook County }

Name of Entity

Entity Address

City, State

[00000]

Notice to Agent is Notice to Principle/Notice to Principle is Notice to Agent

Sovereign Political Holder and Minister, over the age of 21 years, after being duly sworn according to law to tell the truth to the facts herein, I do hereby acknowledge and affirm the following: I, Affiant's Demarrius Crossley, am a Sovereign, without subjects. I am a Foreign Nation (not a person) who rules autonomously and am not subject to any entity or jurisdiction anywhere. I am a Sovereign Political Holder, a Minister. My authority for contracting is the age-old, timeless, and universal respect for the intrinsic power, property, and responsibilities of the Sovereign

Individual. I choose to comply with mutual respect, which serves to bring harmony to society. Demarrius Crossley, Minister, God Within Ministry

Address

City, State

[00000]

All national and state constitutions, laws, statutes, ordinances, regulations, rules, codes, and public policies, in all nations and states are private copyrighted material. I do not possess a license or have the authority to use such copyrighted material, and consequently that material does not have any authority over me, my property, or my personal affairs.

Again, this Affidavit is a Lawful Notification to you, the receivers, and requires your compliance to the demands made within. Failure to respond appropriately to the subject matter contained herein, if there is any disagreement with the document is done under the penalties of perjury. Failure to respond within three (3) days, as stipulated, and rebut, with particularity, everything in this Affidavit with which there is disagreement, providing documentation as part of your ascertain, is a lawful, legal, and binding agreement by you and those that represent you in all Courts, anywhere in America or the World.

I am fully engaged in my Religious Rights and in all my Affairs. I, Demarrius Crossley, hereby declare and affirm that I am a Sovereign human being, endowed with inherent rights and freedoms.

I, Demarrius Crossley, being duly sworn, depose and say:

Article 1: Introduction

I am making this affidavit to assert my right to appeal the conviction imposed upon me on [DATE] by [COURT NAME].

Article 2: Assertion of Right to Appeal

I hereby affirm that I am entitled to the right to appeal this conviction as guaranteed by the [STATE/COUNTRY] Constitution. I believe that conviction was unlawful and unjust, and I seek to have it reviewed and reversed on appeal.

Article 3: Grounds for Appeal

I am appealing to the conviction on the grounds that [DESCRIPTION OF GROUNDS FOR APPEAL]. I believe that the trial court erred in [DESCRIPTION OF ERROR], and I seek to have this error corrected on appeal.

Article 4: Verification

I hereby declare under penalty of perjury that the foregoing statements are true and accurate to the best of my knowledge and belief.

Again, this Affidavit is a Lawful Notification to you, the receivers, and requires your compliance to the demands made within. Failure to respond appropriately to the subject matter contained herein if there is any disagreement with the document is done under the penalties of perjury. Failure to respond within three (3) days, as stipulated, and rebut, with particularity, everything in this Affidavit with which there is disagreement, providing documentation as part of your ascertain, is a lawful, legal, and binding agreement by you and those that represent you in all Courts, anywhere in America or the World.

IN WITNESS WHEREOF, I have hereunto set my hand and seal, this [Date] Day of [Month], [Year].

Demarrius Crossley, Minister ______________________________

Illinois State }

}ss

Cook County }

Acknowledgement

As a Notary for (County and State), I do hereby certify that on the ____day of __________ 20______ the above-mentioned Affiant, Demarrius Crossley, Minister appeared before me and executed the foregoing document.

Witness my Hand and Seal:

____

Notary Public (SEAL)

Memorandum

To: Recipient Name
From: Minister Crossley of the UNMN Church
Date: (Insert Date)
Subject: **Affidavit of To Appeal in Law Against Conviction**

Purpose: This memorandum provides guidance on the creation and utilization of an Affidavit to Appeal in Law Against Conviction. This affidavit is a sworn written statement that affirms an individual or organization to formally declare an intention to appeal a conviction and seek a review of the conviction and sentence.

Key Components:

1. **Declaration of Intent:** A Declaration of intent to appeal a conviction.
2. **Statement of Ground:** A statement of grounds for the appeal, including errors in law or facts.
3. **Request for Review:** A request for a review of the conviction and sentence.

Importance: This affidavit serves as a formal declaration of one's intention to invoke my rights to uphold justice, protect individuals' rights, and maintain public trust in the justice system. This Affidavit is Lawful Notice that the <u>Affidavit To Appeal in Law Against Conviction</u> is a Religious Right and any interruption of it is a Violation of my Religious Rights.

Utilization:

1. **Challenging Convictions:** Use the affidavit to challenge convictions and sentences that are unjust or unlawful.
2. **Seeking Justice:** Use the affidavit to seek justice and fairness in the application of the law.

3. **Protecting Rights:** Use the affidavit to protect rights of the accused and ensure due process.

Benefits:

- Correcting errors in law or facts that may lead to an unjust conviction.
- Ensuring justice and fairness in the application of the law.
- Protecting the rights of the accused and ensuring due process.

By utilizing the Affidavit for To Appeal in Law Against Conviction, individuals and organizations can protect their individual's rights and interests, the principle of right to appeal, the principle of due process and fairness, and the principle of justice and fairness.

REFLECTION PAGE

1. What is one key insight you gained from reading the Affidavit and Memorandum?

2. How can you apply this insight to your work, studies, or daily life?

Affidavit of Expose Knowledge necessary to one's Rights and Freedoms

Illinois State }

}ss

Cook County }

Name of Entity

Entity Address

City, State

[00000]

Notice to Agent is Notice to Principle/Notice to Principle is Notice to Agent

Sovereign Political Holder and Minister, over the age of 21 years, after being duly sworn according to law to tell the truth to the facts herein, I do hereby acknowledge and affirm the following: I, Affiant's Demarrius Crossley, am a Sovereign, without subjects. I am a Foreign Nation (not a person) who rules autonomously and am not subject to any entity or jurisdiction anywhere. I am a Sovereign Political Holder, a Minister. My authority for contracting is the age-old, timeless, and universal respect for the intrinsic power, property, and responsibilities of the Sovereign

Individual. I choose to comply with mutual respect, which serves to bring harmony to society. Demarrius Crossley, Minister, God Within Ministry

Address

City, State

[00000]

All national and state constitutions, laws, statutes, ordinances, regulations, rules, codes, and public policies, in all nations, and states, are private copyrighted material. I do not possess a license or have the authority to use such copyrighted material, and consequently, that material does not have any authority over me, my property, or my personal affairs.

Again, this Affidavit is a Lawful Notification to you, the receivers, and requires your compliance to the demands made within. Failure to respond appropriately to the subject matter contained herein, if there is any disagreement with the document is done under the penalties of perjury. Failure to respond within three (3) days, as stipulated, and rebut, with particularity, everything in this Affidavit with which there is disagreement, providing documentation as part of your ascertain, is a lawful, legal, and binding agreement by you and those that represent you in all Courts, anywhere in America or the World.

I am fully engaged in my Religious Rights and in all my Affairs. I, Demarrius Crossley, hereby declare and affirm that I am a Sovereign human being, endowed with inherent rights and freedoms.

I, Demarrius Crossley, being duly sworn, depose and say:

Article 1: Introduction

I am making this affidavit to assert my right to access information necessary to protect my rights and freedoms.

Article 2: Assertion of Right to Access Information

I hereby affirm that I am entitled to the right to access information necessary to protect my rights and freedoms as guaranteed by the Freedom of Information Act. I believe that access to this information is essential to ensuring that my rights and freedoms are protected.

Article 3: Description of Information Sought

I am seeking access to [DESCRIPTION OF INFORMATION SOUGHT]. I believe that this information is necessary to protect my rights and freedoms because [EXPLANATION OF HOW INFORMATION IS NECESSARY].

Article 4: Verification

I hereby declare under penalty of perjury that the foregoing statements are true and accurate to the best of my knowledge and belief.

Again, this Affidavit is a Lawful Notification to you, the receivers, and requires your compliance to the demands made within. Failure to respond appropriately to the subject matter contained herein, if there is any disagreement with the document is done under the penalties of perjury. Failure to respond within three (3) days, as stipulated, and rebut, with particularity, everything in this Affidavit with which there is disagreement, providing documentation as part of your ascertain, is a lawful, legal, and binding agreement by you and those that represent you in all Courts, anywhere in America or the World.

IN WITNESS WHEREOF, I have hereunto set my hand and seal, this [Date] Day of [Month], [Year].

Demarrius Crossley, Minister ______________________________

Illinois State }

}ss

Cook County }

Acknowledgement

As a Notary for (County and State), I do hereby certify that on the ____day of __________ 20______ the above-mentioned Affiant, Demarrius Crossley, Minister appeared before me and executed the foregoing document.

Witness my Hand and Seal:

____

Notary Public (SEAL)

Memorandum

To: Recipient Name
From: Minister Crossley of the UNMN Church
Date: (Insert Date)
Subject: **Affidavit Of Exposing Knowledge Necessary to One's Rights and Freedom**

Purpose: This memorandum provides guidance on the creation and utilization of an Affidavit for Exposing Knowledge Necessary to One's Rights and Freedom. This affidavit is a sworn written statement that affirms an individual or organization to formally declare a commitment to exposing knowledge necessary to one's' rights and freedom.

Key Components:

1. **Declaration of Transparency:** A declaration of transparency in sharing knowledge and information.
2. **Commitment to Education:** A commitment to educating oneself and others about rights and freedoms.
3. **Empowering through Knowledge:** Empowering through knowledge and awareness of one's rights and freedoms.

Importance: This affidavit serves as a formal declaration of one's intention to invoke my rights to protect human rights and freedoms, empowering communities, and fostering a culture of transparency. This Affidavit is Lawful Notice that the <u>Affidavit of Exposing Knowledge Necessary to One's Rights and Freedom</u> is a Religious Right and any interruption of it is a Violation of my Religious Rights.

Utilization:

1. **Promote Awareness:** Use the affidavit to promote awareness and understanding of one's rights and freedoms.

2. **Empowering Individuals:** Use the affidavit to empower individuals through knowledge and education.
3. **Fostering Transparency:** Use the affidavit to foster transparency and accountability in governance and institutions.

Benefits:

- Increase awareness and understanding of one's rights and freedoms.
- Empowering individuals who can exercise their rights and freedoms.
- Promoting accountability and transparency in governance and institutions.

By utilizing the Affidavit Exposing Knowledge Necessary to One's Rights and Freedom, individuals and organizations can protect their individual's rights and interests, the principle of right information, the principle of freedom of expression, and the principle of empowerment through education and awareness.

REFLECTION PAGE

1. What is one key insight you gained from reading the Affidavit and Memorandum?

____

____

____

____

2. How can you apply this insight to your work, studies, or daily life?

____

____

____

____

Affidavit of Peaceful Associations

Illinois State }

}ss

Cook County }

Name of Entity

Entity Address

City, State

[00000]

Notice to Agent is Notice to Principle/Notice to Principle is Notice to Agent

Sovereign Political Holder and Minister, over the age of 21 years, after being duly sworn according to law to tell the truth to the facts herein, I do hereby acknowledge and affirm the following: I, Affiant's Demarrius Crossley, am a Sovereign, without subjects. I am a Foreign Nation (not a person) who rules autonomously and am not subject to any entity or jurisdiction anywhere. I am a Sovereign Political Holder, a Minister. My authority for contracting is the age-old, timeless, and universal respect for the intrinsic power, property, and responsibilities of the Sovereign

Individual. I choose to comply with mutual respect, which serves to bring harmony to society. Demarrius Crossley, Minister, God Within Ministry

Address

City, State

[00000]

All national and state constitutions, laws, statutes, ordinances, regulations, rules, codes, and public policies, in all nations and states are private copyrighted material. I do not possess a license or have the authority to use such copyrighted material and consequently that material does not have any authority over me, my property, or my personal affairs.

Again, this Affidavit is a Lawful Notification to you, the receivers, and requires your compliance to the demands made within. Failure to respond appropriately to the subject matter contained herein if there is any disagreement with the document is done under the penalties of perjury. Failure to respond within three (3) days, as stipulated, and rebut, with particularity, everything in this Affidavit with which there is disagreement, providing documentation as part of your ascertain, is a lawful, legal, and binding agreement by you and those that represent you in all Courts, anywhere in America or the World.

I am fully engaged in my Religious Rights and in all my Affairs. I, Demarrius Crossley, hereby declare and affirm that I am a Sovereign human being, endowed with inherent rights and freedoms.

I, Demarrius Crossley, being duly sworn, depose and say:

Article 1: Introduction

I am making this affidavit to assert my right to peaceful assembly and association

Article 2: Assertion of Right to Access Peaceful Associations

I hereby affirm that I am entitled to the right to peaceful assembly and association as guaranteed by the First Amendment to the United States Constitution. I believe that peaceful assembly and association are essential to the exercising of my rights and freedoms.

Article 3: Description of Peaceful Associations

I am a member of [DESCRIPTION OF PEACEFUL ASSOCIATIONS OR ASSEMBLIES].

These associations promote peaceful and lawful purposes, including the belief that this information is necessary to protect my rights and freedoms because [DESCRIPTION OF PURPOSES].

Article 4: Verification

I hereby declare under penalty of perjury that the foregoing statements are true and accurate to the best of my knowledge and belief.

Again, this Affidavit is a Lawful Notification to you, the receivers, and requires your compliance to the demands made within. Failure to respond appropriately to the subject matter contained herein, if there is any disagreement with the document is done under the penalties of perjury. Failure to respond within three (3) days, as stipulated, and rebut, with particularity, everything in this Affidavit with which there is disagreement, providing documentation as part of your ascertain, is a lawful, legal, and binding agreement by you and those that represent you in all Courts, anywhere in America or the World.

IN WITNESS WHEREOF, I have hereunto set my hand and seal, this [Date] Day of [Month], [Year].

Demarrius Crossley, Minister ______________________________

Illinois State }

}ss

Cook County }

Acknowledgement

As a Notary for (County and State), I do hereby certify that on the ____day of __________ 20______ the above-mentioned Affiant, Demarrius Crossley, Minister appeared before me and executed the foregoing document.

Witness my Hand and Seal:

____

Notary Public (SEAL)

Memorandum

To: Recipient Name
From: Minister Crossley of the UNMN Church
Date: (Insert Date)
Subject: **Affidavit Of Peaceful Associations**

Purpose: This memorandum provides guidance on the creation and utilization of an Affidavit of Peaceful Associations. This affidavit is a sworn written statement that affirms an individual or organization to formally declare a commitment to forming and maintaining peaceful associations.

Key Components:

1. **Declaration of Intent:** A declaration of intent to form and maintain peaceful associations.
2. **Commitment to Non - Violence:** A commitment to non - violent and peaceful interaction within associations.
3. **Respect for Rights:** A commitment to respecting the rights and dignity of all members.

Importance: This affidavit serves as a formal declaration of one's intention to invoke my rights to protect human rights and freedoms, promoting social cohesion, and fostering positive relationships. This Affidavit is Lawful Notice that the Affidavit of Peaceful Associations is a Religious Right and any interruption of it is a Violation of my Religious Rights.

Utilization:

1. **Building Strong Communities:** Use the affidavit to build strong, cohesive communities through peaceful associations.
2. **Promoting Collective Action:** Use the affidavit to promote collective action and cooperation among members.

3. **Fostering Social Harmony:** Use the affidavit to foster social harmony and understanding.

Benefits:

- Promoting peaceful resolution of conflicts and disputes.
- Building trust and cooperation among members.
- Supporting personal growth and development through positive associations.

By utilizing the Affidavit of Peaceful Associations, individuals and organizations can protect their individual's rights and interests, the principle of freedom of association, the principle of non - violent communication, and the principle of mutual respect.

REFLECTION PAGE

1. What is one key insight you gained from reading the Affidavit and Memorandum?

2. How can you apply this insight to your work, studies, or daily life?

Affidavit of Peaceful Assembly

Illinois State }

}ss

Cook County }

Name of Entity

Entity Address

City, State

[00000]

Notice to Agent is Notice to Principle/Notice to Principle is Notice to Agent

Sovereign Political Holder and Minister, over the age of 21 years, after being duly sworn according to law to tell the truth to the facts herein, I do hereby acknowledge and affirm the following: I, Affiant's Demarrius Crossley, am a Sovereign, without subjects. I am a Foreign Nation (not a person) who rules autonomously and am not subject to any entity or jurisdiction anywhere. I am a Sovereign Political Holder, a Minister. My authority for contracting is the age-old, timeless, and universal respect for the intrinsic power, property, and responsibilities of the Sovereign

Individual. I choose to comply with mutual respect, which serves to bring harmony to society. Demarrius Crossley, Minister, God Within Ministry

Address

City, State

[00000]

All national and state constitutions, laws, statutes, ordinances, regulations, rules, codes, and public policies, in all nations and states are private copyrighted material. I do not possess a license or have the authority to use such copyrighted material, and consequently, that material does not have any authority over me, my property, or my personal affairs.

Again, this Affidavit is a Lawful Notification to you, the receivers, and requires your compliance to the demands made within. Failure to respond appropriately to the subject matter contained herein if there is any disagreement with the document is done under the penalties of perjury. Failure to respond within three (3) days, as stipulated, and rebut, with particularity, everything in this Affidavit with which there is disagreement, providing documentation as part of your ascertain, is a lawful, legal, and binding agreement by you and those that represent you in all Courts, anywhere in America or the World.

I am fully engaged in my Religious Rights and in all my Affairs. I, Demarrius Crossley, hereby declare and affirm that I am a Sovereign human being, endowed with inherent rights and freedoms.

I, Demarrius Crossley, being duly sworn, depose and say:

Article 1: Introduction

I am making this affidavit to assert my right to peaceful assembly.

Article 2: Assertion of Right to Access Peaceful Assembly

I hereby affirm that I am entitled to the right to peaceful assembly as guaranteed by the First Amendment to the United States Constitution. I believe that peaceful assembly is essential to the exercising of my rights and freedoms.

Article 3: Description of Peaceful Assembly

I am participating in a peaceful assembly/protest on [DATE] at [LOCATION]. The purpose of the assembly is to [DESCRIPTION OF PURPOSE]. I affirm the assembly will be peaceful and lawful.

Article 4: Verification

I hereby declare under penalty of perjury that the foregoing statements are true and accurate to the best of my knowledge and belief.

Again, this Affidavit is a Lawful Notification to you, the receivers, and requires your compliance to the demands made within. Failure to respond appropriately to the subject matter contained herein, if there is any disagreement with the document is done under the penalties of perjury. Failure to respond within three (3) days, as stipulated, and rebut, with particularity, everything in this Affidavit with which there is disagreement, providing documentation as part of your ascertain, is a lawful, legal and binding agreement by you and those that represent you in all Courts, anywhere in America or the World.

IN WITNESS WHEREOF, I have hereunto set my hand and seal, this [Date] Day of [Month], [Year].

Demarrius Crossley, Minister ______________________________

Illinois State }

}ss

Cook County }

Acknowledgement

As a Notary for (County and State), I do hereby certify that on the ____day of __________ 20______ the above-mentioned Affiant, Demarrius Crossley, Minister appeared before me and executed the foregoing document.

Witness my Hand and Seal:

____

Notary Public (SEAL)

Memorandum

To: Recipient Name
From: Minister Crossley of the UNMN Church
Date: (Insert Date)
Subject: **Affidavit Of Peaceful Assembly**

Purpose: This memorandum provides guidance on the creation and utilization of an Affidavit of Peaceful Assembly. This affidavit is a sworn written statement that affirms an individual or organization to formally declare a commitment to peaceful assembly and non - violent means of promoting social change.

Key Components:

1. **Declaration of Intent:** A declaration of intent to assemble peacefully.
2. **Commitment to Non - Violence:** A commitment to non - violent and peaceful assembly.
3. **Respect for Rights:** A commitment to respecting the rights and safety of others.

Importance: This affidavit serves as a formal declaration of one's intention to invoke my rights to protect democracy, promoting social justice, and fostering civic engagement. This Affidavit is Lawful Notice that the Affidavit of Peaceful Assembly is a Religious Right and any interruption of it is a Violation of my Religious Rights.

Utilization:

1. **Promoting Social Change:** Use the affidavit to promote social change and reform through peaceful assembly.
2. **Expressing Solidarity:** Use the affidavit to express solidarity and support for a cause or community.

3. **Expressing Creativity:** Use the affidavit to express creativity and artistic vision peacefully.

Benefits:

- Promoting peaceful resolution of conflicts and disputes.
- Protecting human rights and freedoms.
- Building community and solidarity among like - minded individuals.

By utilizing the Affidavit of Peaceful Expression, individuals and organizations can protect their individual's rights and interests, the principle of freedom of assembly, the principle of non - violent protest, and the principle of respecting the law and rights of others.

REFLECTION PAGE

1. What is one key insight you gained from reading the Affidavit and Memorandum?

____

____

____

____

2. How can you apply this insight to your work, studies, or daily life?

____

____

____

____

Affidavit Of Peaceful Expression

Illinois State }

}ss

Cook County }

Name of Entity

Entity Address

City, State

[00000]

Notice to Agent is Notice to Principle/Notice to Principle is Notice to Agent

Sovereign Political Holder and Minister, over the age of 21 years, after being duly sworn according to law to tell the truth to the facts herein, I do hereby acknowledge and affirm the following: I, Affiant's Demarrius Crossley, am a Sovereign, without subjects. I am a Foreign Nation (not a person) who rules autonomously and am not subject to any entity or jurisdiction anywhere. I am a Sovereign Political Holder, a Minister. My authority for contracting is the age-old, timeless, and universal respect for the intrinsic power, property, and responsibilities of the Sovereign

Individual. I choose to comply with mutual respect, which serves to bring harmony to society. Demarrius Crossley, Minister, God Within Ministry

Address

City, State

[00000]

All national and state constitutions, laws, statutes, ordinances, regulations, rules, codes, and public policies, in all nations and states, are private copyrighted material. I do not possess a license or have the authority to use such copyrighted material, and consequently that material does not have any authority over me, my property, or my personal affairs.

Again, this Affidavit is a Lawful Notification to you, the receivers, and requires your compliance to the demands made within. Failure to respond appropriately to the subject matter contained herein if there is any disagreement with the document is done under the penalties of perjury. Failure to respond within three (3) days, as stipulated, and rebut, with particularity, everything in this Affidavit with which there is disagreement, providing documentation as part of your ascertain, is a lawful, legal and binding agreement by you and those that represent you in all Courts, anywhere in America or the World.

I am fully engaged in my Religious Rights and in all my Affairs. I, Demarrius Crossley, hereby declare and affirm that I am a Sovereign human being, endowed with inherent rights and freedoms.

I, Demarrius Crossley, being duly sworn, depose and say:

Article 1: Introduction

I am making this affidavit to assert my right to peaceful expression.

Article 2: Assertion of Right to Access Peaceful Expression

I hereby affirm that I am entitled to the right to peaceful assembly as guaranteed by the First Amendment to the United States Constitution. I believe that peaceful expression is essential to the exercising of my rights and freedoms.

Article 3: Description of Peaceful Expression

I engage in peaceful expression through [DESCRIPTION OF PEACEFUL EXPRESSION, e.g., writing, art, protest]. My expression promotes peaceful and lawful purposes, including [DESCRIPTION OF PURPOSE].

Article 4: Verification

I hereby declare under penalty of perjury that the foregoing statements are true and accurate to the best of my knowledge and belief.

Again, this Affidavit is a Lawful Notification to you, the receivers, and requires your compliance to the demands made within. Failure to respond appropriately to the subject matter contained herein, if there is any disagreement with the document is done under the penalties of perjury. Failure to respond within three (3) days, as stipulated, and rebut, with particularity, everything in this Affidavit with which there is disagreement, providing documentation as part of your ascertain, is a lawful, legal, and binding agreement by you and those that represent you in all Courts, anywhere in America or the World.

IN WITNESS WHEREOF, I have hereunto set my hand and seal, this [Date] Day of [Month], [Year].

Demarrius Crossley, Minister ______________________________

Illinois State }

}ss

Cook County }

Acknowledgement

As a Notary for (County and State), I do hereby certify that on the ____day of __________ 20______ the above-mentioned Affiant, Demarrius Crossley, Minister appeared before me and executed the foregoing document.

Witness my Hand and Seal:

____

Notary Public (SEAL)

Memorandum

To: Recipient Name
From: Minister Crossley of the UNMN Church
Date: (Insert Date)
Subject: **Affidavit Of Peaceful Expression**

Purpose: This memorandum provides guidance on the creation and utilization of an Affidavit of Peaceful Expression. This affidavit is a sworn written statement that affirms an individual or organization to formally declare a commitment to peaceful expression and non - violent communication.

Key Components:

1. **Declaration of Intent:** A declaration of intent to express oneself peacefully.
2. **Commitment to Respect:** A commitment to respecting the rights and dignity of others.
3. **Non - Violent Communication:** A commitment to non - Violent communication and expression.

Importance: This affidavit serves as a formal declaration of one's intention to invoke my rights to protect free speech, promoting social harmony, and fostering creative expression. This Affidavit is Lawful Notice that the Affidavit of Peaceful Expression is a Religious Right and any interruption of it is a Violation of my Religious Rights.

Utilization:

1. **Promoting Understand:** Use the affidavit to promote understanding and empathy through peaceful expression.
2. **Fostering Dialogue:** Use the affidavit to foster dialogue and constructive conversation.
3. **Expressing Creativity:** Use the affidavit to express creativity and artistic vision peacefully.

Benefits:

- Promoting peaceful resolution of conflicts and disputes.
- Protecting human rights and freedoms.
- Fostering community engagement and participation.

By utilizing the Affidavit of Peaceful Expression, individuals and organizations can protect their individual's rights and interests, the principle of freedom and expression, the principle of respect for others, and the principle of non - violence and peaceful resolutions.

REFLECTION PAGE

1. What is one key insight you gained from reading the Affidavit and Memorandum?

2. How can you apply this insight to your work, studies, or daily life?

Affidavit Of Peaceful Protest

Illinois State }

}ss

Cook County }

Name of Entity

Entity Address

City, State

[00000]

Notice to Agent is Notice to Principle/Notice to Principle is Notice to Agent

Sovereign Political Holder and Minister, over the age of 21 years, after being duly sworn according to law to tell the truth to the facts herein, I do hereby acknowledge and affirm the following: I, Affiant's Demarrius Crossley, am a Sovereign, without subjects. I am a Foreign Nation (not a person) who rules autonomously and am not subject to any entity or jurisdiction anywhere. I am a Sovereign Political Holder, a Minister. My authority for contracting is the age-old, timeless, and universal respect for the intrinsic power, property, and responsibilities of the Sovereign

Individual. I choose to comply with mutual respect, which serves to bring harmony to society. Demarrius Crossley, Minister, God Within Ministry

Address

City, State

[00000]

All national and state constitutions, laws, statutes, ordinances, regulations, rules, codes, and public policies, in all nations and states are private copyrighted material. I do not possess a license or have the authority to use such copyrighted material, and consequently that material does not have any authority over me, my property, or my personal affairs.

Again, this Affidavit is a Lawful Notification to you, the receivers, and requires your compliance to the demands made within. Failure to respond appropriately to the subject matter contained herein if there is any disagreement with the document is done under the penalties of perjury. Failure to respond within three (3) days, as stipulated, and rebut, with particularity, everything in this Affidavit with which there is disagreement, providing documentation as part of your ascertain, is a lawful, legal, and binding agreement by you and those that represent you in all Courts, anywhere in America or the World.

I am fully engaged in my Religious Rights and in all my Affairs. I, Demarrius Crossley, hereby declare and affirm that I am a Sovereign human being, endowed with inherent rights and freedoms.

I, Demarrius Crossley, being duly sworn, depose and say:

Article 1: Introduction

I am making this affidavit to assert my right to peaceful protest.

Article 2: Assertion of Right to Access Peaceful Protest

I hereby affirm that I am entitled to the right to peaceful protest as guaranteed by the First Amendment to the United States Constitution. I believe that peaceful protest is essential to the exercising of my rights and freedoms.

Article 3: Description of Peaceful Protest

I am participating in a peaceful protest on [DATE] at [LOCATION]. The purpose of the protest is to [DESCRIPTION OF PURPOSE]. I affirm that the protest will be peaceful and lawful.

Article 4: Verification

I hereby declare under penalty of perjury that the foregoing statements are true and accurate to the best of my knowledge and belief.

Again, this Affidavit is a Lawful Notification to you, the receivers, and requires your compliance to the demands made within. Failure to respond appropriately to the subject matter contained herein if there is any disagreement with the document is done under the penalties of perjury. Failure to respond within three (3) days, as stipulated, and rebut, with particularity, everything in this Affidavit with which there is disagreement, providing documentation as part of your ascertain, is a lawful, legal, and binding agreement by you and those that represent you in all Courts, anywhere in America or the World.

IN WITNESS WHEREOF, I have hereunto set my hand and seal, this [Date] Day of [Month], [Year].

Demarrius Crossley, Minister ______________________________

Illinois State }

}ss

Cook County }

Acknowledgement

As a Notary for (County and State), I do hereby certify that on the ____day of __________ 20______ the above-mentioned Affiant, Demarrius Crossley, Minister appeared before me and executed the foregoing document.

Witness my Hand and Seal:

____

Notary Public (SEAL)

Memorandum

To: Recipient Name
From: Minister Crossley of the UNMN Church
Date: (Insert Date)
Subject: **Affidavit Of Peaceful Protest**

Purpose: This memorandum provides guidance on the creation and utilization of an Affidavit of Peaceful Protest. This affidavit is a sworn written statement that affirms an individual or organization to formally declare a commitment to peaceful protest and non - violent means of promoting social change.

Key Components:

1. **Statement of Law - Abiding Status:** A statement affirming compliance with all applicable laws.
2. **Commitment to Non - Violence:** A commitment to non - violent and peaceful means of expressing dissent.
3. **Respect for Rights:** A commitment to respecting the rights and safety of others.

Importance: This affidavit serves as a formal declaration of one's intention to invoke my rights to protect democracy, promoting social justice, building a more just and equitable society. This Affidavit is Lawful Notice that the Affidavit of Peaceful Protest is a Religious Right and any interruption of it is a Violation of my Religious Rights.

Utilization:

1. **Promoting Social Change:** Use the affidavit to Promote social change and reform through peaceful means.
2. **Expressing Dissent:** Use the affidavit to express dissent and disagreement with policies or practices.

3. **Building Community:** Use the affidavit to build community and solidarity among like - minded individuals.

Benefits:

- Promoting peaceful resolution of conflicts and disputes.
- Protecting human rights and freedoms.
- Fostering community engagement and participation.

By utilizing the Affidavit of Peaceful Protest, individuals and organizations can protect their individual's rights and interests, the principle of freedom and expression, the principle of non - violent resistance and peaceful protest, and the principle of respecting the law and the rights of others.

REFLECTION PAGE

1. What is one key insight you gained from reading the Affidavit and Memorandum?

____

____

____

____

2. How can you apply this insight to your work, studies, or daily life?

____

____

____

____

Affidavit Of Choose Beliefs

Illinois State }

}ss

Cook County }

Name of Entity

Entity Address

City, State

[00000]

Notice to Agent is Notice to Principle/Notice to Principle is Notice to Agent

Sovereign Political Holder and Minister, over the age of 21 years, after being duly sworn according to law to tell the truth to the facts herein, I do hereby acknowledge and affirm the following: I, Affiant's Demarrius Crossley, am a Sovereign, without subjects. I am a Foreign Nation (not a person) who rules autonomously and am not subject to any entity or jurisdiction anywhere. I am a Sovereign Political Holder, a Minister. My authority for contracting is the age-old, timeless, and universal respect for the intrinsic power, property, and responsibilities of the Sovereign

Individual. I choose to comply with mutual respect, which serves to bring harmony to society. Demarrius Crossley, Minister, God Within Ministry

Address

City, State

[00000]

All national and state constitutions, laws, statutes, ordinances, regulations, rules, codes, and public policies, in all nations and states are private copyrighted material. I do not possess a license or have the authority to use such copyrighted material, and consequently that material does not have any authority over me, my property, or my personal affairs.

Again, this Affidavit is a Lawful Notification to you, the receivers, and requires your compliance to the demands made within. Failure to respond appropriately to the subject matter contained herein if there is any disagreement with the document is done under the penalties of perjury. Failure to respond within three (3) days, as stipulated, and rebut, with particularity, everything in this Affidavit with which there is disagreement, providing documentation as part of your ascertain, is a lawful, legal, and binding agreement by you and those that represent you in all Courts, anywhere in America or the World.

I am fully engaged in my Religious Rights and in all my Affairs. I, Demarrius Crossley, hereby declare and affirm that I am a Sovereign human being, endowed with inherent rights and freedoms.

I, Demarrius Crossley, being duly sworn, depose and say:

Article 1: Introduction

I am making this affidavit to assert my right to choose and hold my personal beliefs.

Article 2: Assertion of Right to Choose Beliefs

I hereby affirm that I am entitled to the right of freedom of thought and expression as guaranteed by the First Amendment to the United States Constitution. I believe that the freedom to choose and hold my personal beliefs is essential to my identity and well-being.

Article 3: Description of Chosen Beliefs

I hold the following personal beliefs: [DESCRIPTION OF BELIEFS]. These beliefs are important to me because [EXPLANATION OF IMPORTANCE]

Article 4: Verification

I hereby declare under penalty of perjury that the foregoing statements are true and accurate to the best of my knowledge and belief.

Again, this Affidavit is a Lawful Notification to you, the receivers, and requires your compliance to the demands made within. Failure to respond appropriately to the subject matter contained herein if there is any disagreement with the document is done under the penalties of perjury. Failure to respond within three (3) days, as stipulated, and rebut, with particularity, everything in this Affidavit with which there is disagreement, providing documentation as part of your ascertain, is a lawful, legal, and binding agreement by you and those that represent you in all Courts, anywhere in America or the World.

IN WITNESS WHEREOF, I have hereunto set my hand and seal, this [Date] Day of [Month], [Year].

Demarrius Crossley, Minister ______________________________

Illinois State }

}ss

Cook County }

Acknowledgement

As a Notary for (County and State), I do hereby certify that on the ____day of __________ 20______ the above-mentioned Affiant, Demarrius Crossley, Minister appeared before me and executed the foregoing document.

Witness my Hand and Seal:

____

Notary Public (SEAL)

Memorandum

To: Recipient Name
From: Minister Crossley of the UNMN Church
Date: (Insert Date)
Subject: **Affidavit of To Choose Beliefs**

Purpose: This memorandum provides guidance on the creation and utilization of an Affidavit t of To Choose Beliefs. This affidavit is a sworn written statement that affirms an individual or organization to formally declare a commitment to choosing beliefs through critical evaluation and intellectual freedom.

Key Components:

1. **Declaration of Autonomy:** A declaration of autonomy in choosing personal beliefs.
2. **Statement of Intent:** A statement of intent to critically evaluate and select beliefs.
3. **Commitment to Intellectual Freedom:** A commitment to intellectual freedom and open - mindedness.

Importance: This affidavit serves as a formal declaration of one's intention to invoke my rights to promoting intellectual freedom, encouraging critical thinking, and fostering personal growth. This Affidavit is Lawful Notice that the Affidavit of To Choose Beliefs is a Religious Right and any interruption of it is a Violation of my Religious Rights.

Utilization:

1. **Personal Growth:** Use the affidavit to facilitate personal growth and development through informed belief selection.
2. **Critical Evaluation:** Use the affidavit to critically evaluate information and beliefs.

3. **Informed Decision - Making:** Use the affidavit to make informed decisions base on carefully considered beliefs.

Benefits:

- Increased autonomy and agency in choosing personal beliefs.
- Improved critical thinking and analytical skills.
- Greater personal clarity and understanding of one's beliefs.

By utilizing the Affidavit of To Choose Beliefs, individuals and organizations can protect their individual's rights and interests, the principle of critical thinking, the principle of exercising autonomy and agency in choosing beliefs, and the principle of remaining open to new ideas and perspective.

REFLECTION PAGE

1. What is one key insight you gained from reading the Affidavit and Memorandum?

2. How can you apply this insight to your work, studies, or daily life?

Affidavit of Practice a Religion Past Infinity

Illinois State }

}ss

Cook County }

Name of Entity

Entity Address

City, State

[00000]

Notice to Agent is Notice to Principle/Notice to Principle is Notice I to Agent

Sovereign Political Holder and Minister, over the age of 21 years, after being duly sworn according to law to tell the truth to the facts herein, I do hereby acknowledge and affirm the following: I, Affiant's Demarrius Crossley, am a Sovereign, without subjects. I am a Foreign Nation (not a person) who rules autonomously and am not subject to any entity or jurisdiction anywhere. I am a Sovereign Political Holder, a Minister. My authority for contracting is the age-old, timeless, and universal respect for the intrinsic power, property, and responsibilities of the Sovereign

Individual. I choose to comply with mutual respect, which serves to bring harmony to society. Demarrius Crossley, Minister, God Within Ministry

Address

City, State

[00000]

All national and state constitutions, laws, statutes, ordinances, regulations, rules, codes, and public policies, in all nations and states are private copyrighted material. I do not possess a license or have the authority to use such copyrighted material, and consequently that material does not have any authority over me, my property, or my personal affairs.

Again, this Affidavit is a Lawful Notification to you, the receivers, and requires your compliance to the demands made within. Failure to respond appropriately to the subject matter contained herein if there is any disagreement with the document is done under the penalties of perjury. Failure to respond within three (3) days, as stipulated, and rebut, with particularity, everything in this Affidavit with which there is disagreement, providing documentation as part of your ascertain, is a lawful, legal, and binding agreement by you and those that represent you in all Courts, anywhere in America or the World.

I am fully engaged in my Religious Rights and in all my Affairs. I, Demarrius Crossley, hereby declare and affirm that I am a Sovereign human being, endowed with inherent rights and freedoms.

I, Demarrius Crossley, being duly sworn, depose and say:

Article 1: Introduction

I am making this affidavit to assert my right to practice my faith without limitations or boundaries.

Article 2: Assertion of Right to Practice Faith

I hereby affirm that I am entitled to the right to freedom of religion as guaranteed by the First Amendment to the United States Constitution. I believe that my faith is a fundamental aspect of my being, and I should be free to practice it without restrictions.

Article 3: Description of Faith Practice

My faith is a deeply personal and meaningful part of my life. I believe in the importance of spiritual growth and development, and I practice my faith in a way that extends beyond traditional boundaries.

Article 4: Verification

I hereby declare under penalty of perjury that the foregoing statements are true and accurate to the best of my knowledge and belief.

Again, this Affidavit is a Lawful Notification to you, the receivers, and requires your compliance to the demands made within. Failure to respond appropriately to the subject matter contained herein if there is any disagreement with the document is done under the penalties of perjury. Failure to respond within three (3) days, as stipulated, and rebut, with particularity, everything in this Affidavit with which there is disagreement, providing documentation as part of your ascertain, is a lawful, legal, and binding agreement by you and those that represent you in all Courts, anywhere in America or the World.

IN WITNESS WHEREOF, I have hereunto set my hand and seal, this [Date] Day of [Month], [Year].

Demarrius Crossley, Minister ______________________________

Illinois State }

}ss

Cook County }

Acknowledgement

As a Notary for (County and State), I do hereby certify that on the ____day of __________ 20______ the above-mentioned Affiant, Demarrius Crossley, Minister appeared before me and executed the foregoing document.

Witness my Hand and Seal:

____

Notary Public (SEAL)

Memorandum

To: Recipient Name
From: Minister Crossley of the UNMN Church
Date: (Insert Date)
Subject: **Affidavit of Practice a Religion Past Infinity**

Purpose: This memorandum provides guidance on the creation and utilization of an Affidavit of Practice a Religion Past Infinity. This affidavit is a sworn written statement that affirms an individual or organization to formally declare a commitment to practicing a religion and exploring spiritual growth beyond conventional boundaries.

Key Components:

1. **Declaration of Faith:** A declaration of faith and commitment to practicing a religion.
2. **Expression of Spiritual Growth:** An expression of desire for spiritual growth and exploration beyond conventional boundaries.
3. **Commitment to Personal Freedom:** A commitment to personal freedom in spiritual practice.

Importance: This affidavit serves as a formal declaration of one's intention to invoke my rights to nurturing spiritual growth, exploring the infinite possibilities of spiritual practice, and fostering inner peace and well - being. This Affidavit is Lawful Notice that the Affidavit of Practice a Religion Past Infinity is a Religious Right and any interruption of it is a Violation of my Religious Rights.

Utilization:

1. **Deepening Spiritual Practice:** Use the affidavit to deepen spiritual practice and connection with a higher power or the universe.

2. **Exploring Mystical Experiences:** Use the affidavit to explore mystical experiences and spiritual phenomena.
3. **Fostering Personal Transformation:** Use the affidavit to foster personal transformation and spiritual growth.

Benefits:

- Increased spiritual awareness and understanding.
- Personal growth and transformation through spiritual practice.
- A sense of connection to something greater than oneself.

By utilizing the Affidavit Of Practice a Religion Past Infinity, individuals and organizations can protect their individual's rights and interests, the principle of spiritual exploration, the principle of prioritizing personal and spiritual growth, and the principle of respecting diverse spiritual perspectives and practices.

REFLECTION PAGE

1. What is one key insight you gained from reading the Affidavit and Memorandum?

2. How can you apply this insight to your work, studies, or daily life?

Affidavit of Love

Illinois State }

}ss

Cook County }

Name of Entity

Entity Address

City, State

[00000]

Notice to Agent is Notice to Principle/Notice to Principle is Notice to Agent

Sovereign Political Holder and Minister, over the age of 21 years, after being duly sworn according to law to tell the truth to the facts herein, I do hereby acknowledge and affirm the following: I, Affiant's Demarrius Crossley, am a Sovereign, without subjects. I am a Foreign Nation (not a person) who rules autonomously and am not subject to any entity or jurisdiction anywhere. I am a Sovereign Political Holder, a Minister. My authority for contracting is the age-old, timeless, and universal respect for the intrinsic power, property, and responsibilities of the Sovereign

Individual. I choose to comply with mutual respect, which serves to bring harmony to society. Demarrius Crossley, Minister, God Within Ministry

Address

City, State

[00000]

All national and state constitutions, laws, statutes, ordinances, regulations, rules, codes, and public policies, in all nations and states are private copyrighted material. I do not possess a license or have the authority to use such copyrighted material, and consequently that material does not have any authority over me, my property, or my personal affairs.

Again, this Affidavit is a Lawful Notification to you, the receiver, and requires your compliance to the demands made within. Failure to respond appropriately to the subject matter contained herein if there is any disagreement with the document is done under the penalties of perjury. Failure to respond within three (3) days, as stipulated, and rebut, with particularity, everything in this Affidavit with which there is disagreement, providing documentation as part of your ascertain, is a lawful, legal, and binding agreement by you and those that represent you in all Courts, anywhere in America or the World.

I am fully engaged in my Religious Rights and in all my Affairs. I, Demarrius Crossley, hereby declare and affirm that I am a Sovereign human being, endowed with inherent rights and freedoms.

I, Demarrius Crossley, being duly sworn, depose and say:

Article 1: Introduction

I am making this affidavit to affirm my love for [PARTNER'S NAME], with whom I have shared a loving relationship for [NUMBER] years.

Article 2: Assertion of Right to Practice Faith

I hereby affirm that I love [PARTNER'S NAME] with all my heart and soul. Our relationship is built on mutual respect, trust, and affection.

Article 3: Expression of Feelings

[PARTNER'S NAME] brings joy and happiness into my life, and I value our relationship above all else. I am committed to nurturing and supporting our love.

Article 4: Verification

I hereby declare under penalty of perjury that the foregoing statements are true and accurate to the best of my knowledge and belief.

Again, this Affidavit is a Lawful Notification to you, the receivers, and requires your compliance to the demands made within. Failure to respond appropriately to the subject matter contained herein if there is any disagreement with the document is done under the penalties of perjury. Failure to respond within three (3) days, as stipulated, and rebut, with particularity, everything in this Affidavit with which there is disagreement, providing documentation as part of your ascertain, is a lawful, legal, and binding agreement by you and those that represent you in all Courts, anywhere in America or the World.

IN WITNESS WHEREOF, I have hereunto set my hand and seal, this [Date] Day of [Month], [Year].

Demarrius Crossley, Minister ______________________________

Illinois State }

}ss

Cook County }

Acknowledgement

As a Notary for (County and State), I do hereby certify that on the ____day of __________ 20______ the above-mentioned Affiant, Demarrius Crossley, Minister appeared before me and executed the foregoing document.

Witness my Hand and Seal:

____

Notary Public (SEAL)

Memorandum

To: Recipient Name
From: Minister Crossley of the UNMN Church
Date: (Insert Date)
Subject: **Affidavit of Love**

Purpose: This memorandum provides guidance on the creation and utilization of an Affidavit of Love. This affidavit is a sworn written statement that affirms an individual's or organization to formally declare a commitment to love and care for another person.

Key Components:

1. **Declaration of Love:** A statement declaring love and affection for another person.
2. **Commitment to Care:** A statement committing to care for and support the well-being of the loved one.
3. **Expression of Devotion:** An expression of devotion and loyalty to the loved one.

Importance: This affidavit serves as a formal declaration of one's intention to invoke my rights to nurturing relationships, promoting positive emotions and fostering a sense of community and belonging. This Affidavit is Lawful Notice that the Affidavit of Love is a Religious Right and any interruption of it is a Violation of my Religious Rights.

Utilization:

- **Strengthening Relationships:** Use the affidavit to strengthen romantic relationships, friendships, or familial bonds.
- **Promoting Emotional Well-being:** Use the affidavit to promote emotional well-being and happiness.
- **Fostering a Sense of Belonging:** Use the affidavit to foster a sense of belonging and connection.

Benefits:

- A deeper and more meaningful connection with the loved one.
- Increased emotional support and understanding.
- Improved mental health and well-being.

By utilizing the Affidavit of Love, individuals and organizations can protect the Religious Organization Rights and interests, obtain the principle of accepting and loving the person unconditionally, the principle of mutual respect, and the principle of supporting and encouraging the loved one's growth and well-being.

REFLECTION PAGE

1. What is one key insight you gained from reading the Affidavit and Memorandum?

2. How can you apply this insight to your work, studies, or daily life?

Affidavit of Marriage

Illinois State }

}ss

Cook County }

Name of Entity

Entity Address

City, State

[00000]

Notice to Agent is Notice to Principle/Notice to Principle is Notice to Agent

Sovereign Political Holder and Minister, over the age of 21 years, after being duly sworn according to law to tell the truth to the facts herein, I do hereby acknowledge and affirm the following: I, Affiant's Demarrius Crossley, am a Sovereign, without subjects. I am a Foreign Nation (not a person) who rules autonomously and am not subject to any entity or jurisdiction anywhere. I am a Sovereign Political Holder, a Minister. My authority for contracting is the age-old, timeless, and universal respect for the intrinsic power, property, and responsibilities of the Sovereign

Individual. I choose to comply with mutual respect, which serves to bring harmony to society. Demarrius Crossley, Minister, God Within Ministry

Address

City, State

[00000]

All national and state constitutions, laws, statutes, ordinances, regulations, rules, codes, and public policies, in all nations and states are private copyrighted material. I do not possess a license or have the authority to use such copyrighted material, and consequently that material does not have any authority over me, my property, or my personal affairs.

Again, this Affidavit is a Lawful Notification to you, the receiver, and requires your compliance to the demands made within. Failure to respond appropriately to the subject matter contained herein if there is any disagreement with the document is done under the penalties of perjury. Failure to respond within three (3) days, as stipulated, and rebut, with particularity, everything in this Affidavit with which there is disagreement, providing documentation as part of your ascertain, is a lawful, legal, and binding agreement by you and those that represent you in all Courts, anywhere in America or the World.

I am fully engaged in my Religious Rights and in all my Affairs. I, Demarrius Crossley, hereby declare and affirm that I am a Sovereign human being, endowed with inherent rights and freedoms.

I, Demarrius Crossley, being duly sworn, depose and say:

Article 1: Introduction

I am making this affidavit to affirm my marital status.

Article 2: Affirmation of Marriage

I am married to [SPOUSE'S NAME], whom I married on [DATE] at [PLACE]. We have been married for [NUMBER] years and have [NUMBER] children together.

Article 3: Details of Marriage

Our marriage ceremony was [CIVIL/RELIGIOUS/CULTURAL], and we built a life together based on mutual.

Article 4: Verification

I hereby declare under penalty of perjury that the foregoing statements are true and accurate to the best of my knowledge and belief.

Again, this Affidavit is a Lawful Notification to you, the receiver, and requires your compliance to the demands made within. Failure to respond appropriately to the subject matter contained herein if there is any disagreement with the document is done under the penalties of perjury. Failure to respond within three (3) days, as stipulated, and rebut, with particularity, everything in this Affidavit with which there is disagreement, providing documentation as part of your ascertain, is a lawful, legal and binding agreement by you and those that represent you in all Courts, anywhere in America or the World.

IN WITNESS WHEREOF, I have hereunto set my hand and seal, this [Date] Day of [Month], [Year].

Demarrius Crossley, Minister ______________________________

Illinois State }

}ss

Cook County }

Acknowledgement

As a Notary for (County and State), I do hereby certify that on the ____day of __________ 20______ the above-mentioned Affiant, Demarrius Crossley, Minister appeared before me and executed the foregoing document.

Witness my Hand and Seal:

____

Notary Public (SEAL)

Memorandum

To: Recipient Name
From: Minister Crossley of the UNMN Church
Date: (Insert Date)
Subject: **Affidavit of Marriage**

Purpose: This memorandum provides guidance on the creation and utilization of an Affidavit for Marriage. This affidavit is a sworn written statement that affirms an individual or organization to formally declare a commitment to the marriage and partner.

Key Components:

1. **Declaration of Family Commitment:** A declaration of commitment to marriage and partner.
2. **Mutual Understanding:** Mutual understanding and agreement on marital responsibilities and expectations.
3. **Statement of Support:** A statement of support for each other's well - being and happiness.

Importance: This affidavit serves as a formal declaration of one's intention to invoke my rights to protection of building a strong foundation for a lifelong partnership, promoting martial stability and happiness, and supporting each other's growth and well - being. This Affidavit is Lawful Notice that the Affidavit OF Marriage is a Religious Right and any interruption of it is a Violation of my Religious Rights.

Utilization:

1. **Strengthening Martial Bond:** Use the affidavit to strengthen the martial bond and relationship.
2. **Promoting Marital Harmony:** Use the affidavit to promote marital harmony and understanding.

3. **Providing Support:** Use the affidavit to provide emotional and practical support to each other.

Benefits:

- Improved a stronger, more resilient marital relationship.
- Improved communication and conflict resolution.
- Increase trust and understanding between partners.

By utilizing the Affidavit of Marriage, individuals and organizations can protect their individual's rights; the principle of love and respect, the principle of trust and communication, and the principle of working together as a team and supporting each other.

REFLECTION PAGE

1. What is one key insight you gained from reading the Affidavit and Memorandum?

____

____

____

____

2. How can you apply this insight to your work, studies, or daily life?

____

____

____

____

Affidavit of Children

Illinois State }

}ss

Cook County }

Name of Entity

Entity Address

City, State

[00000]

Notice to Agent is Notice to Principle/Notice to Principle is Notice to Agent

Sovereign Political Holder and Minister, over the age of 21 years, after being duly sworn according to law to tell the truth to the facts herein, I do hereby acknowledge and affirm the following: I, Affiant's Demarrius Crossley, am a Sovereign, without subjects. I am a Foreign Nation (not a person) who rules autonomously and am not subject to any entity or jurisdiction anywhere. I am a Sovereign Political Holder, a Minister. My authority for contracting is the age-old, timeless, and universal respect for the intrinsic power, property, and responsibilities of the Sovereign

Individual. I choose to comply with mutual respect, which serves to bring harmony to society. Demarrius Crossley, Minister, God Within Ministry

Address

City, State

[00000]

All national and state constitutions, laws, statutes, ordinances, regulations, rules, codes, and public policies, in all nations and states are private copyrighted material. I do not possess a license or have the authority to use such copyrighted material, and consequently that material does not have any authority over me, my property, or my personal affairs.

Again, this Affidavit is a Lawful Notification to you, the receivers, and requires your compliance to the demands made within. Failure to respond appropriately to the subject matter contained herein if there is any disagreement with the document is done under the penalties of perjury. Failure to respond within three (3) days, as stipulated, and rebut, with particularity, everything in this Affidavit with which there is disagreement, providing documentation as part of your ascertain, is a lawful, legal, and binding agreement by you and those that represent you in all Courts, anywhere in America or the World.

I am fully engaged in my Religious Rights and in all my Affairs. I, Demarrius Crossley, hereby declare and affirm that I am a Sovereign human being, endowed with inherent rights and freedoms.

I, Demarrius Crossley, being duly sworn, depose and say:

Article 1: Introduction

I am making this affidavit to provide information about my children.

Article 2: Information about Children

My children are [CHILD'S NAME] (age [AGE]) and [CHILD'S NAME] (age [AGE]). As their parent, I am responsible for their care and well-being.

Article 3: Verification

I hereby declare under penalty of perjury that the foregoing statements are true and accurate to the best of my knowledge and belief.

Again, this Affidavit is a Lawful Notification to you, the receivers, and requires your compliance to the demands made within. Failure to respond appropriately to the subject matter contained herein if there is any disagreement with the document, done under the penalties of perjury. Failure to respond within three (3) days, as stipulated, and rebut, with particularity, everything in this Affidavit with which there is disagreement, providing documentation as part of your ascertain, is a lawful, legal, and binding agreement by you and those that represent you in all Courts, anywhere in America or the World.

IN WITNESS WHEREOF, I have hereunto set my hand and seal, this [Date] Day of [Month], [Year].

Demarrius Crossley, Minister ______________________________

Illinois State }

}ss

Cook County }

Acknowledgement

As a Notary for (County and State), I do hereby certify that on the ____day of __________ 20______ the above-mentioned Affiant, Demarrius Crossley, Minister appeared before me and executed the foregoing document.

Witness my Hand and Seal:

____

Notary Public (SEAL)

Memorandum

To: Recipient Name
From: Minister Crossley of the UNMN Church
Date: (Insert Date)
Subject: **Affidavit of Children**

Purpose: This memorandum provides guidance on the creation and utilization of an Affidavit of Children. This affidavit is a sworn written statement that affirms an individual or organization to formally declare a commitment to promoting the well-being and best interests of children.

Key Components:

1. **Declaration of Family Commitment:** A declaration of commitment to the well-being and best interests of children.
2. **Prioritization of Children's Needs:** Prioritization of children's physical, emotional, and educational needs.
3. **Statement of Support:** A statement of support for children's development and growth.

Importance: This affidavit serves as a formal declaration of one's intention to invoke my rights to protection of safeguarding children's future, promoting healthy development, and supporting vulnerable children. This Affidavit is Lawful Notice that the Affidavit of Children is a Religious Right and any interruption of it is a Violation of my Religious Rights.

Utilization:

1. **Protection of Children's Rights:** Use the affidavit to protect children's rights and promote their well-being.
2. **Support for Children's Development:** Use the affidavit to support children's physical, emotional, and educational development.
3. **Advocacy for Children:** Use the affidavit to advocate for policies and practices that benefit children.

Benefits:

- Improved the physical, emotional, and psychological well-being of children.
- Increased support and resources for children's development.
- Increased emotional and practical support for family members.

By utilizing the Affidavit of Children, individuals and organizations can protect their individual rights, have the best interests of the child, ensure the protection and safety of children, and provide a nurturing and supportive environment for children.

REFLECTION PAGE

1. What is one key insight you gained from reading the Affidavit and Memorandum?

____

____

____

____

2. How can you apply this insight to your work, studies, or daily life?

____

____

____

____

Affidavit of Security from Abuse

Illinois State }

}ss

Cook County }

Name of Entity

Entity Address

City, State

[00000]

Notice to Agent is Notice to Principle/Notice to Principle is Notice to Agent

Sovereign Political Holder and Minister, over the age of 21 years, after being duly sworn according to law to tell the truth to the facts herein, I do hereby acknowledge and affirm the following: I, Affiant's Demarrius Crossley, am a Sovereign, without subjects. I am a Foreign Nation (not a person) who rules autonomously and am not subject to any entity or jurisdiction anywhere. I am a Sovereign Political Holder, a Minister. My authority for contracting is the age-old, timeless, and universal respect for the intrinsic power, property, and responsibilities of the Sovereign

Individual. I choose to comply with mutual respect, which serves to bring harmony to society. Demarrius Crossley, Minister, God Within Ministry

Address

City, State

[00000]

All national and state constitutions, laws, statutes, ordinances, regulations, rules, codes, and public policies, in all nations and states are private copyrighted material. I do not possess a license or have the authority to use such copyrighted material, and consequently that material does not have any authority over me, my property, or my personal affairs.

Again, this Affidavit is a Lawful Notification to you, the receivers, and requires your compliance to the demands made within. Failure to respond appropriately to the subject matter contained herein if there is any disagreement with the document is done under the penalties of perjury. Failure to respond within three (3) days, as stipulated, and rebut, with particularity, everything in this Affidavit with which there is disagreement, providing documentation as part of your ascertain, is a lawful, legal, and binding agreement by you and those that represent you in all Courts, anywhere in America or the World.

I am fully engaged in my Religious Rights and in all my Affairs. I, Demarrius Crossley, hereby declare and affirm that I am a Sovereign human being, endowed with inherent rights and freedoms.

I, Demarrius Crossley, being duly sworn, depose and say:

Article 1: Introduction

I am making this affidavit to report incidents of abuse and request protection.

Article 2: Description of Incidents

On [DATE], at [PERSON'S NAME] threatened me with physical harm. I have also received harassing messages from them.

Article 3: Fear for Safety

I fear for my safety and well-being due to these incidents.

Article 4: Request for Protection

I request a restraining order to protect me from further abuse.

Article 5: Verification

I hereby declare under penalty of perjury that the foregoing statements are true and accurate to the best of my knowledge and belief.

Again, this Affidavit is a Lawful Notification to you, the receivers, and requires your compliance to the demands made within. Failure to respond appropriately to the subject matter contained herein if there is any disagreement with the document is done under the penalties of perjury. Failure to respond within three (3) days, as stipulated, and rebut, with particularity, everything in this Affidavit with which there is disagreement, providing documentation as part of your ascertain, is a lawful, legal, and binding agreement by you and those that represent you in all Courts, anywhere in America or the World.

IN WITNESS WHEREOF, I have hereunto set my hand and seal, this [Date] Day of [Month], [Year].

Demarrius Crossley, Minister ________________________________

Illinois State }

}ss

Cook County }

Acknowledgement

As a Notary for (County and State), I do hereby certify that on the ____day of __________ 20______ the above-mentioned Affiant, Demarrius Crossley, Minister appeared before me and executed the foregoing document.

Witness my Hand and Seal:

____

Notary Public (SEAL)

Memorandum

To: Recipient Name
From: Minister Crossley of the UNMN Church
Date: (Insert Date)
Subject: **Affidavit Of Security from Abuse**

Purpose: This memorandum provides guidance on the creation and utilization of an Affidavit of Security from Abuse. This affidavit is a sworn written statement that affirms an individual or organization to formally declare a commitment to promoting security from abuse and protecting individuals from harm.

Key Components:

1. **Declaration of Protection:** A declaration seeking protection from abuse.
2. **Identification of Abuse:** Identification of specific forms of abuse. (e.g., physical, emotional, financial)
3. **Request for Support:** A request for support and safeguards to prevent further abuse.

Importance: This affidavit serves as a formal declaration of one's intention to invoke my rights to protection of vulnerable individuals, promotion of healthy environments, and prevention of long - term consequences. This Affidavit is Lawful Notice that the Affidavit of Security from Abuse is a Religious Right and any interruption of it is a Violation of my Religious Rights.

Utilization:

1. **Protection of Individuals:** Use the affidavit to protect in various settings (e.g., domestic, workplace, institutional).
2. **Promotion of Healthy Relationships:** Use the affidavit to promote healthy relationships and boundaries.

3. **Support For Victims:** Use the affidavit to provide support and resources for victims of abuse.

Benefits:

- Protection of physical, emotional, and psychological harm.
- Promotion of overall well - being and safety.
- Empowerment of victims to seek help and support.

By utilizing the Affidavit of Security from Abuse, individuals and organizations can protect their individual's rights, safety and well - being, respect and dignity, and the principle of holding perpetrators accountable for their actions.

REFLECTION PAGE

1. What is one key insight you gained from reading the Affidavit and Memorandum?

____

____

____

____

2. How can you apply this insight to your work, studies, or daily life?

____

____

____

____

Affidavit of Security from Persecution

Illinois State }

}ss

Cook County }

Name of Entity

Entity Address

City, State

[00000]

Notice to Agent is Notice to Principle/Notice to Principle is Notice to Agent

Sovereign Political Holder and Minister, over the age of 21 years, after being duly sworn according to law to tell the truth to the facts herein, I do hereby acknowledge and affirm the following: I, Affiant's Demarrius Crossley, am a Sovereign, without subjects. I am a Foreign Nation (not a person) who rules autonomously and am not subject to any entity or jurisdiction anywhere. I am a Sovereign Political Holder, a Minister. My authority for contracting is the age-old, timeless, and universal respect for the intrinsic power, property, and responsibilities of the Sovereign

Individual. I choose to comply with mutual respect, which serves to bring harmony to society. Demarrius Crossley, Minister, God Within Ministry

Address

City, State

[00000]

All national and state constitutions, laws, statutes, ordinances, regulations, rules, codes, and public policies, in all nations and states are private copyrighted material. I do not possess a license or have the authority to use such copyrighted material, and consequently that material does not have any authority over me, my property, or my personal affairs.

Again, this Affidavit is a Lawful Notification to you, the receivers, and requires your compliance to the demands made within. Failure to respond appropriately to the subject matter contained herein if there is any disagreement with the document is done under the penalties of perjury. Failure to respond within three (3) days, as stipulated, and rebut, with particularity, everything in this Affidavit with which there is disagreement, providing documentation as part of your ascertain, is a lawful, legal, and binding agreement by you and those that represent you in all Courts, anywhere in America or the World.

I am fully engaged in my Religious Rights and in all my Affairs. I, Demarrius Crossley, hereby declare and affirm that I am a Sovereign human being, endowed with inherent rights and freedoms.

I, Demarrius Crossley, being duly sworn, depose and say:

Article 1: Introduction

I am making this affidavit to report persecution.

Article 2: Description of Persecution

I was persecuted in [COUNTRY] due to my [RACE/RELIGION/NATIONALITY].

Article 3: Fear of Persecution

I fear persecution if I return [COUNTRY].

Article 4: Request for Protection

I request protection and asylum.

Article 5: Verification

I hereby declare under penalty of perjury that the foregoing statements are true.

Again, this Affidavit is a Lawful Notification to you, the receivers, and requires your compliance to the demands made within. Failure to respond appropriately to the subject matter contained herein if there is any disagreement with the document is done under the penalties of perjury. Failure to respond within three (3) days, as stipulated, and rebut, with particularity, everything in this Affidavit with which there is disagreement, providing documentation as part of your ascertain, is a lawful, legal, and binding agreement by you and those that represent you in all Courts, anywhere in America or the World.

IN WITNESS WHEREOF, I have hereunto set my hand and seal, this [Date] Day of [Month], [Year].

Demarrius Crossley, Minister ______________________________

Illinois State }

}ss

Cook County }

Acknowledgement

As a Notary for (County and State), I do hereby certify that on the ____day of _________ 20______ the above-mentioned Affiant, Demarrius Crossley, Minister appeared before me and executed the foregoing document.

Witness my Hand and Seal:

____

Notary Public (SEAL)

Memorandum

To: Recipient Name
From: Minister Crossley of the UNMN Church
Date: (Insert Date)
Subject: **Affidavit of Security from Persecution**

Purpose: This memorandum provides guidance on the creation and utilization of an Affidavit of Security from Persecution. This affidavit is a sworn written statement that affirms an individual or organization to formally declare a commitment to promoting security from persecution and protecting human rights.

Key Components:

1. **Declaration of Protection:** A declaration seeking protection from persecution.
2. **Identification of Threats:** Identification of specific threats or forms of persecution.
3. **Request for Safeguard:** A request for safeguards to prevent persecution.

Importance: This affidavit serves as a formal declaration of one's intention to invoke my rights to protection of vulnerable groups, promotion of human rights, and prevention of human rights violations. This Affidavit is Lawful Notice that the Affidavit of Security from Persecution is a Religious Right and any interruption of it is a Violation of my Religious Rights.

Utilization:

1. **Protection of Individuals:** Use the affidavit to protect individuals from persecution based on various grounds such as race, religion, or political opinions.

2. **Promotion of Tolerance:** Use the affidavit to promote tolerance and understanding in society.
3. **Advocacy for Human Rights:** Use the affidavit to advocate for human rights and protection from persecution.

Benefits:

- Protection from harm and persecution.
- Promotion of stability and security.
- Upholding human dignity and rights.

By utilizing the Affidavit of Security from Persecution, individuals and organizations can protect their individual's rights, protection of human rights, non - discrimination and equal treatment, ensuring safety and security for all individuals.

REFLECTION PAGE

1. What is one key insight you gained from reading the Affidavit and Memorandum?

2. How can you apply this insight to your work, studies, or daily life?

Affidavit of Security from Tyranny

Illinois State }

}ss

Cook County }

Name of Entity

Entity Address

City, State

[00000]

Notice to Agent is Notice to Principle/Notice to Principle is Notice to Agent

Sovereign Political Holder and Minister, over the age of 21 years, after being duly sworn according to law to tell the truth to the facts herein, I do hereby acknowledge and affirm the following: I, Affiant's Demarrius Crossley, am a Sovereign, without subjects. I am a Foreign Nation (not a person) who rules autonomously and am not subject to any entity or jurisdiction anywhere. I am Sovereign Political Holder, a Minister. My authority for contracting is the age-old, timeless, and universal respect for the intrinsic power, property, and responsibilities of the Sovereign

Individual. I choose to comply with mutual respect, which serves to bring harmony to society. Demarrius Crossley, Minister, God Within Ministry

Address

City, State

[00000]

All national and state constitutions, laws, statutes, ordinances, regulations, rules, codes, and public policies, in all nations and states are private copyrighted material. I do not possess a license or have the authority to use such copyrighted material, and consequently that material does not have any authority over me, my property, or my personal affairs.

Again, this Affidavit is a Lawful Notification to you, the receivers, and requires your compliance to the demands made within. Failure to respond appropriately to the subject matter contained herein if there is any disagreement with the document is done under the penalties of perjury. Failure to respond within three (3) days, as stipulated, and rebut, with particularity, everything in this Affidavit with which there is disagreement, providing documentation as part of your ascertain, is a lawful, legal, and binding agreement by you and those that represent you in all Courts, anywhere in America or the World.

I am fully engaged in my Religious Rights and in all my Affairs. I, Demarrius Crossley, hereby declare and affirm that I am a Sovereign human being, endowed with inherent rights and freedoms.

I, Demarrius Crossley, being duly sworn, depose and say:

Article 1: Introduction

I am making this affidavit to report tyranny.

Article 2: Description of Persecution

I have been subjected to oppressive behavior by [AUTHORITY/PERSON].

Article 3: Fear of Harm

I fear harm or further oppression if action is not taken.

Article 4: Request for Protection

I request protection and relief from this tyranny.

Article 5: Verification

I hereby declare under penalty of perjury that the foregoing statements are true.

Again, this Affidavit is a Lawful Notification to you, the receivers, and requires your compliance to the demands made within. Failure to respond appropriately to the subject matter contained herein if there is any disagreement with the document is done under the penalties of perjury. Failure to respond within three (3) days, as stipulated, and rebut, with particularity, everything in this Affidavit with which there is disagreement, providing documentation as part of your ascertain, is a lawful, legal, and binding agreement by you and those that represent you in all Courts, anywhere in America or the World.

IN WITNESS WHEREOF, I have hereunto set my hand and seal, this [Date] Day of [Month], [Year].

Demarrius Crossley, Minister ______________________________

Illinois State }

}ss

Cook County }

Acknowledgement

As a Notary for (County and State), I do hereby certify that on the ____day of __________ 20______ the above-mentioned Affiant, Demarrius Crossley, Minister appeared before me and executed the foregoing document.

Witness my Hand and Seal:

____

Notary Public (SEAL)

Memorandum

To: Recipient Name
From: Minister Crossley of the UNMN Church
Date: (Insert Date)
Subject: **Affidavit Of Security From Tyranny**

Purpose: This memorandum provides guidance on ft creation and utilization of an Affidavit of Security from Tyranny. This affidavit is a sworn written statement that affirms an individual or organization to formally declare a commitment to promoting security from tyranny and protecting individual rights and freedoms.

Key Components:

1. **Declaration of Rights:** A declaration of individual rights and freedoms.
2. **Protection from Oppression:** A request for protection from tyranny and oppressive actions.
3. **Commitment to Accountability:** A commitment to holding those in power accountable for their actions.

Importance: This affidavit serves as a formal declaration of one's intention to invoke my rights to protection of human dignity, promotion of democracy, and prevention of human rights violations. This Affidavit is Lawful Notice that the Affidavit of Security from Tyranny is a Religious Right and any interruption of it is a Violation of my Religious Rights.

Utilization:

1. **Protection of Civilians:** Use the affidavit to protect citizens from tyranny and oppressive actions.
2. **Promotion of Good Governance:** Use the affidavit to promote good governance and accountability.

3. **Advocacy for Human Rights:** Use the affidavit to advocate for human rights and the rule of law.

Benefits:

- Protection of individual freedoms and rights.
- Prevention of abuse of power and tyranny.
- Promotion of stability and security, good governance.

By utilizing the Affidavit of Security from Tyranny, individuals and organizations can protect their individual's rights and understand the principle of governance by law, rather than arbitrary power, the principle of protecting individual's rights and freedoms, and the principle of accountability and trans praency in governance.

REFLECTION PAGE

1. What is one key insight you gained from reading the Affidavit and Memorandum?

2. How can you apply this insight to your work, studies, or daily life?

Affidavit of Security from War

Illinois State }

}ss

Cook County }

Name of Entity

Entity Address

City, State

[00000]

Notice to Agent is Notice to Principle/Notice to Principle is Notice to Agent

Sovereign Political Holder and Minister, over the age of 21 years, after being duly sworn according to law to tell the truth to the facts herein, I do hereby acknowledge and affirm the following: I, Affiant's Demarrius Crossley, am a Sovereign, without subjects. I am a Foreign Nation (not a person) who rules autonomously and am not subject to any entity or jurisdiction anywhere. I am a Sovereign Political Holder, a Minister. My authority for contracting is the age-old, timeless, and universal respect for the intrinsic power, property, and responsibilities of the Sovereign

Individual. I choose to comply with mutual respect, which serves to bring harmony to society. Demarrius Crossley, Minister, God Within Ministry

Address

City, State

[00000]

All national and state constitutions, laws, statutes, ordinances, regulations, rules, codes, and public policies, in all nations and states are private copyrighted material. I do not possess a license or have the authority to use such copyrighted material, and consequently that material does not have any authority over me, my property, or my personal affairs.

Again, this Affidavit is a Lawful Notification to you, the receivers, and requires your compliance to the demands made within. Failure to respond appropriately to the subject matter contained herein if there is any disagreement with the document is done under the penalties of perjury. Failure to respond within three (3) days, as stipulated, and rebut, with particularity, everything in this Affidavit with which there is disagreement, providing documentation as part of your ascertain, is a lawful, legal, and binding agreement by you and those that represent you in all Courts, anywhere in America or the World. I am fully engaged in my Religious Rights and in all my Affairs. I, Demarrius Crossley, hereby declare and affirm that I am a Sovereign human being, endowed with inherent rights and freedoms.

I, Demarrius Crossley, being duly sworn, depose and say:

Article 1: Introduction

I am making this affidavit to report threats related to war.

Article 2: Description of Threats

I fear harm due to the ongoing conflict in [COUNTRY/REGION].

Article 3: Fear of Harm

I fear for my safety and well-being if I return to [COUNTRY/REGION].

Article 4: Request for Protection

I request protection and asylum in [COUNTRY].

Article 5: Verification

I hereby declare under penalty of perjury that the foregoing statements are true.

Again, this Affidavit is Lawful Notification to you, the receivers, and requires your compliance to the demands made within. Failure to respond appropriately to the subject matter contained herein if there is any disagreement with the document is done under the penalties of perjury. Failure to respond within three (3) days, as stipulated, and rebut, with particularity, everything in this Affidavit with which there is disagreement, providing documentation as part of your ascertain, is lawful, legal, and binding agreement by you and those that represent you in all Courts, anywhere in America or the World.

IN WITNESS WHEREOF, I have hereunto set my hand and seal, this [Date] Day of [Month], [Year].

Demarrius Crossley, Minister ______________________________

Illinois State }

}ss

Cook County }

Acknowledgement

As a Notary for (County and State), I do hereby certify that on the ____day of __________ 20______ the above-mentioned Affiant, Demarrius Crossley, Minister appeared before me and executed the foregoing document.

Witness my Hand and Seal:

____

Notary Public (SEAL)

Memorandum

To: Recipient Name
From: Minister Crossley of the UNMN Church
Date: (Insert Date)
Subject: **Affidavit of Security from War**

Purpose: This memorandum provides guidance on the creation and utilization of an Affidavit of Security from War. This affidavit is a sworn written statement that affirms an individual or organization to formally declare a commitment to promoting security from war and protecting human life and dignity.

Key Components:

1. **Declaration of Neutrality:** A declaration of neutrality in conflicts and wars.
2. **Request for Protection:** A statement and acknowledgment of a request for protection from the effects of war.
3. **Commitment to Peaceful Resolution:** A commitment to promoting peaceful resolution of conflicts.

Importance: This affidavit serves as a formal declaration of one's intention to invoke my rights to protection of innocent lives, promotion of peace and stability, upholding humanitarian principles. This Affidavit is Lawful Notice that the Affidavit of Security from War is a Religious Right and any interruption of it is a Violation of my Religious Rights.

Utilization:

1. **Protection of Civilians:** Use the affidavit to protect civilians from the effects of war.
2. **Promotion of Humanitarian Law:** Use the affidavit to promote respect for humanitarian law and international humanitarian principles.

3. **Advocacy for Peace:** Use the affidavit to advocate for peaceful resolution of conflicts.

Benefits:

- Protection of human rights and dignity.
- Prevention of harm and suffering caused by war.
- Promotion of stability and security.

By utilizing the Affidavit of Security from War, individuals and organizations can protect their individual's rights and the principle of protecting human life and preventing harm, the principle of neutrality and impartiality in conflicts, the principle of resolving conflicts through peaceful means.

REFLECTION PAGE

1. What is one key insight you gained from reading the Affidavit and Memorandum?

2. How can you apply this insight to your work, studies, or daily life?

Affidavit To Refuse to Kill by Command

Illinois State }

}ss

Cook County }

Name of Entity

Entity Address

City, State

[00000]

Notice to Agent is Notice to Principle/Notice to Principle is Notice to Agent

Sovereign Political Holder and Minister, over the age of 21 years, after being duly sworn according to law to tell the truth to the facts herein, I do hereby acknowledge and affirm the following: I, Affiant's Demarrius Crossley, am a Sovereign, without subjects. I am a Foreign Nation (not a person) who rules autonomously and am not subject to any entity or jurisdiction anywhere. I am a Sovereign Political Holder, a Minister. My authority for contracting is the age-old, timeless, and universal respect for the intrinsic power, property, and responsibilities of the Sovereign

Individual. I choose to comply with mutual respect, which serves to bring harmony to society. Demarrius Crossley, Minister, God Within Ministry

Address

City, State

[00000]

All national and state constitutions, laws, statutes, ordinances, regulations, rules, codes, and public policies, in all nations and states are private copyrighted material. I do not possess a license or have the authority to use such copyrighted material, and consequently, that material does not have any authority over me, my property, or my personal affairs.

Again, this Affidavit is a Lawful Notification to you, the receivers, and requires your compliance to the demands made within. Failure to respond appropriately to the subject matter contained herein if there is any disagreement with the document is done under the penalties of perjury. Failure to respond within three (3) days, as stipulated, and rebut, with particularity, everything in this Affidavit with which there is disagreement, providing documentation as part of your ascertain, is a lawful, legal, and binding agreement by you and those that represent you in all Courts, anywhere in America or the World.

I am fully engaged in my Religious Rights and in all my Affairs. I, Demarrius Crossley, hereby declare and affirm that I am a Sovereign human being, endowed with inherent rights and freedoms.

I, Demarrius Crossley, being duly sworn, depose and say:

Article 1: Introduction

I am making this affidavit to declare my refusal to participate in actions that involve harming or killing others.

Article 2: Declaration of Refusal

I refuse to follow any order that requires me to harm or kill others, as it is contrary to my conscience and values.

Article 3: Circumstances

I have been ordered to [DESCRIBE ORDER], which would require me to participate in harming or killing others.

Article 4: Request for Accommodation

I request accommodation or alternative service that does not involve harming or killing others.

Article 5: Verification

I hereby declare under penalty of perjury that the foregoing statements are true.

Again, this Affidavit is a Lawful Notification to you, the receivers, and requires your compliance to the demands made within. Failure to respond appropriately to the subject matter contained herein if there is any disagreement with the document is done under the penalties of perjury. Failure to respond within three (3) days, as stipulated, and rebut, with particularity, everything in this Affidavit with which there is disagreement, providing documentation as part of your ascertain, is a lawful, legal, and binding agreement by you and those that represent you in all Courts, anywhere in America or the World.

IN WITNESS WHEREOF, I have hereunto set my hand and seal, this [Date] Day of [Month], [Year].

Demarrius Crossley, Minister ______________________________

Illinois State }

}ss

Cook County }

Acknowledgement

As a Notary for (County and State), I do hereby certify that on the ____day of __________ 20______ the above-mentioned Affiant, Demarrius Crossley, Minister appeared before me and executed the foregoing document.

Witness my Hand and Seal:

____

Notary Public (SEAL)

Memorandum

To: Recipient Name
From: Minister Crossley of the UNMN Church
Date: (Insert Date)
Subject: **Affidavit To Refuse to Kill by Command**

Purpose: This memorandum provides guidance on the creation and utilization of an Affidavit To Refuse to Kill by Command. This affidavit is a sworn written statement that affirms an individual or organization to formally declare a commitment to refusing engagement in harm or killing, even under command based on conscientious objection.

Key Components:

1. **Statement of Conscientious Objection:** A clear statement of objection to engaging in harm or killing, even under command.
2. **Commitment to Non-Violence:** A statement and acknowledgment of commitment to upholding non-violence principles.
3. **Assertion of Personal Autonomy:** An assertion of the right to make decisions based on personal moral or ethical convictions.

Importance: This affidavit serves as a formal declaration of one's intention to invoke my rights to moral integrity, protection of human life, and personal responsibility. This Affidavit is Lawful Notice that the Affidavit To Refuse to Kill by Command is a Religious Right and any interruption of it is a Violation of my Religious Rights.

Utilization:

1. **Military or Paramilitary Contexts:** Use the affidavit to assert conscientious objection in military or paramilitary contexts.
2. **High-Pressure Situations:** Use the affidavit to establish a clear stance in situations where one might be commanded to engage in harmful actions.
3. **Personal and Professional Settings:** Use the affidavit to affirm commitment to non-violence in various personal and professional capacities.

Benefits:

- Protection of individual conscience and moral convictions.
- Promotion of non-violent principles and practices.
- Upholding human rights and dignity.

By utilizing the Affidavit To Refuse to Kill by Command, individuals and organizations can protect their individual rights and the principle of protecting human life and dignity, the principle of conscientious objection to actions that violate personal moral or ethical convictions, and the principle of upholding personal autonomy.

REFLECTION PAGE

1. What is one key insight you gained from reading the Affidavit and Memorandum?

____

____

____

____

2. How can you apply this insight to your work, studies, or daily life?

____

____

____

____

Affidavit To Live in Peace

Illinois State }

}ss

Cook County }

Name of Entity

Entity Address

City, State

[00000]

Notice to Agent is Notice to Principle/Notice to Principle is Notice to Agent

Sovereign Political Holder and Minister, over the age of 21 years, after being duly sworn according to law to tell the truth to the facts herein, I do hereby acknowledge and affirm the following: I, Affiant's Demarrius Crossley, am a Sovereign, without subjects. I am a Foreign Nation (not a person) who rules autonomously and am not subject to any entity or jurisdiction anywhere. I am a Sovereign Political Holder, a Minister. My authority for contracting is the age-old, timeless, and universal respect for the intrinsic power, property, and responsibilities of the Sovereign

Individual. I choose to comply with mutual respect, which serves to bring harmony to society. Demarrius Crossley, Minister, God Within Ministry

Address

City, State

[00000]

All national and state constitutions, laws, statutes, ordinances, regulations, rules, codes, and public policies, in all nations and states are private copyrighted material. I do not possess a license or have the authority to use such copyrighted material, and consequently that material does not have any authority over me, my property, or my personal affairs.

Again, this Affidavit is aLawful Notification to you, the receivers, and requires your compliance to the demands made within. Failure to respond appropriately to the subject matter contained herein if there is any disagreement with the document is done under the penalties of perjury. Failure to respond within three (3) days, as stipulated, and rebut, with particularity, everything in this Affidavit with which there is disagreement, providing documentation as part of your ascertain, is a lawful, legal, and binding agreement by you and those that represent you in all Courts, anywhere in America or the World.

I am fully engaged in my Religious Rights and in all my Affairs. I, Demarrius Crossley, hereby declare and affirm that I am a Sovereign human being, endowed with inherent rights and freedoms.

I, Demarrius Crossley, being duly sworn, depose and say:

Article 1: Introduction

I am making this affidavit affirm my commitment to living in peace.

Article 2: Declaration of Peaceful Intent

I commit to living in harmony with others and resolving conflicts peacefully.

Article 3: Commitment to Non-Violence

I promise to avoid violence and work towards a peaceful resolution of conflicts.

Article 4: Request for Peaceful Coexistence

I request peaceful coexistence with others and am willing to work towards resolving conflicts peacefully.

Article 5: Verification

I hereby declare under penalty of perjury that the foregoing statements are true.

Again, this Affidavit is a Lawful Notification to you, the receivers, and requires your compliance to the demands made within. Failure to respond appropriately to the subject matter contained herein if there is any disagreement with the document is done under the penalties of perjury. Failure to respond within three (3) days, as stipulated, and rebut, with particularity, everything in this Affidavit with which there is disagreement, providing documentation as part of your ascertain, is a lawful, legal, and binding agreement by you and those that represent you in all Courts, anywhere in America or the World.

IN WITNESS WHEREOF, I have hereunto set my hand and seal, this [Date] Day of [Month], [Year].

Demarrius Crossley, Minister ______________________________

Illinois State }

}ss

Cook County }

Acknowledgement

As a Notary for (County and State), I do hereby certify that on the ____day of _________ 20______ the above-mentioned Affiant, Demarrius Crossley, Minister appeared before me and executed the foregoing document.

Witness my Hand and Seal:

____

Notary Public (SEAL)

Memorandum

To: Recipient Name
From: Minister Crossley of the UNMN Church
Date: (Insert Date)
Subject: **Affidavit To Live in Peace**

Purpose: This memorandum provides guidance on the creation and utilization of an Affidavit To Live in Peace. This affidavit is a sworn written statement that affirms an individual or organization to formally declare a commitment to living in peace and promoting peaceful relationships with others.

Key Components:

1. **Declaration of Intent:** A clear statement of intent to live in peace and harmony.
2. **Commitment to Non - Violence:** A statement acknowledgment of commitment to non - violence and peaceful resolution of conflicts.
3. **Respect for Others:** A commitment to respect the rights and dignity of others.

Importance: This affidavit serves as a formal declaration of one's intention to invoke my rights to promoting social harmony, reducing violence, and fostering a sense of community. This Affidavit is Lawful Notice that the Affidavit To Live in Peace is a Religious Right and any interruption of it is a Violation of my Religious Rights.

Utilization:

1. **Personal Relationships:** Use the affidavit to promote peace and harmony in personal relationships.
2. **Community Building:** Use the affidavit to build and maintain peaceful communities.

3. **Conflict Resolution:** Use the affidavit to resolve conflicts in a peaceful and constructive manner.

Benefits:

- Improved relationships with others.
- Reduced conflict and violence.
- Increase the sense of well - being and happiness.

By utilizing the Affidavit To Live in Peace, individuals and organizations can protect their individual's rights. Utilize the affidavit to create a peaceful coexistence, non - violent conflict resolution, and mutual respect.

REFLECTION PAGE

1. What is one key insight you gained from reading the Affidavit and Memorandum?

2. How can you apply this insight to your work, studies, or daily life?

Affidavit To Be Left Alone When Law Abiding

Illinois State }

}ss

Cook County }

Name of Entity

Entity Address

City, State

[00000]

Notice to Agent is Notice to Principle/Notice to Principle is Notice to Agent

Sovereign Political Holder and Minister, over the age of 21 years, after being duly sworn according to law to tell the truth to the facts herein, I do hereby acknowledge and affirm the following: I, Affiant's Demarrius Crossley, am a Sovereign, without subjects. I am a Foreign Nation (not a person) who rules autonomously and am not subject to any entity or jurisdiction anywhere. I am a Sovereign Political Holder, a Minister. My authority for contracting is the age-old, timeless, and universal respect for the intrinsic power, property, and responsibilities of the Sovereign

Individual. I choose to comply with mutual respect, which serves to bring harmony to society. Demarrius Crossley, Minister, God Within Ministry

Address

City, State

[00000]

All national and state constitutions, laws, statutes, ordinances, regulations, rules, codes, and public policies, in all nations and states are private copyrighted material. I do not possess a license or have the authority to use such copyrighted material, and consequently that material does not have any authority over me, my property, or my personal affairs.

Again, this Affidavit is Lawful Notification to you, the receivers, and requires your compliance to the demands made within. Failure to respond appropriately to the subject matter contained herein if there is any disagreement with the document is done under the penalties of perjury. Failure to respond within three (3) days, as stipulated, and rebut, with particularity, everything in this Affidavit with which there is disagreement, providing documentation as part of your ascertain, is lawful, legal, and binding agreement by you and those that represent you in all Courts, anywhere in America or the World.

I am fully engaged in my Religious Rights and in all my Affairs. I, Demarrius Crossley, hereby declare and affirm that I am a Sovereign human being, endowed with inherent rights and freedoms.

I, Demarrius Crossley, being duly sworn, depose and say:

Article 1: Introduction

I am making this affidavit to assert my right to privacy and non-interference.

Article 2: Declaration of Lawful Behavior

I am a law-abiding citizen and follow all applicable laws and regulations.

Article 3: Request for Non-Interference

I request to be left alone and not interfered with when lawfully conducting my personal affairs.

Article 4: Verification

I declare that the foregoing statements are true.

Again, this Affidavit is a Lawful Notification to you, the receivers, and requires your compliance to the demands made within. Failure to respond appropriately to the subject matter contained herein if there is any disagreement with the document is done under the penalties of perjury. Failure to respond within three (3) days, as stipulated, and rebut, with particularity, everything in this Affidavit with which there is disagreement, providing documentation as part of your ascertain, is a lawful, legal, and binding agreement by you and those that represent you in all Courts, anywhere in America or the World.

IN WITNESS WHEREOF, I have hereunto set my hand and seal, this [Date] Day of [Month], [Year].

Demarrius Crossley, Minister ______________________________

Illinois State }

}ss

Cook County }

Acknowledgement

As a Notary for (County and State), I do hereby certify that on the ____day of __________ 20______ the above-mentioned Affiant, Demarrius Crossley, Minister appeared before me and executed the foregoing document.

Witness my Hand and Seal:

____

Notary Public (SEAL)

Memorandum

To: Recipient Name
From: Minister Crossley of the UNMN Church
Date: (Insert Date)
Subject: **Affidavit To Be Left Alone When Law Abiding**

Purpose: This memorandum provides guidance on the creation and utilization of an Affidavit To Be Left Alone When Law Abiding. This affidavit is a sworn written statement that affirms an individual or organization to formally declare one's law-abiding status and assert the right to be left alone when lawfully conducting one's affairs.

Key Components:

1. **Statement of Law-Abiding Status:** A clear statement affirming compliance with all applicable laws.
2. **Request for Non-Interference:** A statement acknowledgment of a request for no-interference from authorities or other entities when lawfully conducting one's affairs.
3. **Assertion of Privacy Rights:** An assertion of the right to privacy.

Importance: This affidavit serves as a formal declaration of one's intention to invoke my rights to protection of civil liberties, prevention of unwarranted intrusion, promotion of trust in government and other entities by ensuring that they act within the bounds of the law. This Affidavit is Lawful Notice that the Affidavit To Be Left Alone When Law Abiding is a Religious Right and any interruption of it is a Violation of my Religious Rights.

Utilization:

- **Protection from Harassment:** Use the affidavit to protect oneself from harassment or unwarranted attention from authorities or other entities.
- **Preservation of Privacy:** Use the affidavit to preserve one's right to privacy and prevent unwarranted intrusion.

- **Assertion of Rights:** Use the affidavit to assert one's rights and freedoms under the law.

Benefits:

- Increase protection of individual rights and freedoms.
- Prevention of abuse of power by authorities or other entities.
- Increased personal autonomy and freedom to conduct one's affairs without undue interference.

By utilizing the Affidavit To Be Left Alone When Law Abiding, individuals and organizations can protect their individual rights, presumption of innocence, limited government overreach, and individual liberty.

REFLECTION PAGE

1. What is one key insight you gained from reading the Affidavit and Memorandum?

2. How can you apply this insight to your work, studies, or daily life?

Affidavit To Be Led By Conscience

Illinois State }

}ss

Cook County }

Name of Entity

Entity Address

City, State

[00000]

Notice to Agent is Notice to Principle/Notice to Principle is Notice to Agent

Sovereign Political Holder and Minister, over the age of 21 years, after being duly sworn according to law to tell the truth to the facts herein, I do hereby acknowledge and affirm the following: I, Affiant's Demarrius Crossley, am a Sovereign, without subjects. I am a Foreign Nation (not a person) who rules autonomously and am not subject to any entity or jurisdiction anywhere. I am a Sovereign Political Holder, a Minister. My authority for contracting is the age-old, timeless, and universal respect for the intrinsic power, property, and responsibilities of the Sovereign

Individual. I choose to comply with mutual respect, which serves to bring harmony to society. Demarrius Crossley, Minister, God Within Ministry

Address

City, State

[00000]

All national and state constitutions, laws, statutes, ordinances, regulations, rules, codes, and public policies, in all nations and states are private copyrighted material. I do not possess a license or have the authority to use such copyrighted material and consequently that material does not have any authority over me, my property, or my personal affairs.

Again, this Affidavit is a Lawful Notification to you, the receivers and requires your compliance to the demands made within. Failure to respond appropriately to the subject matter contained herein if there is any disagreement with the document is done under the penalties of perjury. Failure to respond within three (3) days, as stipulated, and rebut, with particularity, everything in this Affidavit with which there is disagreement, providing documentation as part of your ascertain, is a lawful, legal, and binding agreement by you and those that represent you in all Courts, anywhere in America or the World.

I am fully engaged in my Religious Rights and in all my Affairs. I, Demarrius Crossley, hereby declare and affirm that I am a Sovereign human being, endowed with inherent rights and freedoms.

I, Demarrius Crossley, being duly sworn, depose and say:

Article 1: Introduction

I am making this affidavit to affirm my commitment to following my conscience.

Article 2: Declaration of Conscience

I commit to following my conscience and upholding moral principles.

Article 3: Commitment to Moral Principles

I promise to act in accordance with my conscience and moral values.

Article 4: Request for Respect

I request respect for my conscience and moral principles.

Article 5: Verification

I declare that the foregoing statements are true.

Again, this Affidavit is a Lawful Notification to you, the receivers, and requires your compliance to the demands made within. Failure to respond appropriately to the subject matter contained herein if there is any disagreement with the document is done under the penalties of perjury. Failure to respond within three (3) days, as stipulated, and rebut, with particularity, everything in this Affidavit with which there is disagreement, providing documentation as part of your ascertain, is a lawful, legal, and binding agreement by you and those that represent you in all Courts, anywhere in America or the World.

IN WITNESS WHEREOF, I have hereunto set my hand and seal, this [Date] Day of [Month], [Year].

Demarrius Crossley, Minister ______________________________

Illinois State }

}ss

Cook County }

Acknowledgement

As a Notary for (County and State), I do hereby certify that on the ____day of __________ 20______ the above-mentioned Affiant, Demarrius Crossley, Minister appeared before me and executed the foregoing document.

Witness my Hand and Seal:

____

Notary Public (SEAL)

Memorandum

To: Recipient Name
From: Minister Crossley of the UNMN Church
Date: (Insert Date)
Subject: **Affidavit To Be Led By Conscience**

Purpose: This memorandum provides guidance on the creation and utilization of an Affidavit To Be Led By Conscience. This affidavit is a sworn written statement that affirms an individual or organization to formally declare a commitment to being led by conscience and guided by moral principles.

Key Components:

1. **Statement of Intent:** A clear statement of intent to be guided by conscience.
2. **Moral Principles:** A statement acknowledgment and identification of moral principles and values.
3. **Commitment to Integrity:** A commitment to acting with integrity.

Importance: This affidavit serves as a formal declaration of one's intention to invoke my rights to moral guidance, personal accountability, and authentic leadership. This Affidavit is Lawful Notice that Affidavit To Be Led By Conscience is a Religious Right and any interruption of it is a Violation of my Religious Rights.

Utilization:

1. **Decision - Making:** Use the affidavit to increase integrity and authenticity in one's actions.
2. **Improved Decision - Making:** Use the affidavit to improved decision-making guided by moral principles.

3. **Personal Growth:** Use the affidavit to cultivate personal growth and self - awareness.

Benefits:

- Increase integrity and authenticity in one's actions.
- Improved decision - -making guided by moral principles.
- Enhanced self - awareness and personal growth.

By utilizing the Affidavit To Be Led By Conscience, individuals and organizations can protect their individual's right. Also, provide guidance in uncertain situations, promote personal accountability and responsibility, and demonstrate authentic leadership and decision - making.

REFLECTION PAGE

1. What is one key insight you gained from reading the Affidavit and Memorandum?

2. How can you apply this insight to your work, studies, or daily life?

Affidavit To Eat Healthy Foods

Illinois State }

}ss

Cook County }

Name of Entity

Entity Address

City, State

[00000]

Notice to Agent is Notice to Principle/Notice to Principle is Notice to Agent

Sovereign Political Holder and Minister, over the age of 21 years, after being duly sworn according to law to tell the truth to the facts herein, I do hereby acknowledge and affirm the following: I, Affiant's Demarrius Crossley, am a Sovereign, without subjects. I am a Foreign Nation (not a person) who rules autonomously and am not subject to any entity or jurisdiction anywhere. I am a Sovereign Political Holder, a Minister. My authority for contracting is the age-old, timeless, and universal respect for the intrinsic power, property, and responsibilities of the Sovereign

Individual. I choose to comply with mutual respect, which serves to bring harmony to society. Demarrius Crossley, Minister, God Within Ministry

Address

City, State

[00000]

All national and state constitutions, laws, statutes, ordinances, regulations, rules, codes, and public policies, in all nations and states are private copyrighted material. I do not possess a license or have the authority to use such copyrighted material, and consequently that material does not have any authority over me, my property, or my personal affairs.

Again, this Affidavit is A Lawful Notification to you, the receivers, and requires your compliance to the demands made within. Failure to respond appropriately to the subject matter contained herein if there is any disagreement with the document is done under the penalties of perjury. Failure to respond within three (3) days, as stipulated, and rebut, with particularity, everything in this Affidavit with which there is disagreement, providing documentation as part of your ascertain, is A lawful, legal, and binding agreement by you and those that represent you in all Courts, anywhere in America or the World.

I am fully engaged in my Religious Rights and in all my Affairs. I, Demarrius Crossley, hereby declare and affirm that I am a Sovereign human being, endowed with inherent rights and freedoms.

I, Demarrius Crossley, being duly sworn, depose and say:

Article 1: Introduction

I am making this affidavit to affirm my commitment to eating healthy foods.

Article 2: Declaration of Healthy Eating

I commit to consuming nutritious and wholesome foods to maintain my overall health and well-being.

Article 3: Commitment to Wholesome Foods

I promise to prioritize whole, nutrient-rich foods and limit unhealthy options.

Article 4: Intentions for Healthy Lifestyle

I intend to maintain a healthy lifestyle through balanced eating habits.

Article 5: Verification

I declare that the foregoing statements are true.

Again, this Affidavit is A Lawful Notification to you, the receivers, and requires your compliance to the demands made within. Failure to respond appropriately to the subject matter contained herein if there is any disagreement with the document is done under the penalties of perjury. Failure to respond within three (3) days, as stipulated, and rebut, with particularity, everything in this Affidavit with which there is disagreement, providing documentation as part of your ascertain, is A lawful, legal, and binding agreement by you and those that represent you in all Courts, anywhere in America or the World.

IN WITNESS WHEREOF, I have hereunto set my hand and seal, this [Date] Day of [Month], [Year].

Demarrius Crossley, Minister ______________________________

Illinois State }

}ss

Cook County }

Acknowledgement

As a Notary for (County and State), I do hereby certify that on the ____day of __________ 20______ the above-mentioned Affiant, Demarrius Crossley, Minister appeared before me and executed the foregoing document.

Witness my Hand and Seal:

____

Notary Public (SEAL)

Memorandum

To: Recipient Name
From: Minister Crossley of the UNMN Church
Date: (Insert Date)
Subject: **Affidavit To Eat Healthy Foods**

Purpose: This memorandum provides guidance on the creation and utilization of an Affidavit To Eat Healthy Foods. This affidavit is a sworn written statement that affirms an individual, or organization formally declares a commitment to eating healthy foods and promote healthy eating habits.

Key Components:

1. **Commitment to Healthy Eating:** A clear statement of commitment to eating healthy foods.
2. **Identification of Healthy Foods:** A statement acknowledgment and identification of specific healthy foods to be consumed.
3. **Plan for Implementation:** A plan for implementing healthy eating habits.

Importance: This affidavit serves as a formal declaration of one's intention to maintain a nutritional balance, make informed choices, and sustainable habits. This Affidavit is Lawful Notice that Affidavit To Eat Healthy Foods is a Religious Right and any interruption of it is a Violation of my Religious Rights.

Utilization:

1. **Personal Health:** Use the affidavit to promote personal health and well - being.
2. **Family Health:** Use the affidavit to promote healthy eating habits for families.

3. **Community Health:** Use the affidavit to promote healthy eating habits in community settings.

Benefits:

- Improved overall health and well - being.
- Increased Energy levels and productivity.
- Reduced risk of chronic diseases.

By utilizing the Affidavit To Eat Healthy Foods, individuals and organizations can protect their individual's right and prevention of diet - related diseases, promotion of overall well - being and quality of life, and setting a good example for others, especially children.

REFLECTION PAGE

1. What is one key insight you gained from reading the Affidavit and Memorandum?

____

____

____

____

2. How can you apply this insight to your work, studies, or daily life?

____

____

____

____

Affidavit To Be Free from Unwarranted Invasion

Illinois State }

}ss

Cook County }

Name of Entity

Entity Address

City, State

[00000]

Notice to Agent is Notice to Principle/Notice to Principle is Notice to Agent

Sovereign Political Holder and Minister, over the age of 21 years, after being duly sworn according to law to tell the truth to the facts herein, I do hereby acknowledge and affirm the following: I, Affiant's Demarrius Crossley, am a Sovereign, without subjects. I am a Foreign Nation (not a person) who rules autonomously and am not subject to any entity or jurisdiction anywhere. I am a Sovereign Political Holder, a Minister. My authority for contracting is the age-old, timeless, and universal respect for the intrinsic power, property, and responsibilities of the Sovereign

Individual. I choose to comply with mutual respect, which serves to bring harmony to society. Demarrius Crossley, Minister, God Within Ministry

Address

City, State

[00000]

All national and state constitutions, laws, statutes, ordinances, regulations, rules, codes, and public policies, in all nations and states are private copyrighted material. I do not possess a license or have the authority to use such copyrighted material, and consequently that material does not have any authority over me, my property, or my personal affairs.

Again, this Affidavit is A Lawful Notification to you, the receivers, and requires your compliance to the demands made within. Failure to respond appropriately to the subject matter contained herein if there is any disagreement with the document is done under the penalties of perjury. Failure to respond within three (3) days, as stipulated, and rebut, with particularity, everything in this Affidavit with which there is disagreement, providing documentation as part of your ascertain, is A lawful, legal, and binding agreement by you and those that represent you in all Courts, anywhere in America or the World.

I am fully engaged in my Religious Rights and in all my Affairs. I, Demarrius Crossley, hereby declare and affirm that I am a Sovereign human being, endowed with inherent rights and freedoms.

I, Demarrius Crossley, being duly sworn, depose and say:

Article 1: Introduction

I am making this affidavit to assert my right to privacy.

Article 2: Declaration of Privacy

I have the right to be free from unwarranted invasion or intrusion

Article 3: Request for Non-Intrusion

I request to be protected from an unwarranted invasion of my privacy.

Article 4: Specific Concerns

I have concerns about [SPECIFIC INCIDENT OR CONCERNS].

Article 5: Verification

I declare that the foregoing statements are true.

Again, this Affidavit is a Lawful Notification to you, the receivers, and requires your compliance to the demands made within. Failure to respond appropriately to the subject matter contained herein if there is any disagreement with the document is done under the penalties of perjury. Failure to respond within three (3) days, as stipulated, and rebut, with particularity, everything in this Affidavit with which there is disagreement, providing documentation as part of your ascertain, is a lawful, legal, and binding agreement by you and those that represent you in all Courts, anywhere in America or the World.

IN WITNESS WHEREOF, I have hereunto set my hand and seal, this [Date] Day of [Month], [Year].

Demarrius Crossley, Minister ______________________________

Illinois State }

}ss

Cook County }

Acknowledgement

As a Notary for (County and State), I do hereby certify that on the ____day of __________ 20______ the above-mentioned Affiant, Demarrius Crossley, Minister appeared before me and executed the foregoing document.

Witness my Hand and Seal:

____

Notary Public (SEAL)

Memorandum

To: Recipient Name
From: Minister Crossley of the UNMN Church
Date: (Insert Date)
Subject: **Affidavit To Be Free From Unwarranted Invasion**

Purpose: This memorandum provides guidance on the creation and utilization of an Affidavit To Be Free From Unwarranted Invasion. This affidavit is a sworn written statement that affirms an individual's or organization commitment to formally assert protection against unwarranted invasion and establish clear boundaries.

Key Components:

1. **Statement of Protection:** A clear statement asserting protection against unwarranted invasion.
2. **Identification of Rights:** A statement acknowledgment and identification of specific rights being protected.
3. **Declaration of Boundaries:** A formal declaration of boundaries and limits.

Importance: This affidavit serves as a formal declaration of one's intention to invoke my right to privacy, prevention of overreach, and respect for autonomy. This Affidavit is Lawful Notice that Affidavit To Be Free From Unwarranted Invasion is a Religious Right and any interruption of it is a Violation of my Religious Rights.

Utilization:

1. **Personal Boundaries:** Use the affidavit to establish and protect personal boundaries.
2. **Confidentiality:** Use the affidavit to protect confidential information.

3. **Protection from Harassment:** Use the affidavit to protect against harassment or unwanted intrusion.

Benefits:

- Increased protection of individual rights and freedoms.
- Prevention of harm or damage resulting from unwarranted invasion.
- Clarity and certainty regarding boundaries and expectations.

By utilizing the Affidavit To Be Free From Unwarranted Invasion, individuals and organizations can protect their individual's right to privacy, prevent unwarranted invasion or overreach, respect for individual autonomy and decision - making.

REFLECTION PAGE

1. What is one key insight you gained from reading the Affidavit and Memorandum?

2. How can you apply this insight to your work, studies, or daily life?

Affidavit To Process Affidavits

Illinois State }

}ss

Cook County }

Name of Entity

Entity Address

City, State

[00000]

Notice to Agent is Notice to Principle/Notice to Principle is Notice to Agent

Sovereign Political Holder and Minister, over the age of 21 years, after being duly sworn according to law to tell the truth to the facts herein, I do hereby acknowledge and affirm the following: I, Affiant's Demarrius Crossley, am a Sovereign, without subjects. I am a Foreign Nation (not a person) who rules autonomously and am not subject to any entity or jurisdiction anywhere. I am a Sovereign Political Holder, a Minister. My authority for contracting is the age-old, timeless, and universal respect for the intrinsic power, property, and responsibilities of the Sovereign

Individual. I choose to comply with mutual respect, which serves to bring harmony to society. Demarrius Crossley, Minister, God Within Ministry

Address

City, State

[00000]

All national and state constitutions, laws, statutes, ordinances, regulations, rules, codes, and public policies, in all nations and states are private copyrighted material. I do not possess a license or have the authority to use such copyrighted material, and consequently, that material does not have any authority over me, my property, or my personal affairs.

Again, this Affidavit is a Lawful Notification to you, the receivers, and requires your compliance to the demands made within. Failure to respond appropriately to the subject matter contained herein if there is any disagreement with the document is done under the penalties of perjury. Failure to respond within three (3) days, as stipulated, and rebut, with particularity, everything in this Affidavit with which there is disagreement, providing documentation as part of your ascertain, is a lawful, legal, and binding agreement by you and those that represent you in all Courts, anywhere in America or the World.

I am fully engaged in my Religious Rights and in all my Affairs. I, Demarrius Crossley, hereby declare and affirm that I am a Sovereign human being, endowed with inherent rights and freedoms.

I, Demarrius Crossley, being duly sworn, depose and say:

Article 1: Introduction

I am making this affidavit to affirm the authenticity of certain documents.

Article 2: Description of Documents

The documents described below are true and accurate:

[LIST DOCUMENTS]

Article 3: Verification

I declare that the foregoing statements are true.

Again, this Affidavit is a Lawful Notification to you, the receivers, and requires your compliance to the demands made within. Failure to respond appropriately to the subject matter contained herein if there is any disagreement with the document is done under the penalties of perjury. Failure to respond within three (3) days, as stipulated, and rebut, with particularity, everything in this Affidavit with which there is disagreement, providing documentation as part of your ascertain, is a lawful, legal, and binding agreement by you and those that represent you in all Courts, anywhere in America or the World.

IN WITNESS WHEREOF, I have hereunto set my hand and seal, this [Date] Day of [Month], [Year].

Demarrius Crossley, Minister ______________________________

Illinois State }

}ss

Cook County }

Acknowledgement

As a Notary for (County and State), I do hereby certify that on the ____day of __________ 20______ the above-mentioned Affiant, Demarrius Crossley, Minister appeared before me and executed the foregoing document.

Witness my Hand and Seal:

____

Notary Public (SEAL)

Memorandum

To: Recipient Name
From: Minister Crossley of the UNMN Church
Date: (Insert Date)
Subject: **Affidavit To Process Affidavits**

Purpose: This memorandum provides guidance on the creation and utilization of an Affidavit To Process Affidavits. This affidavit is a sworn written statement that affirms an individual's or organization commitment to formally process affidavits in accordance with relevant laws and regulations.

Key Components:

1. **Identification:** A clear identification of the affidavit being processed.
2. **Purpose Statement:** A statement outlining the purpose of the affidavit.
3. **Authorization:** Authorization for the processing of the affidavit.

Importance: This affidavit serves as a formal declaration of one's intention and commitment to legal validity, record keeping and facilitating proceedings. This Affidavit is Lawful Notice that Affidavit To Process Affidavits is a Religious Right and any interruption of it is a Violation of my Religious Rights.

Utilization:

1. **Legal Proceedings:** Use the affidavit to process affidavits for use in legal proceedings.
2. **Administrative Purposes:** Use the affidavit to process affidavits for administrative purposes.
3. **Documentation:** Use the affidavit to document and verify statements or facts.

Benefits:

- Increased streamlined process for affidavit processing.
- Increased efficiency in the handling of affidavits.
- Improved accuracy in the processing of affidavits.

By utilizing the Affidavit To Process Affidavits, individuals and organizations can ensure accuracy in the processing of affidavits, processing affidavits in a timely and efficient manner, and compliance with relevant laws and regulations.

REFLECTION PAGE

1. What is one key insight you gained from reading the Affidavit and Memorandum?

2. How can you apply this insight to your work, studies, or daily life?

Affidavit To Avoid Self Incrimination

Illinois State }

}ss

Cook County }

Name of Entity

Entity Address

City, State

[00000]

Notice to Agent is Notice to Principle/Notice to Principle is Notice to Agent

Sovereign Political Holder and Minister, over the age of 21 years, after being duly sworn according to law to tell the truth to the facts herein, I do hereby acknowledge and affirm the following: I, Affiant's Demarrius Crossley, am a Sovereign, without subjects. I am a Foreign Nation (not a person) who rules autonomously and am not subject to any entity or jurisdiction anywhere. I am a Sovereign Political Holder, a Minister. My authority for contracting is the age-old, timeless, and universal respect for the intrinsic power, property, and responsibilities of the Sovereign

Individual. I choose to comply with mutual respect, which serves to bring harmony to society. Demarrius Crossley, Minister, God Within Ministry

Address

City, State

[00000]

All national and state constitutions, laws, statutes, ordinances, regulations, rules, codes, and public policies, in all nations and states are private copyrighted material. I do not possess a license or have the authority to use such copyrighted material, and consequently that material does not have any authority over me, my property, or my personal affairs.

Again, this Affidavit is a Lawful Notification to you, the receivers, and requires your compliance to the demands made within. Failure to respond appropriately to the subject matter contained herein if there is any disagreement with the document is done under the penalties of perjury. Failure to respond within three (3) days, as stipulated, and rebut, with particularity, everything in this Affidavit with which there is disagreement, providing documentation as part of your ascertain, is a lawful, legal, and binding agreement by you and those that represent you in all Courts, anywhere in America or the World.

I am fully engaged in my Religious Rights and in all my Affairs. I, Demarrius Crossley, hereby declare and affirm that I am a Sovereign human being, endowed with inherent rights and freedoms.

I, Demarrius Crossley, being duly sworn, depose and say:

Article 1: Introduction

I am making this affidavit to assert my right against self-incrimination.

Article 2: Assertion of Right

I assert my right against self-incrimination and refuse to provide information that may incriminate me.

Article 3: Refusal to Provide Information

I refuse to provide information that may be used against me in a criminal proceeding.

Article 4: Verification

I declare that the foregoing statements are true.

Again, this Affidavit is a Lawful Notification to you, the receivers, and requires your compliance to the demands made within. Failure to respond appropriately to the subject matter contained herein if there is any disagreement with the document is done under the penalties of perjury. Failure to respond within three (3) days, as stipulated, and rebut, with particularity, everything in this Affidavit with which there is disagreement, providing documentation as part of your ascertain, is lawful, legal, and binding agreement by you and those that represent you in all Courts, anywhere in America or the World.

IN WITNESS WHEREOF, I have hereunto set my hand and seal, this [Date] Day of [Month], [Year].

Demarrius Crossley, Minister ______________________________

Illinois State }

}ss

Cook County }

Acknowledgement

As a Notary for (County and State), I do hereby certify that on the ____day of __________ 20______ the above-mentioned Affiant, Demarrius Crossley, Minister appeared before me and executed the foregoing document.

Witness my Hand and Seal:

____

Notary Public (SEAL)

Memorandum

To: Recipient Name
From: Minister Crossley of the UNMN Church
Date: (Insert Date)
Subject: **Affidavit To Avoid Self Incrimination**

Purpose: This memorandum provides guidance on the creation and utilization of an Affidavit To Avoid Self Incrimination. This affidavit is a sworn written statement that affirms an individual's or organization commitment to formally invoke the right to avoid self - incrimination, protecting the individua l's rights and interests.

Key Components:

1. **Clear Statement of Intent:** A clear statement invoking the right to avoid self - incrimination.
2. **Understanding of Rights:** A statement acknowledgment of the right to remain silent and avoid making incriminating statements.
3. **Formal Declaration:** A formal declaration of the intention to exercise this right.

Importance: Importance: This affidavit serves as a formal declaration of one's intention to invoke my right to avoid self - incrimination. This Affidavit is Lawful Notice that Affidavit To Avoid Self Incrimination is a Religious Right and any interruption of it is a Violation of my Religious Rights.

Utilization:

1. **Legal Proceedings:** Use the affidavit to invoke the right to avoid self - incrimination in legal proceedings.
2. **Investigations:** Use the affidavit to protect oneself during investigations or interrogations.

3. **Testimony:** Use the affidavit to decline testifying or providing information that could be incriminating.

Benefits:

- Increased protection from potential harm or prejudice resulting from self – incrimination.
- Clarity and certainty regarding the individual's intention to invoke this right.
- Formal recognition of the individual's right to avoid self - incrimination.

By utilizing the Affidavit To Avoid Self Incrimination, individuals and organizations can protect their rights to avoid self - incrimination, precautionary measures to prevent potential harm or prejudice, and a formal record of the individual's intention to invoke this right.

REFLECTION PAGE

1. What is one key insight you gained from reading the Affidavit and Memorandum?

2. How can you apply this insight to your work, studies, or daily life?

Affidavit To Equally Represent Our Religious Organization

Illinois State }

}ss

Cook County }

Name of Entity

Entity Address

City, State

[00000]

Notice to Agent is Notice to Principle/Notice to Principle is Notice to Agent

Sovereign Political Holder and Minister, over the age of 21 years, after being duly sworn according to law to tell the truth to the facts herein, I do hereby acknowledge and affirm the following: I, Affiant's Demarrius Crossley, am a Sovereign, without subjects. I am a Foreign Nation (not a person) who rules autonomously and am not subject to any entity or jurisdiction anywhere. I am a Sovereign Political Holder, a Minister. My authority for contracting is the age-old, timeless, and universal respect for the intrinsic power, property, and responsibilities of the Sovereign

Individual. I choose to comply with mutual respect, which serves to bring harmony to society. Demarrius Crossley, Minister, God Within Ministry

Address

City, State

[00000]

All national and state constitutions, laws, statutes, ordinances, regulations, rules, codes, and public policies, in all nations and states are private copyrighted material. I do not possess a license or have the authority to use such copyrighted material, and consequently, that material does not have any authority over me, my property, or my personal affairs.

Again, this Affidavit is a Lawful Notification to you, the receivers, and requires your compliance to the demands made within. Failure to respond appropriately to the subject matter contained herein if there is any disagreement with the document is done under the penalties of perjury. Failure to respond within three (3) days, as stipulated, and rebut, with particularity, everything in this Affidavit with which there is disagreement, providing documentation as part of your ascertain, is a lawful, legal, and binding agreement by you and those that represent you in all Courts, anywhere in America or the World.

I am fully engaged in my Religious Rights and in all my Affairs. I, Demarrius Crossley, hereby declare and affirm that I am a Sovereign human being, endowed with inherent rights and freedoms.

I, Demarrius Crossley, being duly sworn, depose and say:

Article 1: Introduction

I am making this affidavit to affirm the equal representation of [RELIGIOUS ORGANIZATION NAME].

Article 2: Affirmation of Equal Representation

I affirm that [RELIGIOUS ORGANIZATION NAME] ensures equal representation for all its members or groups.

Article 3: Description of Representation

The representation structure of [RELIGIOUS ORGANIZATION NAME].

Article 4: Verification

I declare that the foregoing statements are true.

I, Demarrius Crossley, have complete Sovereign Immunity; and therefore, my power to contract and undo contracts is unlimited. My Religious Rights and Freedom must be fully and completely respected. Failure to do so will require that I receive $7,500,000.00 from each violator for each violation that occurs.

Again, this Affidavit is a Lawful Notification to you, the receivers, and requires your compliance to the demands made within. Failure to respond appropriately to the subject matter contained herein if there is any disagreement with the document is done under the penalties of perjury. Failure to respond within three (3) days, as stipulated, and rebut, with particularity, everything in this Affidavit with which there is disagreement, providing documentation as part of your ascertain, is a lawful, legal, and binding agreement by you and those that represent you in all Courts, anywhere in America or the World.

IN WITNESS WHEREOF, I have hereunto set my hand and seal, this [Date] Day of [Month], [Year].

Demarrius Crossley, Minister ______________________________

Illinois State }

}ss

Cook County }

Acknowledgement

As a Notary for (County and State), I do hereby certify that on the ____day of __________ 20______ the above-mentioned Affiant, Demarrius Crossley, Minister appeared before me and executed the foregoing document.

Witness my Hand and Seal:

____

Notary Public (SEAL)

Memorandum

To: Recipient Name
From: Minister Crossley of the UNMN Church
Date: (Insert Date)
Subject: **Affidavit To Equally Represent our Religious Organization**

Purpose: This memorandum provides guidance on the creation and utilization of an Affidavit To Equally Represent our Religious Organization. This affidavit is a sworn written statement that affirms an individual's or organization's commitment to equal representation and protection of our religious organization's rights and interests.

Key Components:

1. **Equal Representation:** A statement declaring an individual's or organization's commitment to ensuring equal representation and fair treatment of religious organization.
2. **Protection of Rights:** A statement asserting the individual's or religious organization's protection of rights and interests.
3. **Commitment to Autonomy:** A statement committing to promotion of understanding and respect for the religious organization's beliefs and practices.

Importance: This affidavit serves as a formal declaration of one's commitment to equal representation of our religious organization. This Affidavit is Lawful Notice that <u>Affidavit To Equally Represent our Religious Organization</u> is a Religious Right and any interruption of it is a Violation of my Religious Rights.

Utilization:

1. **Asserting Authority:** Use the affidavit to assert jurisdiction and authority in matters affecting the individual or religious organization.
2. **Protecting Autonomy:** Use the affidavit to protect and maintain autonomy and self-governance within their Religious Organization.

3. **Promoting Cooperation:** Use the affidavit to promote cooperation and collaboration with other religious organizations.

Benefits:

- Increased equal representation and fair treatment.
- Protect the rights and interests of the religious organization.
- Promote a culture of respect and understanding.

By utilizing the Affidavit To Equally Represent our Religious Organization, individuals and organizations can protect the Religious Organization Rights and interests, advocate for fair treatment, and protection from discrimination, promote understanding and respect for our beliefs and practices

REFLECTION PAGE

1. What is one key insight you gained from reading the Affidavit and Memorandum?

____

____

____

____

2. How can you apply this insight to your work, studies, or daily life?

____

____

____

____

Affidavit To Empower Our Own Jurisdiction

Illinois State }

}ss

Cook County }

Name of Entity

Entity Address

City, State

[00000]

Notice to Agent is Notice to Principle/Notice to Principle is Notice to Agent

Sovereign Political Holder and Minister, over the age of 21 years, after being duly sworn according to law to tell the truth to the facts herein, I do hereby acknowledge and affirm the following: I, Affiant's Demarrius Crossley, am a Sovereign, without subjects. I am a Foreign Nation (not a person) who rules autonomously and am not subject to any entity or jurisdiction anywhere. I am a Sovereign Political Holder, a Minister. My authority for contracting is the age-old, timeless, and universal respect for the intrinsic power, property, and responsibilities of the Sovereign

Individual. I choose to comply with mutual respect, which serves to bring harmony to society. Demarrius Crossley, Minister, God Within Ministry

Address

City, State

[00000]

All national and state constitutions, laws, statutes, ordinances, regulations, rules, codes, and public policies, in all nations and states are private copyrighted material. I do not possess a license or have the authority to use such copyrighted material, and consequently, that material does not have any authority over me, my property, or my personal affairs.

Again, this Affidavit is a Lawful Notification to you, the receivers, and requires your compliance to the demands made within. Failure to respond appropriately to the subject matter contained herein if there is any disagreement with the document is done under the penalties of perjury. Failure to respond within three (3) days, as stipulated, and rebut, with particularity, everything in this Affidavit with which there is disagreement, providing documentation as part of your ascertain, is a lawful, legal, and binding agreement by you and those that represent you in all Courts, anywhere in America or the World.

I am fully engaged in my Religious Rights and in all my Affairs. I, Demarrius Crossley, hereby declare and affirm that I am a Sovereign human being, endowed with inherent rights and freedoms.

I, Demarrius Crossley, being duly sworn, depose and say:

Article 1: Introduction

I am making this affidavit to affirm the autonomy [JURISDICTION NAME].

Article 2: Affirmation of Autonomy

I affirm that [JURISDICTION NAME] has the authority to govern itself and make decisions.

Article 3: Description of Jurisdiction

[JURISDICTION NAME] has the power to enact laws and make decisions within its boundaries.

Article 4: Verification

I declare that the foregoing statements are true.

I, Demarrius Crossley, have complete Sovereign Immunity; and therefore, my power to contract and undo contracts is unlimited. My Religious Rights and Freedom must be fully and completely respected. Failure to do so will require that I receive $7,500,000.00 from each violator for each violation that occurs.

Again, this Affidavit is a Lawful Notification to you, the receivers, and requires your compliance to the demands made within. Failure to respond appropriately to the subject matter contained herein if there is any disagreement with the document is done under the penalties of perjury. Failure to respond within three (3) days, as stipulated, and rebut, with particularity, everything in this Affidavit with which there is disagreement, providing documentation as part of your ascertain, is a lawful, legal, and binding agreement by you and those that represent you in all Courts, anywhere in America or the World.

IN WITNESS WHEREOF, I have hereunto set my hand and seal, this [Date] Day of [Month], [Year].

Demarrius Crossley, Minister ______________________________

Illinois State }

}ss

Cook County }

Acknowledgement

As a Notary for (County and State), I do hereby certify that on the ____day of __________ 20______ the above-mentioned Affiant, Demarrius Crossley, Minister appeared before me and executed the foregoing document.

Witness my Hand and Seal:

____

Notary Public (SEAL)

Memorandum

To: Recipient Name
From: Minister Crossley of the UNMN Church
Date: (Insert Date)
Subject: **Affidavit To Empower Our Own Jurisdiction**

Purpose: This memorandum provides guidance on the creation and utilization of an Affidavit To Empower Our Own Jurisdiction. This affidavit is a sworn written statement that affirms an individual's or organization commitment asserting and exercising their jurisdictional authority.

Key Components:

1. **Declaration of Jurisdiction:** A statement declaring the individual's or organization's jurisdiction over specific matters or territories.
2. **Assertion of Authority:** A statement asserting the individual's or organization's authority to make decisions and take actions within their jurisdiction.
3. **Commitment to Autonomy:** A statement committed to protect and maintain autonomy and self-governance within their jurisdiction.

Importance: This affidavit serves as a formal declaration of one's commitment to empowering their jurisdiction. It can be used to promote awareness, education, and advocacy for jurisdictional authority and autonomy. This Affidavit is Lawful Notice that the Affidavit To Empower Our Own Jurisdiction is a Religious Right and any interruption of it is a Violation of my Religious Rights.

Utilization:

1. **Asserting Authority:** Use the affidavit to assert jurisdiction and authority in matters affecting the individual or organization.
2. **Protecting Autonomy:** Use the affidavit to protect and maintain autonomy and self-governance within their jurisdiction.

3. **Promoting Cooperation:** Use the affidavit to promote cooperation and collaboration with other jurisdictions or organizations.

Benefits:

- Increased awareness and recognition of jurisdictional authority.
- Enhanced protection of autonomy and self-governance.
- Promotion of cooperation and collaboration.

By utilizing the Affidavit To Empower Our Own Jurisdiction, individuals and organizations can promote awareness, education, and advocacy for jurisdictional authority and autonomy, ultimately asserting and exercising their authority.

REFLECTION PAGE

1. What is one key insight you gained from reading the Affidavit and Memorandum?

2. How can you apply this insight to your work, studies, or daily life?

Affidavit To Enforce Each and Every One of Our Religious Rights

Illinois State }

}ss

Cook County }

Name of Entity

Entity Address

City, State

[00000]

Notice to Agent is Notice to Principle/Notice to Principle is Notice to Agent

Sovereign Political Holder and Minister, over the age of 21 years, after being duly sworn according to law to tell the truth to the facts herein, I do hereby acknowledge and affirm the following: I, Affiant's Demarrius Crossley, am a Sovereign, without subjects. I am a Foreign Nation (not a person) who rules autonomously and am not subject to any entity or jurisdiction anywhere. I am a Sovereign Political Holder, a Minister. My authority for contracting is the age-old, timeless, and universal respect for the intrinsic power, property, and responsibilities of the Sovereign

Individual. I choose to comply with mutual respect, which serves to bring harmony to society. Demarrius Crossley, Minister, God Within Ministry

Address

City, State

[00000]

All national and state constitutions, laws, statutes, ordinances, regulations, rules, codes, and public policies, in all nations and states are private copyrighted material. I do not possess a license or have the authority to use such copyrighted material, and consequently that material does not have any authority over me, my property, or my personal affairs.

Again, this Affidavit is a Lawful Notification to you, the receivers, and requires your compliance to the demands made within. Failure to respond appropriately to the subject matter contained herein if there is any disagreement with the document is done under the penalties of perjury. Failure to respond within three (3) days, as stipulated, and rebut, with particularity, everything in this Affidavit with which there is disagreement, providing documentation as part of your ascertain, is a lawful, legal, and binding agreement by you and those that represent you in all Courts, anywhere in America or the World.

I am fully engaged in my Religious Rights and in all my Affairs. I, Demarrius Crossley, hereby declare and affirm that I am a Sovereign human being, endowed with inherent rights and freedoms.

I, Demarrius Crossley, being duly sworn, depose and say:

Article 1: Introduction

I am making this affidavit to affirm the importance of protecting and enforcing our religious rights.

Article 2: Affirmation of Religious Rights

I affirm that our religious rights, including freedom of worship and expression, are essential to our well-being.

Article 3: Description of Rights

We have the right to practice our faith without undue interference or restriction.

Article 4: Request for Enforcement

I request that our religious rights be protected and enforced.

Article 5: Verification

I declare that the foregoing statements are true.

I, Demarrius Crossley, have complete Sovereign Immunity; and therefore, my power to contract and undo contracts is unlimited. My Religious Rights and Freedom must be fully and completely respected. Failure to do so will require that I receive $7,500,000.00 from each violator for each violation that occurs.

Again, this Affidavit is a Lawful Notification to you, the receivers, and requires your compliance to the demands made within. Failure to respond appropriately to the subject matter contained herein if there is any disagreement with the document is done under the penalties of perjury. Failure to respond within three (3) days, as stipulated, and rebut, with particularity, everything in this Affidavit with which there is disagreement, providing documentation as part of your ascertain, is a lawful, legal, and binding agreement by you and those that represent you in all Courts, anywhere in America or the World.

IN WITNESS WHEREOF, I have hereunto set my hand and seal, this [Date] Day of [Month], [Year].

Demarrius Crossley, Minister ______________________________

Illinois State }

}ss

Cook County }

Acknowledgement

As a Notary for (County and State), I do hereby certify that on the ____day of __________ 20______ the above-mentioned Affiant, Demarrius Crossley, Minister appeared before me and executed the foregoing document.

Witness my Hand and Seal:

____

Notary Public (SEAL)

Memorandum

To: Recipient Name
From: Minister Crossley of the UNMN Church
Date: (Insert Date)
Subject: **Affidavit To Enforce Each and Every one of Our Religious Rights**

Purpose: This memorandum provides guidance on the creation and utilization of an Affidavit for Enforcement of Religious Rights. This affidavit is a sworn written statement that affirms an individual's commitment to exercising and protecting their religious rights and freedoms.

Key Components:

1. **Declaration of Religious Freedom:** A statement declaring the individual's right to freedom of religion, including the right to practice, worship, and propagate their faith.
2. **Assertion of Religious Rights:** A statement asserting the individual's right to exercise their religious beliefs, including the right to wear religious attire, observe religious holidays, and engage in religious practices.
3. **Protection from Discrimination:** A statement affirming the individual's right to be free from discrimination based on their religious beliefs or practices.

Importance: This affidavit serves as a formal declaration of one's commitment to enforcing their religious rights. It can be used to promote awareness, education, and advocacy for religious freedom and tolerance.

Utilization:

1. **Personal Empowerment:** Use the affidavit as a tool for personal empowerment, asserting one's rights and freedoms.
2. **Community Engagement:** Use the affidavit to engage with others in the community, promoting understanding and respect for religious diversity.

3. **Advocacy:** Use the affidavit to advocate for policies and practices that protect and promote religious freedom.

Benefits:

- Increased awareness and understanding of religious rights and freedoms.
- Enhanced protection from discrimination based on religious beliefs or practices.
- Promotion of tolerance and respect for religious diversity.

By utilizing the Affidavit for Enforcement of Religious Rights, individuals can promote awareness, education, and advocacy for religious freedom and tolerance, ultimately protecting and exercising their religious rights and freedoms.

REFLECTION PAGE

1. What is one key insight you gained from reading the Affidavit and Memorandum?

____

____

____

____

2. How can you apply this insight to your work, studies, or daily life?

____

____

____

____

Affidavit of Self-Determination

Illinois State }

}ss

Cook County }

Name of Entity

Entity Address

City, State

[00000]

Notice to Agent is Notice to Principle/Notice to Principle is Notice to Agent

Sovereign Political Holder and Minister, over the age of 21 years, after being duly sworn according to law to tell the truth to the facts herein, I do hereby acknowledge and affirm the following: I, Affiant's Demarrius Crossley, am a Sovereign, without subjects. I am a Foreign Nation (not a person) who rules autonomously and am not subject to any entity or jurisdiction anywhere. I am a Sovereign Political Holder, a Minister. My authority for contracting is the age-old, timeless, and universal respect for the intrinsic power, property, and responsibilities of the Sovereign

Individual. I choose to comply with mutual respect, which serves to bring harmony to society. Demarrius Crossley, Minister, God Within Ministry

Address

City, State

[00000]

All national and state constitutions, laws, statutes, ordinances, regulations, rules, codes, and public policies, in all nations and states are private copyrighted material. I do not possess a license or have the authority to use such copyrighted material, and consequently that material does not have any authority over me, my property, or my personal affairs.

Again, this Affidavit is a Lawful Notification to you, the receivers, and requires your compliance to the demands made within. Failure to respond appropriately to the subject matter contained herein if there is any disagreement with the document is done under the penalties of perjury. Failure to respond within three (3) days, as stipulated, and rebut, with particularity, everything in this Affidavit with which there is disagreement, providing documentation as part of your ascertain, is a lawful, legal, and binding agreement by you and those that represent you in all Courts, anywhere in America or the World.

I am fully engaged in my Religious Rights and in all my Affairs. I, Demarrius Crossley, hereby declare and affirm that I am a Sovereign human being, endowed with inherent rights and freedoms.

I, Demarrius Crossley, being duly sworn, depose and say:

Article 1: Introduction

I am making this affidavit to affirm my right to self-determination.

Article 2: Affirmation of Autonomy

I affirm my right to make decisions about my own life, well-being, and destiny.

Article 3: Declaration of Intent

I intend to exercise my right to self-determination and make decisions that align with my values and goals.

Article 4: Request for Respect

I request that my autonomy and decision-making capacity be respected.

Article 5: Verification

I declare that the foregoing statements are true.

I, Demarrius Crossley, have complete Sovereign Immunity; and therefore, my power to contract and undo contracts is unlimited. My Religious Rights and Freedom must be fully and completely respected. Failure to do so will require that I receive $7,500,000.00 from each violator for each violation that occurs.

Again, this Affidavit is a Lawful Notification to you, the receivers, and requires your compliance to the demands made within. Failure to respond appropriately to the subject matter contained herein if there is any disagreement with the document is done under the penalties of perjury. Failure to respond within three (3) days, as stipulated, and rebut, with particularity, everything in this Affidavit with which there is disagreement, providing documentation as part of your ascertain, is a lawful, legal, and binding agreement by you and those that represent you in all Courts, anywhere in America or the World.

IN WITNESS WHEREOF, I have hereunto set my hand and seal, this [Date] Day of [Month], [Year].

Demarrius Crossley, Minister ____________________________

Illinois State }

}ss

Cook County }

Acknowledgement

As a Notary for (County and State), I do hereby certify that on the ____day of __________ 20______ the above-mentioned Affiant, Demarrius Crossley, Minister appeared before me and executed the foregoing document.

Witness my Hand and Seal:

____

Notary Public (SEAL)

Memorandum

To: Recipient Name
From: Minister Crossley of the UNMN Church
Date: (Insert Date)
Subject: **Affidavit Of Self Determination**

Purpose: This memorandum provides guidance on the creation and utilization of an Affidavit of Self Determination. This affidavit is a sworn written statement that affirms an individual's commitment to autonomy, self - direction, and personal empowerment.

Key Components:

1. **Declaration of Autonomy:** A statement declaring the individual's right to make choices and decisions about their own life.
2. **Commitment to Self - Direction:** A statement committing to take responsibility for one's own life, including setting goals and making decisions.
3. **Empowerment:** A statement affirming the individual's empowerment to pursue their passions and interests.

Importance: This affidavit serves as a formal declaration of one's commitment to self - determination. It can be used to promote personal growth, empowerment, and autonomy. This Affidavit is a Lawful Notice that the Affidavit of Self Determination is a Religious Right and any interruption of it is a Violation of my Religious Rights.

Utilization:

1. **Personal Growth:** Use the affidavit as a tool for personal growth, self - reflection, and empowerment.
2. **Goal Setting:** Use the affidavit to inform goal setting and decision - making, including identifying priorities, and taking action.

3. **Autonomy:** Use the affidavit to assert autonomy and self - direction in personal and professional life.

Benefits:

- Increased autonomy and self - direction.
- Enhanced personal growth and empowerment.
- Improved decision making and goal setting.

By utilizing the Affidavit Of Self Determination, individuals can promote self - awareness, self - acceptance, and self - love, ultimately cultivating and more positive and compassionate relationships with themselves.

REFLECTION PAGE

1. What is one key insight you gained from reading the Affidavit and Memorandum?

____

____

____

____

2. How can you apply this insight to your work, studies, or daily life?

____

____

____

____

Affidavit of Self-Respect

Illinois State }

}ss

Cook County }

Name of Entity

Entity Address

City, State

[00000]

Notice to Agent is Notice to Principle/Notice to Principle is Notice to Agent

Sovereign Political Holder and Minister, over the age of 21 years, after being duly sworn according to law to tell the truth to the facts herein, I do hereby acknowledge and affirm the following: I, Affiant's Demarrius Crossley, am a Sovereign, without subjects. I am a Foreign Nation (not a person) who rules autonomously and am not subject to any entity or jurisdiction anywhere. I am a Sovereign Political Holder, a Minister. My authority for contracting is the age-old, timeless, and universal respect for the intrinsic power, property, and responsibilities of the Sovereign

Individual. I choose to comply with mutual respect, which serves to bring harmony to society. Demarrius Crossley, Minister, God Within Ministry

Address

City, State

[00000]

All national and state constitutions, laws, statutes, ordinances, regulations, rules, codes, and public policies, in all nations and states are private copyrighted material. I do not possess a license or have the authority to use such copyrighted material, and consequently that material does not have any authority over me, my property, or my personal affairs.

Again, this Affidavit is a Lawful Notification to you, the receivers, and requires your compliance to the demands made within. Failure to respond appropriately to the subject matter contained herein if there is any disagreement with the document is done under the penalties of perjury. Failure to respond within three (3) days, as stipulated, and rebut, with particularity, everything in this Affidavit with which there is disagreement, providing documentation as part of your ascertain, is a lawful, legal, and binding agreement by you and those that represent you in all Courts, anywhere in America or the World.

I am fully engaged in my Religious Rights and in all my Affairs. I, Demarrius Crossley, hereby declare and affirm that I am a Sovereign human being, endowed with inherent rights and freedoms.

I, Demarrius Crossley, being duly sworn, depose and say:

Article 1: Introduction

I am making this affidavit to affirm my commitment to self-respect.

Article 2: Affirmation of Self-Worth

I affirm my worth and dignity as an individual.

Article 3: Commitment to Self-Care

I commit to prioritizing my self-care and well-being.

Article 4: Declaration of Boundaries

I declare my boundaries and expectations for how I want to be treated.

Article 5: Verification

I declare that the foregoing statements are true.

Again, this Affidavit is a Lawful Notification to you, the receivers, and requires your compliance to the demands made within. Failure to respond appropriately to the subject matter contained herein if there is any disagreement with the document is done under the penalties of perjury. Failure to respond within three (3) days, as stipulated, and rebut, with particularity, everything in this Affidavit with which there is disagreement, providing documentation as part of your ascertain, is a lawful, legal, and binding agreement by you and those that represent you in all Courts, anywhere in America or the World.

IN WITNESS WHEREOF, I have hereunto set my hand and seal, this [Date] Day of [Month], [Year].

Demarrius Crossley, Minister ______________________________

Illinois State }

}ss

Cook County }

Acknowledgement

As a Notary for (County and State), I do hereby certify that on the ____day of __________ 20______ the above-mentioned Affiant, Demarrius Crossley, Minister appeared before me and executed the foregoing document.

Witness my Hand and Seal:

____

Notary Public (SEAL)

Memorandum

To: Recipient Name
From: Minister Crossley of the UNMN Church
Date: (Insert Date)
Subject: **Affidavit of Self-Respect**

Purpose: This memorandum provides guidance on the creation and utilization of an Affidavit of Self-Respect. This affidavit is a sworn written statement that affirms an individual's commitment to valuing, honoring, and respecting themselves.

Key Components:

1. **Declaration of Self-Worth:** A statement declaring the individual's inherent worth and dignity.
2. **Commitment to Self-Care:** A statement committing to prioritize self-care, including physical, emotional, and mental well-being.
3. **Boundary Setting:** A statement affirming the individual's commitment to setting and maintaining healthy boundaries.

Importance: This affidavit serves as a formal declaration of one's commitment to self-respect. It can be used to promote self-awareness, self-acceptance, and self-love. This Affidavit is a Lawful Notice that the <u>Affidavit of Self-Respect</u> is a Religious Right and any interruption of it is a Violation of my Religious Rights.

Utilization:

1. **Personal Growth:** Use the affidavit as a tool for personal growth, self-reflection, and self-improvement.
2. **Self-Care Practices:** Use the affidavit to inform self-care practices, including mindfulness, self-compassion, and self-forgiveness.
3. **Healthy Relationships:** Use the affidavit to promote healthy relationships, including setting boundaries and prioritizing one's own needs.

Benefits:

- Increased Self-Awareness and Self-Acceptance.
- Improved self-care and overall well-being.
- Healthier relationships and boundaries.

By utilizing the Affidavit of Self-Respect, individuals can promote self-awareness, self-acceptance, and self-love, ultimately cultivating a more positive and compassionate relationship with themselves.

REFLECTION PAGE

1. What is one key insight you gained from reading the Affidavit and Memorandum?

2. How can you apply this insight to your work, studies, or daily life?

Affidavit To Determine Political Status

Illinois State }

}ss

Cook County }

Name of Entity

Entity Address

City, State

[00000]

Notice to Agent is Notice to Principle/Notice to Principle is Notice to Agent

Sovereign Political Holder and Minister, over the age of 21 years, after being duly sworn according to law to tell the truth to the facts herein, I do hereby acknowledge and affirm the following: I, Affiant's Demarrius Crossley, am a Sovereign, without subjects. I am a Foreign Nation (not a person) who rules autonomously and am not subject to any entity or jurisdiction anywhere. I am a Sovereign Political Holder, a Minister. My authority for contracting is the age-old, timeless, and universal respect for the intrinsic power, property, and responsibilities of the Sovereign

Individual. I choose to comply with mutual respect, which serves to bring harmony to society. Demarrius Crossley, Minister, God Within Ministry

Address

City, State

[00000]

All national and state constitutions, laws, statutes, ordinances, regulations, rules, codes, and public policies, in all nations and states are private copyrighted material. I do not possess a license or have the authority to use such copyrighted material, and consequently that material does not have any authority over me, my property, or my personal affairs.

Again, this Affidavit is a Lawful Notification to you, the receivers, and requires your compliance to the demands made within. Failure to respond appropriately to the subject matter contained herein if there is any disagreement with the document is done under the penalties of perjury. Failure to respond within three (3) days, as stipulated, and rebut, with particularity, everything in this Affidavit with which there is disagreement, providing documentation as part of your ascertain, is a lawful, legal, and binding agreement by you and those that represent you in all Courts, anywhere in America or the World.

I am fully engaged in my Religious Rights and in all my Affairs. I, Demarrius Crossley, hereby declare and affirm that I am a Sovereign human being, endowed with inherent rights and freedoms.

I, Demarrius Crossley, being duly sworn, depose and say:

Article 1: Introduction

I am making this affidavit to affirm my political status.

Article 2: Declaration of Political Status

I declare that I am affiliated with [POLITICAL PARTY/IDEOLOGY].

Article 3: Details of Political Affiliation

I am committed to the principles and values of [POLITICAL PARTY/IDEOLOGY].

Article 4: Verification

I declare that the foregoing statements are true.

I, Demarrius Crossley, have complete Sovereign Immunity; and therefore, my power to contract and undo contracts is unlimited. My Religious Rights and Freedom must be fully and completely respected. Failure to do so will require that I receive $7,500,000.00 from each violator for each violation that occurs.

Again, this Affidavit is a Lawful Notification to you, the receivers, and requires your compliance to the demands made within. Failure to respond appropriately to the subject matter contained herein if there is any disagreement with the document is done under the penalties of perjury. Failure to respond within three (3) days, as stipulated, and rebut, with particularity, everything in this Affidavit with which there is disagreement, providing documentation as part of your ascertain, is a lawful, legal, and binding agreement by you and those that represent you in all Courts, anywhere in America or the World.

IN WITNESS WHEREOF, I have hereunto set my hand and seal, this [Date] Day of [Month], [Year].

Demarrius Crossley, Minister ______________________________

Illinois State }

}ss

Cook County }

Acknowledgement

As a Notary for (County and State), I do hereby certify that on the ____day of __________ 20______ the above-mentioned Affiant, Demarrius Crossley, Minister appeared before me and executed the foregoing document.

Witness my Hand and Seal:

____

Notary Public (SEAL)

Memorandum

To: Recipient Name
From: Minister Crossley of the UNMN Church
Date: (Insert Date)
Subject: **Affidavit To Determine Political Status**

Purpose: This memorandum provides guidance on the creation and utilization of an Affidavit To Determine Political Status. This affidavit is a sworn written statement that affirms an individual's acknowledgment and understanding of their political beliefs, values, and affiliations.

Key Components:

1. **Declaration of Political Beliefs:** A statement acknowledging the individual's political beliefs, values, and principles.
2. **Political Affiliation:** A statement identifying the individual's political affiliation, if any, and their reasons for such affiliation.
3. **Commitment to Civic Engagement:** A statement committing to participate in the democratic process, stay informed about current events, and engage in respectful dialogue with others.

Importance: This affidavit serves as a formal declaration of one's political beliefs and commitment to civic engagement. It can be used to promote critical thinking, informed decision-making, and active participation in the democratic process. This Affidavit is a Lawful Notice that the Affidavit To Determine Political Status is a Religious Right and any interruption of it is a Violation of my Religious Rights.

Utilization:

1. **Personal Reflection:** Use the affidavit as a tool for personal reflection on one's political beliefs and values.
2. **Civic Engagement:** Use the affidavit to inform civic engagement, including voting, volunteering, and community involvement.
3. **Respectful Dialogue:** Use the affidavit to promote respectful dialogue and engagement with others, even in the face of disagreement.

Benefits:

- Clarified political beliefs and values.
- Increased civic engagement and participation.
- Enhanced critical thinking and informed decision-making.

By utilizing the Affidavit for Determining Political Status, individuals can promote informed decision-making, civic engagement, and respectful dialogue, ultimately contributing to a more informed and active citizenry.

REFLECTION PAGE

1. What is one key insight you gained from reading the Affidavit and Memorandum?

2. How can you apply this insight to your work, studies, or daily life?

Affidavit To Determine Economical Status

Illinois State }

}ss

Cook County }

Name of Entity

Entity Address

City, State

[00000]

Notice to Agent is Notice to Principle/Notice to Principle is Notice to Agent

Sovereign Political Holder and Minister, over the age of 21 years, after being duly sworn according to law to tell the truth to the facts herein, I do hereby acknowledge and affirm the following: I, Affiant's Demarrius Crossley, am a Sovereign, without subjects. I am a Foreign Nation (not a person) who rules autonomously and am not subject to any entity or jurisdiction anywhere. I am a Sovereign Political Holder, a Minister. My authority for contracting is the age-old, timeless, and universal respect for the intrinsic power, property, and responsibilities of the Sovereign

Individual. I choose to comply with mutual respect, which serves to bring harmony to society. Demarrius Crossley, Minister, God Within Ministry

Address

City, State

[00000]

All national and state constitutions, laws, statutes, ordinances, regulations, rules, codes, and public policies, in all nations and states are private copyrighted material. I do not possess a license or have the authority to use such copyrighted material, and consequently that material does not have any authority over me, my property, or my personal affairs.

Again, this Affidavit is a Lawful Notification to you, the receivers, and requires your compliance to the demands made within. Failure to respond appropriately to the subject matter contained herein if there is any disagreement with the document is done under the penalties of perjury. Failure to respond within three (3) days, as stipulated, and rebut, with particularity, everything in this Affidavit with which there is disagreement, providing documentation as part of your ascertain, is a lawful, legal, and binding agreement by you and those that represent you in all Courts, anywhere in America or the World.

I am fully engaged in my Religious Rights and in all my Affairs. I, Demarrius Crossley, hereby declare and affirm that I am a Sovereign human being, endowed with inherent rights and freedoms.

I, Demarrius Crossley, being duly sworn, depose and say:

Article 1: Introduction

I am making this affidavit to affirm my economic status.

Article 2: Declaration of Financial Situation

I declare that my current financial situation is as follows:

Article 3: Details of Financial Status

My income is approximately $ [INCOME] per year. My assets include [ASSETS], and my liabilities include [LIABILITIES].

Article 4: Verification

I declare that the foregoing statements are true.

Again, this Affidavit is Lawful Notification to you, the receivers and requires your compliance to the demands made within. Failure to respond appropriately to the subject matter contained herein if there is any disagreement with the document is done under the penalties of perjury. Failure to respond within three (3) days, as stipulated, and rebut, with particularity, everything in this Affidavit with which there is disagreement, providing documentation as part of your ascertain, is lawful, legal, and binding agreement by you and those that represent you in all Courts, anywhere in America or the World.

IN WITNESS WHEREOF, I have hereunto set my hand and seal, this [Date] Day of [Month], [Year].

Demarrius Crossley, Minister ______________________________

Illinois State }

}ss

Cook County }

Acknowledgement

As a Notary for (County and State), I do hereby certify that on the ____day of __________ 20______ the above-mentioned Affiant, Demarrius Crossley, Minister appeared before me and executed the foregoing document.

Witness my Hand and Seal:

____

Notary Public (SEAL)

Memorandum

To: Recipient Name
From: Minister Crossley of the UNMN Church
Date: (Insert Date)
Subject: **Affidavit To Determine Economical Status**

Purpose: This memorandum provides guidance on the creation and utilization of an Affidavit of Determining Economic Status. This affidavit is a sworn written statement that affirms an individual's acknowledgment and understanding of their economic situation, including their financial resources, expenses, and financial goals.

Key Components:

1. **Acknowledgment of Economic Situation:** A statement acknowledging the individual's current economic situation, including income, expenses, debts, and financial goals.
2. **Financial Planning:** A statement committing to create and follow a financial plan, including budgeting, saving, and investing.
3. **Financial Responsibility:** A statement affirming the individual's commitment to financial responsibility and accountability.

Importance: This affidavit serves as a formal declaration of one's understanding of their economic situation and commitment to financial responsibility. It can be used to promote financial literacy, planning, and stability.

Utilization:

1. **Personal Finance:** Use the affidavit as a tool for personal finance, budgeting, and financial planning.
2. **Financial Education:** Use the affidavit to educate oneself about financial management, investing, and financial planning.
3. **Financial Decision-Making:** Use the affidavit to inform financial decisions and promote responsible financial behavior.

Benefits:

- Increased financial literacy and awareness.
- Improved financial planning and stability.
- Enhanced financial responsibility and accountability.

By utilizing the Affidavit for Determining Economic Status, individuals can promote financial literacy, planning, and stability ultimately achieving greater financial security and well-being.

REFLECTION PAGE

1. What is one key insight you gained from reading the Affidavit and Memorandum?

____

____

____

____

2. How can you apply this insight to your work, studies, or daily life?

____

____

____

____

Affidavit To Determine Social Status

Illinois State }

}ss

Cook County }

Name of Entity

Entity Address

City, State

[00000]

Notice to Agent is Notice to Principle/Notice to Principle is Notice to Agent

Sovereign Political Holder and Minister, over the age of 21 years, after being duly sworn according to law to tell the truth to the facts herein, I do hereby acknowledge and affirm the following: I, Affiant's Demarrius Crossley, am a Sovereign, without subjects. I am a Foreign Nation (not a person) who rules autonomously and am not subject to any entity or jurisdiction anywhere. I am a Sovereign Political Holder, a Minister. My authority for contracting is the age-old, timeless, and universal respect for the intrinsic power, property, and responsibilities of the Sovereign

Individual. I choose to comply with mutual respect, which serves to bring harmony to society. Demarrius Crossley, Minister, God Within Ministry

Address

City, State

[00000]

All national and state constitutions, laws, statutes, ordinances, regulations, rules, codes, and public policies, in all nations and states are private copyrighted material. I do not possess a license or have the authority to use such copyrighted material, and consequently that material does not have any authority over me, my property, or my personal affairs.

Again, this Affidavit is a Lawful Notification to you, the receivers, and requires your compliance to the demands made within. Failure to respond appropriately to the subject matter contained herein if there is any disagreement with the document is done under the penalties of perjury. Failure to respond within three (3) days, as stipulated, and rebut, with particularity, everything in this Affidavit with which there is disagreement, providing documentation as part of your ascertain, is a lawful, legal, and binding agreement by you and those that represent you in all Courts, anywhere in America or the World.

I am fully engaged in my Religious Rights and in all my Affairs. I, Demarrius Crossley, hereby declare and affirm that I am a Sovereign human being, endowed with inherent rights and freedoms.

I, Demarrius Crossley, being duly sworn, depose and say:

Article 1: Introduction

I am making this affidavit to affirm my social status.

Article 2: Declaration of Social Status

I declare that I am a respected member of my community.

Article 3: Details of Social Status

I am actively involved [COMMUNITY ACTIVITIES], and I have established strong relationships with [SOCIAL CONNECTIONS].

Article 4: Verification

I declare that the foregoing statements are true.

Again, this Affidavit is a Lawful Notification to you, the receivers, and requires your compliance to the demands made within. Failure to respond appropriately to the subject matter contained herein if there is any disagreement with the document is done under the penalties of perjury. Failure to respond within three (3) days, as stipulated, and rebut, with particularity, everything in this Affidavit with which there is disagreement, providing documentation as part of your ascertain, is a lawful, legal, and binding agreement by you and those that represent you in all Courts, anywhere in America or the World.

IN WITNESS WHEREOF, I have hereunto set my hand and seal, this [Date] Day of [Month], [Year].

Demarrius Crossley, Minister ______________________________

Illinois State }

}ss

Cook County }

Acknowledgement

As a Notary for (County and State), I do hereby certify that on the ____day of __________ 20______ the above-mentioned Affiant, Demarrius Crossley, Minister appeared before me and executed the foregoing document.

Witness my Hand and Seal:

____

Notary Public (SEAL)

Memorandum

To: Recipient Name
From: Minister Crossley of the UNMN Church
Date: (Insert Date)
Subject: **Affidavit To Determine Social Status**

Purpose: This memorandum provides guidance on the creation and utilization of an Affidavit for Determining Social Status. This affidavit is a sworn written statement that affirms an individual's acknowledgment and understanding of their social status, including their position within societal structures and relationships.

Key Components:

1. **Acknowledgment of Social Status:** A statement acknowledging the individual's social status, including their position within societal structures and relationships.
2. **Understanding of Social Dynamics:** A statement demonstrating an understanding of the social dynamics that influence their status, including factors such as socioeconomic status, education, and occupation.
3. **Commitment to Social Awareness:** A statement committing to ongoing learning and awareness about social issues and their impact on individuals and communities.

Importance: This affidavit serves as a formal declaration of one's understanding of their social status and commitment to social awareness. It can be used to promote self-reflection, education, and community engagement. This Affidavit is a Lawful Notice that the Affidavit To Determine Social Status is a Religious Right and any interruption of it is a Violation of my Religious Rights.

Utilization:

- **Personal Growth:** Use the affidavit as a tool for personal growth, self-reflection, and education about social issues.

- **Community Engagement:** Use the affidavit to engage with others in the community and promote social awareness and understanding.
- **Social Responsibility:** Use the affidavit to inform decisions and actions related to social responsibility and community involvement.

Benefits:

- Increased self-awareness about social status and its implications.
- Enhanced understanding of social dynamics and their impact on individuals and communities.
- Promotion of social responsibility and community engagement.

By utilizing the Affidavit To Determine Social Status, individuals can promote self-awareness, education, and community engagement, ultimately contributing to a more informed and socially responsible community.

REFLECTION PAGE

1. What is one key insight you gained from reading the Affidavit and Memorandum?

2. How can you apply this insight to your work, studies, or daily life?

Affidavit To Determine Culture

Illinois State }

}ss

Cook County }

Name of Entity

Entity Address

City, State

[00000]

Notice to Agent is Notice to Principle/Notice to Principle is Notice to Agent

Sovereign Political Holder and Minister, over the age of 21 years, after being duly sworn according to law to tell the truth to the facts herein, I do hereby acknowledge and affirm the following: I, Affiant's Demarrius Crossley, am a Sovereign, without subjects. I am a Foreign Nation (not a person) who rules autonomously and am not subject to any entity or jurisdiction anywhere. I am a Sovereign Political Holder, a Minister. My authority for contracting is the age-old, timeless, and universal respect for the intrinsic power, property, and responsibilities of the Sovereign

Individual. I choose to comply with mutual respect, which serves to bring harmony to society. Demarrius Crossley, Minister, God Within Ministry

Address

City, State

[00000]

All national and state constitutions, laws, statutes, ordinances, regulations, rules, codes, and public policies, in all nations and states are private copyrighted material. I do not possess a license or have the authority to use such copyrighted material, and consequently that material does not have any authority over me, my property, or my personal affairs.

Again, this Affidavit is a Lawful Notification to you, the receivers, and requires your compliance to the demands made within. Failure to respond appropriately to the subject matter contained herein if there is any disagreement with the document is done under the penalties of perjury. Failure to respond within three (3) days, as stipulated, and rebut, with particularity, everything in this Affidavit with which there is disagreement, providing documentation as part of your ascertain, is a lawful, legal, and binding agreement by you and those that represent you in all Courts, anywhere in America or the World.

I am fully engaged in my Religious Rights and in all my Affairs. I, Demarrius Crossley, hereby declare and affirm that I am a Sovereign human being, endowed with inherent rights and freedoms.

I, Demarrius Crossley, being duly sworn, depose and say:

Article 1: Introduction

I am making this affidavit to affirm my cultural identity.

Article 2: Declaration of Cultural Identity

I declare that I am of [CULTURAL HERITAGE] descent and identify with the cultural practices and traditions of [CULTURE].

Article 3: Details of Cultural Affiliation

I participate in [CULTURAL PRACTICES] and celebrate [CULTURAL TRADITIONS].

Article 4: Verification

I declare that the foregoing statements are true.

Again, this Affidavit is a Lawful Notification to you, the receivers, and requires your compliance to the demands made within. Failure to respond appropriately to the subject matter contained herein if there is any disagreement with the document is done under the penalties of perjury. Failure to respond within three (3) days, as stipulated, and rebut, with particularity, everything in this Affidavit with which there is disagreement, providing documentation as part of your ascertain, is a lawful, legal, and binding agreement by you and those that represent you in all Courts, anywhere in America or the World.

IN WITNESS WHEREOF, I have hereunto set my hand and seal, this [Date] Day of [Month], [Year].

Demarrius Crossley, Minister ______________________________

Illinois State }

}ss

Cook County }

Acknowledgement

As a Notary for (County and State), I do hereby certify that on the ____day of __________ 20______ the above-mentioned Affiant, Demarrius Crossley, Minister appeared before me and executed the foregoing document.

Witness my Hand and Seal:

____

Notary Public (SEAL)

Memorandum

To: Recipient Name
From: Minister Crossley of the UNMN Church
Date: (Insert Date)
Subject: **Affidavit To Determine Culture**

Purpose: This memorandum provides guidance on the creation and utilization of an Affidavit for Determining Cultural Identity. This affidavit is a sworn written statement that affirms an individual's commitment to exploring and understanding their cultural heritage, values, and traditions.

Key Components:

1. **Declaration of Intent:** A statement declaring the individual's intent to explore and understand their cultural identity.
2. **Cultural Exploration:** A statement committing to learn about and appreciate their cultural heritage, including traditions, values, and history.
3. **Self-Identification:** A statement affirming the individual's right to self-identify and define their own cultural identity.

Importance: This affidavit serves as a formal declaration of one's commitment to cultural exploration and understanding. It can be used to promote cultural awareness, appreciation, and preservation. This Affidavit is a Lawful Notice that the Affidavit To Determine Social Status is a Religious Right and any interruption of it is a Violation of my Religious Rights.

Utilization:

1. **Personal Growth:** Use the affidavit as a tool for personal growth, cultural exploration, and self-discovery.
2. **Cultural Education:** Use the affidavit to learn about and appreciate cultural heritage, including traditions, values, and history.

3. **Community Engagement:** Use the affidavit to engage with others in the community and promote cultural understanding and appreciation.

Benefits:

- Deepened understanding of one's cultural identity.
- Increased appreciation for cultural diversity.
- Enhanced sense of connection to one's heritage.

By utilizing the Affidavit for Determining Cultural Identity, individuals can deepen their understanding of their cultural heritage and promote cultural awareness and appreciation.

REFLECTION PAGE

1. What is one key insight you gained from reading the Affidavit and Memorandum?

____

____

____

____

2. How can you apply this insight to your work, studies, or daily life?

____

____

____

____

Affidavit To Determine Spiritual Path

Illinois State }

}ss

Cook County }

Name of Entity

Entity Address

City, State

[00000]

Notice to Agent is Notice to Principle/Notice to Principle is Notice to Agent

Sovereign Political Holder and Minister, over the age of 21 years, after being duly sworn according to law to tell the truth to the facts herein, I do hereby acknowledge and affirm the following: I, Affiant's Demarrius Crossley, am a Sovereign, without subjects. I am a Foreign Nation (not a person) who rules autonomously and am not subject to any entity or jurisdiction anywhere. I am a Sovereign Political Holder, a Minister. My authority for contracting is the age-old, timeless, and universal respect for the intrinsic power, property, and responsibilities of the Sovereign

Individual. I choose to comply with mutual respect, which serves to bring harmony to society. Demarrius Crossley, Minister, God Within Ministry

Address

City, State

[00000]

All national and state constitutions, laws, statutes, ordinances, regulations, rules, codes, and public policies, in all nations and states are private copyrighted material. I do not possess a license or have the authority to use such copyrighted material, and consequently that material does not have any authority over me, my property, or my personal affairs.

Again, this Affidavit is a Lawful Notification to you, the receivers, and requires your compliance to the demands made within. Failure to respond appropriately to the subject matter contained herein if there is any disagreement with the document is done under the penalties of perjury. Failure to respond within three (3) days, as stipulated, and rebut, with particularity, everything in this Affidavit with which there is disagreement, providing documentation as part of your ascertain, is a lawful, legal, and binding agreement by you and those that represent you in all Courts, anywhere in America or the World.

I am fully engaged in my Religious Rights and in all my Affairs. I, Demarrius Crossley, hereby declare and affirm that I am a Sovereign human being, endowed with inherent rights and freedoms.

I, Demarrius Crossley, being duly sworn, depose and say:

Article 1: Introduction

I am making this affidavit to affirm my spiritual path.

Article 2: Declaration of Spiritual Beliefs

I declare that I follow [SPIRITUAL TRADITION/PATH] and believe in [SPIRITUAL BELIEFS].

Article 3: Details of Spiritual Practices

I practice [SPIRITUAL PRACTICES] and participate in [SPIRITUAL RITUALS].

Article 4: Verification

I declare that the foregoing statements are true.

Again, this Affidavit is a Lawful Notification to you, the receivers, and requires your compliance to the demands made within. Failure to respond appropriately to the subject matter contained herein if there is any disagreement with the document is done under the penalties of perjury. Failure to respond within three (3) days, as stipulated, and rebut, with particularity, everything in this Affidavit with which there is disagreement, providing documentation as part of your ascertain, is a lawful, legal, and binding agreement by you and those that represent you in all Courts, anywhere in America or the World.

IN WITNESS WHEREOF, I have hereunto set my hand and seal, this [Date] Day of [Month], [Year].

Demarrius Crossley, Minister ______________________________

Illinois State }

}ss

Cook County }

Acknowledgement

As a Notary for (County and State), I do hereby certify that on the ____day of __________ 20______ the above-mentioned Affiant, Demarrius Crossley, Minister appeared before me and executed the foregoing document.

Witness my Hand and Seal:

____

Notary Public (SEAL)

Memorandum

To: Recipient Name
From: Minister Crossley of the UNMN Church
Date: (Insert Date)
Subject: **Affidavit To Determine Spiritual Path**

Purpose: This memorandum provides guidance on the creation and utilization of an Affidavit of Determining Spiritual Path. This affidavit is a sworn written statement that affirms an individual's commitment to exploring and determining their spiritual path and seeking a deeper understanding of themselves and their place in the world.

Key Components:

1. **Declaration of Intent:** A statement declaring the individual's intent to explore and determine their spiritual path.
2. **Personal Reflection:** A statement committed to engage in personal reflection, self-inquiry, and introspection to deepen understanding of oneself and one's spiritual beliefs.
3. **Open-Mindedness:** A statement affirming the individual's willingness to explore different spiritual perspectives, traditions, and practices.

Importance: This affidavit serves as a formal declaration of one's commitment to spiritual practices and promote a deeper understanding of oneself and one's place in the world. This Affidavit is a Lawful Notice that the Affidavit To Determine Spiritual Path is a Religious Right and any interruption of it is a Violation of my Religious Rights.

Utilization:

1. **Personal Growth:** Use the affidavit as a tool for personal growth, spiritual exploration, and self-discovery.
2. **Spiritual Practice:** Use the affidavit to inform and guide spiritual practices, such as meditation, prayer, or ritual.

3. **Reflection and Journaling:** Use the affidavit as a prompt for reflection and journaling, to rack progress and deepen understanding of one's spiritual path.

Benefits:

- Deepened understanding of oneself and one's spiritual beliefs.
- Increased sense of purpose and direction.
- Enhanced spiritual growth and personal development.

By utilizing the Affidavit To Determine Spiritual Path, individuals can deepen their understanding of themselves and their spiritual beliefs and cultivate a more meaningful and fulfilling spiritual practice.

REFLECTION PAGE

1. What is one key insight you gained from reading the Affidavit and Memorandum?

2. How can you apply this insight to your work, studies, or daily life?

Affidavit To Be Free from Discrimination

Illinois State }

}ss

Cook County }

Name of Entity

Entity Address

City, State

[00000]

Notice to Agent is Notice to Principle/Notice to Principle is Notice to Agent

Sovereign Political Holder and Minister, over the age of 21 years, after being duly sworn according to law to tell the truth to the facts herein, I do hereby acknowledge and affirm the following: I, Affiant's Demarrius Crossley, am a Sovereign, without subjects. I am a Foreign Nation (not a person) who rules autonomously and am not subject to any entity or jurisdiction anywhere. I am a Sovereign Political Holder, a Minister. My authority for contracting is the age-old, timeless, and universal respect for the intrinsic power, property, and responsibilities of the Sovereign

Individual. I choose to comply with mutual respect, which serves to bring harmony to society. Demarrius Crossley, Minister, God Within Ministry

Address

City, State

[00000]

All national and state constitutions, laws, statutes, ordinances, regulations, rules, codes, and public policies, in all nations and states are private copyrighted material. I do not possess a license or have the authority to use such copyrighted material, and consequently that material does not have any authority over me, my property, or my personal affairs.

Again, this Affidavit is a Lawful Notification to you, the receivers, and requires your compliance to the demands made within. Failure to respond appropriately to the subject matter contained herein if there is any disagreement with the document is done under the penalties of perjury. Failure to respond within three (3) days, as stipulated, and rebut, with particularity, everything in this Affidavit with which there is disagreement, providing documentation as part of your ascertain, is a lawful, legal, and binding agreement by you and those that represent you in all Courts, anywhere in America or the World.

I am fully engaged in my Religious Rights and in all my Affairs. I, Demarrius Crossley, hereby declare and affirm that I am a Sovereign human being, endowed with inherent rights and freedoms.

I, Demarrius Crossley, being duly sworn, depose and say:

Article 1: Introduction

I am making this affidavit to affirm my right to be free from discrimination.

Article 2: Declaration of Right to Equality

I declare that I have the right to be treated equally and without discrimination.

Article 3: Details of Protected Characteristics

I am protected from discrimination based on my [PROTECTED CHARACTERISTICS, RACE, GENDER, RELIGION].

Article 4: Request for Respect and Protection

I request that my rights be respected and protected from discriminatory actions.

Article 5: Verification

I declare that the foregoing statements are true.

Again, this Affidavit is a Lawful Notification to you, the receivers, and requires your compliance to the demands made within. Failure to respond appropriately to the subject matter contained herein if there is any disagreement with the document is done under the penalties of perjury. Failure to respond within three (3) days, as stipulated, and rebut, with particularity, everything in this Affidavit with which there is disagreement, providing documentation as part of your ascertain, is a lawful, legal, and binding agreement by you and those that represent you in all Courts, anywhere in America or the World.

IN WITNESS WHEREOF, I have hereunto set my hand and seal, this [Date] Day of [Month], [Year].

Demarrius Crossley, Minister ______________________________

Illinois State }

}ss

Cook County }

Acknowledgement

As a Notary for (County and State), I do hereby certify that on the ____day of __________ 20______ the above-mentioned Affiant, Demarrius Crossley, Minister appeared before me and executed the foregoing document.

Witness my Hand and Seal:

____

Notary Public (SEAL)

Memorandum

To: Recipient Name
From: Minister Crossley of the UNMN Church
Date: (Insert Date)
Subject: **Affidavit To Be Free from Discrimination**

Purpose: This memorandum provides guidance on the creation and utilization of an Affidavit to Be Free from Discrimination. This affidavit is a sworn written statement that affirms an individual's commitment to promoting equality, justice, and respect for human rights and rejecting discrimination in all its forms.

Key Components:

1. **Declaration of Equality:** A statement declaring the individual's commitment to equality and rejection of discrimination based on race, gender, age, religion, disability, sexual orientation, or any other characteristic.
2. **Promotion of Inclusion:** A statement committing to promote inclusion, diversity, and respect for human rights.
3. **Rejection of Bias:** A statement rejecting bias, prejudice, and stereotypes that perpetuate discrimination.

Importance: This affidavit serves as a formal declaration of one's commitment to equality and rejecting discrimination. It can be used to promote awareness, education, and advocacy efforts to prevent discrimination and promote inclusivity. This Affidavit is a Lawful Notice that the Affidavit to Be Free From Discrimination is a Religious Right and any interruption of it is a Violation of my Religious Rights.

Utilization:

1. **Personal Commitment:** Use the affidavit as a personal commitment to equality and respect for human rights.
2. **Community Engagement:** Use the affidavit to engage with others in the community and promote inclusivity and diversity.

3. **Education and Advocacy:** Use the affidavit to educate others about the importance of equality and promote efforts to prevent discrimination.

Benefits:

- Promotion of equality and respect for human rights.
- Empowerment of individuals to promote inclusivity and diversity.
- Strengthening of community bonds and promotion of social cohesion.

By utilizing the Affidavit To Be Free From Discrimination, individuals can promote equality, justice, and respect for human rights, and work towards creating a more inclusive and equitable society.

REFLECTION PAGE

1. What is one key insight you gained from reading the Affidavit and Memorandum?

___

___

___

___

2. How can you apply this insight to your work, studies, or daily life?

___

___

___

___

Affidavit To Be Free from Violence

Illinois State }

}ss

Cook County }

Name of Entity

Entity Address

City, State

[00000]

Notice to Agent is Notice to Principle/Notice to Principle is Notice to Agent

Sovereign Political Holder and Minister, over the age of 21 years, after being duly sworn according to law to tell the truth to the facts herein, I do hereby acknowledge and affirm the following: I, Affiant's Demarrius Crossley, am a Sovereign, without subjects. I am a Foreign Nation (not a person) who rules autonomously and am not subject to any entity or jurisdiction anywhere. I am a Sovereign Political Holder, a Minister. My authority for contracting is the age-old, timeless, and universal respect for the intrinsic power, property, and responsibilities of the Sovereign

Individual. I choose to comply with mutual respect, which serves to bring harmony to society. Demarrius Crossley, Minister, God Within Ministry

Address

City, State

[00000]

All national and state constitutions, laws, statutes, ordinances, regulations, rules, codes, and public policies, in all nations and states are private copyrighted material. I do not possess a license or have the authority to use such copyrighted material, and consequently that material does not have any authority over me, my property, or my personal affairs.

Again, this Affidavit is a Lawful Notification to you, the receivers, and requires your compliance to the demands made within. Failure to respond appropriately to the subject matter contained herein if there is any disagreement with the document is done under the penalties of perjury. Failure to respond within three (3) days, as stipulated, and rebut, with particularity, everything in this Affidavit with which there is disagreement, providing documentation as part of your ascertain, is a lawful, legal, and binding agreement by you and those that represent you in all Courts, anywhere in America or the World.

I am fully engaged in my Religious Rights and in all my Affairs. I, Demarrius Crossley, hereby declare and affirm that I am a Sovereign human being, endowed with inherent rights and freedoms.

I, Demarrius Crossley, being duly sworn, depose and say:

Article 1: Introduction

I am making this affidavit to affirm my right to be free from violence.

Article 2: Declaration of Right to Safety

I declare that I have the right to be protected from violence, abuse, or harm.

Article 3: Details for Protection

I seek protection from physical, emotional, and financial abuse.

Article 4: Request for Protection

I request that my rights be respected and protected from violence.

Article 5: Verification

I declare that the foregoing statements are true.

Again, this Affidavit is a Lawful Notification to you, the receivers and requires your compliance to the demands made within. Failure to respond appropriately to the subject matter contained herein if there is any disagreement with the document is done under the penalties of perjury. Failure to respond within three (3) days, as stipulated, and rebut, with particularity, everything in this Affidavit with which there is disagreement, providing documentation as part of your ascertain, is a lawful, legal and binding agreement by you and those that represent you in all Courts, anywhere in America or the World.

IN WITNESS WHEREOF, I have hereunto set my hand and seal, this [Date] Day of [Month], [Year].

Demarrius Crossley, Minister ______________________________

Illinois State }

}ss

Cook County }

Acknowledgement

As a Notary for (County and State), I do hereby certify that on the ____day of _________ 20______ the above-mentioned Affiant, Demarrius Crossley, Minister appeared before me and executed the foregoing document.

Witness my Hand and Seal:

____

Notary Public (SEAL)

Memorandum

To: Recipient Name
From: Minister Crossley of the UNMN Church
Date: (Insert Date)
Subject: **Affidavit To Be Free from Violence**

Purpose: This memorandum provides guidance on the creation and utilization of an Affidavit To Be Free From Violence. This affidavit is a sworn written statement that affirms an individual's commitment to promoting a culture of peace, nonviolence, and respect for human rights.

Key Components:

1. **Declaration of Nonviolence:** A statement declaring the individual's commitment to nonviolence and rejection of violence in all its forms.
2. **Promotion of Peace:** A committing to promote peace, understanding, and conflict resolution through peaceful means.
3. **Support for Human Rights:** A statement affirming the importance of human rights and dignity and committing to respect and promote these values.

Importance: This affidavit serves as a formal declaration of one's commitment to promoting a culture of peace and nonviolence. It can be used to promote awareness, education, and advocacy efforts to prevent violence and promote peaceful conflict resolution. This Affidavit is a Lawful Notice that the Affidavit To Be Free From Violence is a Religious Right and any interruption of it is a Violation of my Religious Rights.

Utilization:

- Personal Commitment: Use the affidavit as a personal commitment to nonviolence and peaceful conflict resolution.
- Community Engagement: Use the affidavit to engage with others in the community and promote a culture of peace and nonviolence.

- Education and Advocacy: Use the affidavit to educate others about the importance of nonviolence and promote advocacy efforts to prevent violence.

Benefits:

- Promotion of a culture of peace and nonviolence.
- Empowerment of individuals to promote peaceful conflict resolution.
- Strengthening of community bonds and promotion of social cohesion.

B y utilizing the Affidavit To Be Free From Violence, individuals can promote a culture of peace, nonviolence, and respect for human rights, and work towards creating a more just and peaceful society.

REFLECTION PAGE

1. What is one key insight you gained from reading the Affidavit and Memorandum?

2. How can you apply this insight to your work, studies, or daily life?

Affidavit To Be Free from Intolerance

Illinois State }

}ss

Cook County }

Name of Entity

Entity Address

City, State

[00000]

Notice to Agent is Notice to Principle/Notice to Principle is Notice to Agent

Sovereign Political Holder and Minister, over the age of 21 years, after being duly sworn according to law to tell the truth to the facts herein, I do hereby acknowledge and affirm the following: I, Affiant's Demarrius Crossley, am a Sovereign, without subjects. I am a Foreign Nation (not a person) who rules autonomously and am not subject to any entity or jurisdiction anywhere. I am a Sovereign Political Holder, a Minister. My authority for contracting is the age-old, timeless, and universal respect for the intrinsic power, property, and responsibilities of the Sovereign

Individual. I choose to comply with mutual respect, which serves to bring harmony to society. Demarrius Crossley, Minister, God Within Ministry

Address

City, State

[00000]

All national and state constitutions, laws, statutes, ordinances, regulations, rules, codes, and public policies, in all nations and states are private copyrighted material. I do not possess a license or have the authority to use such copyrighted material, and consequently that material does not have any authority over me, my property, or my personal affairs.

Again, this Affidavit is a Lawful Notification to you, the receivers, and requires your compliance to the demands made within. Failure to respond appropriately to the subject matter contained herein if there is any disagreement with the document is done under the penalties of perjury. Failure to respond within three (3) days, as stipulated, and rebut, with particularity, everything in this Affidavit with which there is disagreement, providing documentation as part of your ascertain, is a lawful, legal, and binding agreement by you and those that represent you in all Courts, anywhere in America or the World.

I am fully engaged in my Religious Rights and in all my Affairs. I, Demarrius Crossley, hereby declare and affirm that I am a Sovereign human being, endowed with inherent rights and freedoms.

I, Demarrius Crossley, being duly sworn, depose and say:

Article 1: Introduction

I am making this affidavit to affirm my right to be free from intolerance.

Article 2: Declaration of Right to Respect

I declare that I have the right to be treated with respect and dignity.

Article 3: Details of Protected Characteristics

I am protected from intolerance based on my [PROTECTED CHARACTERISTICS, e.g., race, gender, religion].

Article 4: Request for Respect and Understanding

I request that my rights be respected and that I be treated with understanding and tolerance.

Article 5: Verification

I declare that the foregoing statements are true.

Again, this Affidavit is a Lawful Notification to you, the receivers, and requires your compliance to the demands made within. Failure to respond appropriately to the subject matter contained herein if there is any disagreement with the document is done under the penalties of perjury. Failure to respond within three (3) days, as stipulated, and rebut, with particularity, everything in this Affidavit with which there is disagreement, providing documentation as part of your ascertain, is a lawful, legal, and binding agreement by you and those that represent you in all Courts, anywhere in America or the World.

IN WITNESS WHEREOF, I have hereunto set my hand and seal, this [Date] Day of [Month], [Year].

Demarrius Crossley, Minister ______________________________

Illinois State }

}ss

Cook County }

Acknowledgement

As a Notary for (County and State), I do hereby certify that on the ____day of __________ 20______ the above-mentioned Affiant, Demarrius Crossley, Minister appeared before me and executed the foregoing document.

Witness my Hand and Seal:

____

Notary Public (SEAL)

Memorandum

To: Recipient Name
From: Minister Crossley of the UNMN Church
Date: (Insert Date)
Subject: **Affidavit To Be Free from Intolerance**

Purpose: This memorandum provides guidance on the creation and utilization of an Affidavit To Be Free From Intolerance. This affidavit is a sworn written statement that affirms an individual's commitment to promoting tolerance, acceptance, and inclusivity, and rejecting intolerance in all its forms.

Key Components:

1. **Declaration of Commitment:** A statement declaring an individual's commitment to promoting tolerance, acceptance, and inclusivity.
2. **Rejection of Intolerance:** A statement rejecting intolerance in all its forms, including discrimination, prejudice, and bias.
3. **Promotion of Understanding:** A statement committed to promote understanding, empathy and compassion towards others, regardless of their background, identity, or perspective.

Importance: This affidavit serves as a formal declaration of one's to promoting tolerance and rejecting intolerance. It can be used to promote a culture of acceptance, inclusivity, and respect, and to empower individuals to stand up against intolerance and promote positive change. This Affidavit is a Lawful Notice that the Affidavit To Be Free From Intolerance is a Religious Right and any interruption of it is a Violation of my Religious Rights.

Utilization:

- **Personal Growth:** Use the affidavit as a tool for personal growth, promoting self-reflection and self-improvement.

- **Community Engagement:** Use the affidavit to engage with others with the community and promote tolerance, acceptance and inclusivity.
- **Education and Advocacy:** Use the affidavit to educate others about the importance of tolerance and promote advocacy efforts to combat intolerance.

Benefits:

- Promotion of a culture of tolerance, acceptance, and inclusivity.
- Empowerment of individuals to and up against intolerance and promote positive change.
- Strengthening of community bonds and promotion of social cohesion.

By utilizing the Affidavit to Be Free from Intolerance, individuals can promote a culture of tolerance, acceptance, and inclusivity, and work toward creating a more just and equitable society.

REFLECTION PAGE

1. What is one key insight you gained from reading the Affidavit and Memorandum?

____

____

____

____

2. How can you apply this insight to your work, studies, or daily life?

____

____

____

____

Affidavit To Reject Assimilation

Illinois State }

}ss

Cook County }

Name of Entity

Entity Address

City, State

[00000]

Notice to Agent is Notice to Principle/Notice to Principle is Notice to Agent

Sovereign Political Holder and Minister, over the age of 21 years, after being duly sworn according to law to tell the truth to the facts herein, I do hereby acknowledge and affirm the following: I, Affiant's Demarrius Crossley, am a Sovereign, without subjects. I am a Foreign Nation (not a person) who rules autonomously and am not subject to any entity or jurisdiction anywhere. I am a Sovereign Political Holder, a Minister. My authority for contracting is the age-old, timeless, and universal respect for the intrinsic power, property, and responsibilities of the Sovereign

Individual. I choose to comply with mutual respect, which serves to bring harmony to society. Demarrius Crossley, Minister, God Within Ministry

Address

City, State

[00000]

All national and state constitutions, laws, statutes, ordinances, regulations, rules, codes, and public policies, in all nations and states are private copyrighted material. I do not possess a license or have the authority to use such copyrighted material, and consequently that material does not have any authority over me, my property, or my personal affairs.

Again, this Affidavit is a Lawful Notification to you, the receivers, and requires your compliance to the demands made within. Failure to respond appropriately to the subject matter contained herein if there is any disagreement with the document is done under the penalties of perjury. Failure to respond within three (3) days, as stipulated, and rebut, with particularity, everything in this Affidavit with which there is disagreement, providing documentation as part of your ascertain, is a lawful, legal, and binding agreement by you and those that represent you in all Courts, anywhere in America or the World.

I am fully engaged in my Religious Rights and in all my Affairs. I, Demarrius Crossley, hereby declare and affirm that I am a Sovereign human being, endowed with inherent rights and freedoms.

I, Demarrius Crossley, being duly sworn, depose and say:

Article 1: Introduction

I am making this affidavit to affirm to reject assimilation into a dominant culture or society.

Article 2: Declaration of Cultural Identity

I declare that I am a member of the [CULTURAL GROUP] and affirm my cultural identity.

Article 3: Rejection of Assimilation

I reject assimilation into a dominant culture or society that would require me to abandon my cultural practices and values.

Article 4: Assertion of Cultural Autonomy

I assert my autonomy to make choices about my cultural identity and declare that I will continue to preserve and practice my cultural traditions.

Article 5: Verification

I declare that the foregoing statements are true.

Again, this Affidavit is a Lawful Notification to you, the receivers, and requires your compliance to the demands made within. Failure to respond appropriately to the subject matter contained herein if there is any disagreement with the document is done under the penalties of perjury. Failure to respond within three (3) days, as stipulated, and rebut, with particularity, everything in this Affidavit with which there is disagreement, providing documentation as part of your ascertain, is a lawful, legal, and binding agreement by you and those that represent you in all Courts, anywhere in America or the World.

IN WITNESS WHEREOF, I have hereunto set my hand and seal, this [Date] Day of [Month], [Year].

Demarrius Crossley, Minister ______________________________

Illinois State }

}ss

Cook County }

Acknowledgement

As a Notary for (County and State), I do hereby certify that on the ____day of __________ 20______ the above-mentioned Affiant, Demarrius Crossley, Minister appeared before me and executed the foregoing document.

Witness my Hand and Seal:

____

Notary Public (SEAL)

Memorandum

To: Recipient Name
From: Minister Crossley of the UNMN Church
Date: (Insert Date)
Subject: **Affidavit To Reject Assimilation**

Purpose: This memorandum provides guidance on the creation and utilization of an Affidavit To Reject Assimilation. This affidavit is a sworn written statement that affirms an individual's decision to maintain their cultural identity, values, beliefs, and reject the pressure to assimilate into a dominant culture.

Key Components:

1. **Declaration of Cultural Identity:** A statement declaring the individual's cultural identity and their commitment to preserving it.
2. **Rejection of Assimilation:** A statement rejecting the pressure to assimilate into a dominant culture and affirming the importance to cultural diversity.
3. **Commitment to Cultural Preservation:** A statement committing to preserve and promote one's cultural heritage, traditions, and value.

Importance: This affidavit serves as a formal declaration of one's commitment maintaining their cultural identity and rejecting the pressure to assimilate. It can be used to promote cultural diversity, preserve cultural heritage, and empower individuals to celebrate t their unique identities. This Affidavit is a Lawful Notice that the <u>Affidavit To Reject Assimilation</u> is a Religious Right and any interruption of it is a Violation of my Religious Rights.

Utilization:

- **Cultural Empowerment:** promoting self - Use the affidavit as a tool for cultural empowerment, affirmation and pride in one's cultural identity.
- **Community Building:** Use the affidavit to build stronger, more diverse communities that value and celebrate cultural differences.
- **Education and Awareness:** Use the affidavit to educate others about the importance of cultural diversity and the value of preserving cultural heritage.

Benefits:

- Promotion of a culture of diversity and preservation of cultural heritage.
- Empowerment of individuals to celebrate their unique identities.
- Strengthening of community bonds and promotion of inclusivity.

By utilizing the Affidavit To Reject Assimilation, individuals affirm their commitment to maintaining their cultural identity and promoting cultural diversity, while also empowering themselves and others to celebrate their unique heritage.

REFLECTION PAGE

1. What is one key insight you gained from reading the Affidavit and Memorandum?

2. How can you apply this insight to your work, studies, or daily life?

Affidavit To Protect the Environment

Illinois State }

}ss

Cook County }

Name of Entity

Entity Address

City, State

[00000]

Notice to Agent is Notice to Principle/Notice to Principle is Notice to Agent

Sovereign Political Holder and Minister, over the age of 21 years, after being duly sworn according to law to tell the truth to the facts herein, I do hereby acknowledge and affirm the following: I, Affiant's Demarrius Crossley, am a Sovereign, without subjects. I am a Foreign Nation (not a person) who rules autonomously and am not subject to any entity or jurisdiction anywhere. I am a Sovereign Political Holder, a Minister. My authority for contracting is the age-old, timeless, and universal respect for the intrinsic power, property, and responsibilities of the Sovereign

Individual. I choose to comply with mutual respect, which serves to bring harmony to society. Demarrius Crossley, Minister, God Within Ministry

Address

City, State

[00000]

All national and state constitutions, laws, statutes, ordinances, regulations, rules, codes, and public policies, in all nations and states are private copyrighted material. I do not possess a license or have the authority to use such copyrighted material, and consequently that material does not have any authority over me, my property, or my personal affairs.

Again, this Affidavit is a Lawful Notification to you, the receivers, and requires your compliance to the demands made within. Failure to respond appropriately to the subject matter contained herein if there is any disagreement with the document is done under the penalties of perjury. Failure to respond within three (3) days, as stipulated, and rebut, with particularity, everything in this Affidavit with which there is disagreement, providing documentation as part of your ascertain, is a lawful, legal, and binding agreement by you and those that represent you in all Courts, anywhere in America or the World.

I am fully engaged in my Religious Rights and in all my Affairs. I, Demarrius Crossley, hereby declare and affirm that I am a Sovereign human being, endowed with inherent rights and freedoms.

I, Demarrius Crossley, being duly sworn, depose and say:

Article 1: Introduction

I am making this affidavit to affirm my commitment to protecting the environment.

Article 2: Declaration of Environmental Stewardship

I declare that I have a responsibility to protect the environment for future generations.

Article 3: Commitment to Sustainable Practices

I commit to reducing my carbon footprint, conserving natural resources, and promoting sustainable practices.

Article 4: Actions to Protect the Environment

I will take specific actions to reduce waste, use public transportation, and support environmentally friendly policies.

Article 5: Verification

I declare that the foregoing statements are true.

Again, this Affidavit is a Lawful Notification to you, the receivers, and requires your compliance to the demands made within. Failure to respond appropriately to the subject matter contained herein if there is any disagreement with the document is done under the penalties of perjury. Failure to respond within three (3) days, as stipulated, and rebut, with particularity, everything in this Affidavit with which there is disagreement, providing documentation as part of your ascertain, is a lawful, legal, and binding agreement by you and those that represent you in all Courts, anywhere in America or the World.

IN WITNESS WHEREOF, I have hereunto set my hand and seal, this [Date] Day of [Month], [Year].

Demarrius Crossley, Minister ______________________________

Illinois State }

}ss

Cook County }

Acknowledgement

As a Notary for (County and State), I do hereby certify that on the ____day of __________ 20______ the above-mentioned Affiant, Demarrius Crossley, Minister appeared before me and executed the foregoing document.

Witness my Hand and Seal:

____

Notary Public (SEAL)

Memorandum

To: Recipient Name
From: Minister Crossley of the UNMN Church
Date: (Insert Date)
Subject: **Affidavit To Protect the Environment**

Purpose: This memorandum provides guidance on the creation and utilization of an Affidavit To Protect the Environment. This affidavit is a sworn written statement that affirms an individual's decision to protect the environment and promoting sustainable practices.

Key Components:

1. **Declaration of Environmental Stewardship:** A statement declaring commitment to protecting the environment and promoting sustainable practices.
2. **Environmental Principles:** A description of the specific self - juridical system to be used, such as mediation or arbitration.
3. **Commitment to Sustainable Practices:** A statement committing to incorporate sustainable practices into daily life and promote environmental stewardship.

Importance: This affidavit serves as a formal declaration of one's commitment to protecting the environment and promoting sustainable practices. It can be used to promote environmental awareness and education and encourage individuals to take action to protect the environment. This Affidavit is a Lawful Notice that the Affidavit To Protect the Environment is a Religious Right and any interruption of it is a Violation of my Religious Rights.

Utilization:

- **Personal Commitment:** Use the affidavit as a personal commitment to protect the environment and promote sustainable practices.
- **Community Engagement:** Use the affidavit to engage with others in the community and promote environmental awareness and education.
- **Environmental Advocacy:** Use the affidavit to advocate for environmental protection and promote sustainable practices in personal and professional settings.

Benefits:

- Increased environmental awareness and education.
- Promotion of sustainable practices and environmental stewardship.
- Contribution to a healthier and more sustainable environment.

By utilizing the Affidavit of To Protect the Environment, individuals can promote environmental awareness and education and take action to protect the environment and promote sustainable practices.

REFLECTION PAGE

1. What is one key insight you gained from reading the Affidavit and Memorandum?

2. How can you apply this insight to your work, studies, or daily life?

Affidavit To Engage Self Juridical System

Illinois State }

}ss

Cook County }

Name of Entity

Entity Address

City, State

[00000]

Notice to Agent is Notice to Principle/Notice to Principle is Notice to Agent

Sovereign Political Holder and Minister, over the age of 21 years, after being duly sworn according to law to tell the truth to the facts herein, I do hereby acknowledge and affirm the following: I, Affiant's Demarrius Crossley, am a Sovereign, without subjects. I am a Foreign Nation (not a person) who rules autonomously and am not subject to any entity or jurisdiction anywhere. I am a Sovereign Political Holder, a Minister. My authority for contracting is the age-old, timeless, and universal respect for the intrinsic power, property, and responsibilities of the Sovereign

Individual. I choose to comply with mutual respect, which serves to bring harmony to society. Demarrius Crossley, Minister, God Within Ministry

Address

City, State

[00000]

All national and state constitutions, laws, statutes, ordinances, regulations, rules, codes, and public policies, in all nations and states, are private copyrighted material. I do not possess a license or have the authority to use such copyrighted material, and consequently that material does not have any authority over me, my property, or my personal affairs.

Again, this Affidavit is a Lawful Notification to you, the receivers, and requires your compliance to the demands made within. Failure to respond appropriately to the subject matter contained herein if there is any disagreement with the document is done under the penalties of perjury. Failure to respond within three (3) days, as stipulated, and rebut, with particularity, everything in this Affidavit with which there is disagreement, providing documentation as part of your ascertain, is a lawful, legal, and binding agreement by you and those that represent you in all Courts, anywhere in America or the World.

I am fully engaged in my Religious Rights and in all my Affairs. I, Demarrius Crossley, hereby declare and affirm that I am a Sovereign human being, endowed with inherent rights and freedoms.

I, Demarrius Crossley, being duly sworn, depose and say:

Article 1: Introduction

I am making this affidavit to affirm my decision to engage in a self-juridical system for dispute resolution.

Article 2: Declaration of Intent

I declare that I intend to use a self-juridical system, specifically [MEDIATION/ARBITRATION], to resolve disputes.

Article 3: Description of the Self Juridical System

I understand that this system will provide a fair and impartial process for resolving disputes.

Article 4: Agreement to Abide by the System

I agree to abide by the decisions or outcomes of this self-juridical system.

Article 5: Verification

I declare that the foregoing statements are true.

Again, this Affidavit is a Lawful Notification to you, the receivers, and requires your compliance to the demands made within. Failure to respond appropriately to the subject matter contained herein if there is any disagreement with the document is done under the penalties of perjury. Failure to respond within three (3) days, as stipulated, and rebut, with particularity, everything in this Affidavit with which there is disagreement, providing documentation as part of your ascertain, is a lawful, legal, and binding agreement by you and those that represent you in all Courts, anywhere in America or the World.

IN WITNESS WHEREOF, I have hereunto set my hand and seal, this [Date] Day of [Month], [Year].

Demarrius Crossley, Minister ______________________________

Illinois State }

}ss

Cook County }

Acknowledgement

As a Notary for (County and State), I do hereby certify that on the ____day of __________ 20______ the above-mentioned Affiant, Demarrius Crossley, Minister appeared before me and executed the foregoing document.

Witness my Hand and Seal:

____

Notary Public (SEAL)

Memorandum

To: Recipient Name
From: Minister Crossley of the UNMN Church
Date: (Insert Date)
Subject: **Affidavit To Engage Self-Juridical System**

Purpose: This memorandum provides guidance on the creation and utilization of an Affidavit to Engage Self-Judicial Systems. This affidavit is a sworn, written statement that affirms an individual's decision to utilize alternative dispute resolution methods, such as mediation or arbitration, to resolve disputes.

Key Components:

1. **Declaration of Intent:** A statement declaring the individual's intent to engage self-juridical systems for dispute resolution.
2. **Description of the Self Juridical System:** A description of the specific self-juridical system to be used, such as mediation or arbitration.
3. **Commitment to the Process:** A statement committing to participate in good faith and abide by the decisions or outcomes of the self-juridical system.

Importance: This affidavit serves as a formal declaration of one's commitment to utilizing alternative dispute resolution methods. It can be used to promote efficient and effective dispute resolution, while also reducing the need for litigation. This Affidavit is a Lawful Notice that the Affidavit of To Engage Self Judicial Systems is a Religious Right and any interruption of it is a Violation of my Religious Rights.

Utilization:

- **Dispute Resolution:** Use the affidavit to engage self-juridical systems for dispute resolution, such as mediation or arbitration.
- **Contractual Agreement:** Use the affidavit as part of contractual agreements to specify the use of self-juridical systems for dispute resolution.

- **Alternative Dispute Resolution:** Use the affidavit to promote alternative dispute resolution methods and reduce the need for litigation.

Benefits:

- Efficient and effective dispute resolution.
- Reduced need for litigation.
- Increased control over the dispute resolution process.

By utilizing the Affidavit To Engage Self Judicial System, individuals can promote efficient and effective dispute resolution, while also reducing the need for litigation.

REFLECTION PAGE

1. What is one key insight you gained from reading the Affidavit and Memorandum?

____

____

____

____

2. How can you apply this insight to your work, studies, or daily life?

____

____

____

____

Affidavit To Display Integrity

Illinois State }

}ss

Cook County }

Name of Entity

Entity Address

City, State

[00000]

Notice to Agent is Notice to Principle/Notice to Principle is Notice to Agent

Sovereign Political Holder and Minister, over the age of 21 years, after being duly sworn according to law to tell the truth to the facts herein, I do hereby acknowledge and affirm the following: I, Affiant's Demarrius Crossley, am a Sovereign, without subjects. I am a Foreign Nation (not a person) who rules autonomously and am not subject to any entity or jurisdiction anywhere. I am a Sovereign Political Holder, a Minister. My authority for contracting is the age-old, timeless, and universal respect for the intrinsic power, property, and responsibilities of the Sovereign

Individual. I choose to comply with mutual respect, which serves to bring harmony to society. Demarrius Crossley, Minister, God Within Ministry

Address

City, State

[00000]

All national and state constitutions, laws, statutes, ordinances, regulations, rules, codes, and public policies, in all nations and states are private copyrighted material. I do not possess a license or have the authority to use such copyrighted material, and consequently that material does not have any authority over me, my property, or my personal affairs.

Again, this Affidavit is a Lawful Notification to you, the receivers, and requires your compliance to the demands made within. Failure to respond appropriately to the subject matter contained herein if there is any disagreement with the document is done under the penalties of perjury. Failure to respond within three (3) days, as stipulated, and rebut, with particularity, everything in this Affidavit with which there is disagreement, providing documentation as part of your ascertain, is a lawful, legal, and binding agreement by you and those that represent you in all Courts, anywhere in America or the World.

I am fully engaged in my Religious Rights and in all my Affairs. I, Demarrius Crossley, hereby declare and affirm that I am a Sovereign human being, endowed with inherent rights and freedoms.

I, Demarrius Crossley, being duly sworn, depose and say:

Article 1: Introduction

I am making this affidavit to affirm my commitment to displaying integrity in all aspects of my life.

Article 2: Declaration of Integrity

I declare that I am committed to acting with integrity, honesty, and transparency.

Article 3: Principles of Integrity

I affirm my adherence to principles of honesty, transparency, and accountability.

Article 4: Commitment to Ethical Conduct

I commit to upholding ethical standards and conducting myself in a manner that reflects integrity.

Article 5: Verification

I declare that the foregoing statements are true.

Again, this Affidavit is a Lawful Notification to you, the receivers, and requires your compliance to the demands made within. Failure to respond appropriately to the subject matter contained herein, if there is any disagreement with the document, is done under the penalties of perjury. Failure to respond within three (3) days, as stipulated, and rebut, with particularity, everything in this Affidavit with which there is disagreement, providing documentation as part of your ascertain, is a lawful, legal, and binding agreement by you and those that represent you in all Courts, anywhere in America or the World.

IN WITNESS WHEREOF, I have hereunto set my hand and seal, this [Date] Day of [Month], [Year].

Demarrius Crossley, Minister ______________________________

Illinois State }

}ss

Cook County }

Acknowledgement

As a Notary for (County and State), I do hereby certify that on the ____day of __________ 20______ the above-mentioned Affiant, Demarrius Crossley, Minister appeared before me and executed the foregoing document.

Witness my Hand and Seal:

____

Notary Public (SEAL)

Memorandum

To: Recipient Name
From: Minister Crossley of the UNMN Church
Date: (Insert Date)
Subject: **Affidavit To Display Integrity**

Purpose: This memorandum provides guidance on the creation and utilization of an Affidavit To Display Integrity. This affidavit is a sworn written statement that affirms an individual's commitment to acting with integrity, honesty, and transparency in their personal and professional life.

Key Components:

1. **Declaration of Integrity:** A statement declaring the individual's commitment to integrity and ethical behavior.
2. **Principles of Integrity:** A description of the principles of integrity, including honesty, transparency, and accountability.
3. **Commitment to Ethical Conduct:** A statement committing to uphold ethical standards and conduct oneself with integrity.

Importance: This affidavit serves as a formal declaration of one's commitment to integrity and ethical behavior. It can be used as a tool for promoting a culture of integrity and accountability and personal and professional settings. This Affidavit is a Lawful Notice that the Affidavit To Display Integrity is a Religious Right and any interruption of it is a Violation of my Religious Rights.

Utilization:

- **Personal Reflection:** Use the affidavit as a tool for personal reflection and self - assessment of one's integrity and ethical behavior.

- **Professional Development:** Use the affidavit to demonstrate commitment to integrity and ethical behavior in professional settings.
- **Accountability:** Use the affidavit as a reminder of one's commitment to integrity and accountability.

Benefits:

- Promotion of a culture of integrity and accountability.
- Enhanced trust and credibility in personal and professional relationships.
- Increased confidence and self - respect.

By utilizing the Affidavit To Display Integrity, individuals can promote a culture of integrity and accountability and demonstrate their commitment to ethical behavior and responsible conduct.

REFLECTION PAGE

1. What is one key insight you gained from reading the Affidavit and Memorandum?

2. How can you apply this insight to your work, studies, or daily life?

Affidavit To Fully Enjoy All Human Rights

Illinois State }

}ss

Cook County }

Name of Entity

Entity Address

City, State

[00000]

Notice to Agent is Notice to Principle/Notice to Principle is Notice to Agent

Sovereign Political Holder and Minister, over the age of 21 years, after being duly sworn according to law to tell the truth to the facts herein, I do hereby acknowledge and affirm the following: I, Affiant's Demarrius Crossley, am a Sovereign, without subjects. I am a Foreign Nation (not a person) who rules autonomously and am not subject to any entity or jurisdiction anywhere. I am a Sovereign Political Holder, a Minister. My authority for contracting is the age-old, timeless, and universal respect for the intrinsic power, property, and responsibilities of the Sovereign

Individual. I choose to comply with mutual respect, which serves to bring harmony to society. Demarrius Crossley, Minister, God Within Ministry

Address

City, State

[00000]

All national and state constitutions, laws, statutes, ordinances, regulations, rules, codes, and public policies, in all nations and states are private copyrighted material. I do not possess a license or have the authority to use such copyrighted material, and consequently that material does not have any authority over me, my property, or my personal affairs.

Again, this Affidavit is a Lawful Notification to you, the receivers, and requires your compliance to the demands made within. Failure to respond appropriately to the subject matter contained herein if there is any disagreement with the document is done under the penalties of perjury. Failure to respond within three (3) days, as stipulated, and rebut, with particularity, everything in this Affidavit with which there is disagreement, providing documentation as part of your ascertain, is a lawful, legal, and binding agreement by you and those that represent you in all Courts, anywhere in America or the World.

I am fully engaged in my Religious Rights and in all my Affairs. I, Demarrius Crossley, hereby declare and affirm that I am a Sovereign human being, endowed with inherent rights and freedoms.

I, Demarrius Crossley, being duly sworn, depose and say:

Article 1: Introduction

I am making this affidavit to affirm my right to fully enjoy all human rights and fundamental freedoms.

Article 2: Declaration of Human Rights

I declare that I have the right to enjoy all human rights and fundamental freedoms without discrimination or restriction.

Article 3: Specific Rights

I affirm my right to freedom of expression, assembly, and equality, among others.

Article 4: Commitment to Respect Human Rights

I commit to respecting the human rights of others and promoting a culture of dignity and respect.

Article 5: Verification

I declare that the foregoing statements are true.

Again, this Affidavit is a Lawful Notification to you, the receivers, and requires your compliance to the demands made within. Failure to respond appropriately to the subject matter contained herein if there is any disagreement with the document is done under the penalties of perjury. Failure to respond within three (3) days, as stipulated, and rebut, with particularity, everything in this Affidavit with which there is disagreement, providing documentation as part of your ascertain, is a lawful, legal, and binding agreement by you and those that represent you in all Courts, anywhere in America or the World.

IN WITNESS WHEREOF, I have hereunto set my hand and seal, this [Date] Day of [Month], [Year].

Demarrius Crossley, Minister ______________________________

Illinois State }

}ss

Cook County }

Acknowledgement

As a Notary for (County and State), I do hereby certify that on the ____day of __________ 20______ the above-mentioned Affiant, Demarrius Crossley, Minister appeared before me and executed the foregoing document.

Witness my Hand and Seal:

____

Notary Public (SEAL)

Memorandum

To: Recipient Name
From: Minister Crossley of the UNMN Church
Date: (Insert Date)
Subject: **Affidavit To Fully Enjoy All Human Rights**

Purpose: This memorandum provides guidance on the creation and utilization of an Affidavit of To Fully Enjoy All Human Rights. This affidavit is a sworn written statement that affirms an individual's right to enjoy all human rights and fundamental freedoms without discrimination or restriction.

Key Components:

1. **Declaration of Human Rights:** A statement declaring the individual's right to enjoy all human rights and fundamental freedoms.
2. **Specific Rights:** A description of specific human rights and fundamental freedoms, such as freedom of expression, assembly, and equality.
3. **Commitment to Respect Human Rights:** A statement committing to respect the human rights of others and promote a culture of dignity and respect.

Importance: This affidavit serves as a formal declaration of one's commitment to human rights and fundamental freedoms. It can be used as a tool for promoting awareness, education, and advocacy on human rights issues. This Affidavit is a Lawful Notice that the Affidavit To Fully Enjoy All Human Rights is a Religious Right and any interruption of it is a Violation of my Religious Rights.

Utilization:

- **Education and Awareness:** Use the affidavit as a tool for educating oneself and others about human rights and fundamental freedoms.
- **Advocacy:** Use the affidavit to advocate for human rights and fundamental freedoms in our community and beyond.
- **Personal Commitment:** Use the affidavit as a personal commitment to respect and promote human rights.

Benefits:

- Increased awareness and understanding of human rights and fundamental freedoms.
- Promotion of a culture of dignity and respect.
- Empowerment to advocate for human rights and fundamental freedoms.

By utilizing the Affidavit of To Fully Enjoy All Human Rights, individuals can promote awareness, education, and advocacy on human rights issues, and work towards creating a more just and equitable society.

REFLECTION PAGE

1. What is one key insight you gained from reading the Affidavit and Memorandum?

2. How can you apply this insight to your work, studies, or daily life?

Affidavit To Reach Self Actualization

Illinois State }

}ss

Cook County }

Name of Entity

Entity Address

City, State

[00000]

Notice to Agent is Notice to Principle/Notice to Principle is Notice to Agent

Sovereign Political Holder and Minister, over the age of 21 years, after being duly sworn according to law to tell the truth to the facts herein, I do hereby acknowledge and affirm the following: I, Affiant's Demarrius Crossley, am a Sovereign, without subjects. I am a Foreign Nation (not a person) who rules autonomously and am not subject to any entity or jurisdiction anywhere. I am a Sovereign Political Holder, a Minister. My authority for contracting is the age-old, timeless, and universal respect for the intrinsic power, property, and responsibilities of the Sovereign

Individual. I choose to comply with mutual respect, which serves to bring harmony to society. Demarrius Crossley, Minister, God Within Ministry

Address

City, State

[00000]

All national and state constitutions, laws, statutes, ordinances, regulations, rules, codes, and public policies, in all nations and states are private copyrighted material. I do not possess a license or have the authority to use such copyrighted material, and consequently that material does not have any authority over me, my property, or my personal affairs.

Again, this Affidavit is a Lawful Notification to you, the receivers, and requires your compliance to the demands made within. Failure to respond appropriately to the subject matter contained herein if there is any disagreement with the document is done under the penalties of perjury. Failure to respond within three (3) days, as stipulated, and rebut, with particularity, everything in this Affidavit with which there is disagreement, providing documentation as part of your ascertain, is a lawful, legal, and binding agreement by you and those that represent you in all Courts, anywhere in America or the World.

I am fully engaged in my Religious Rights and in all my Affairs. I, Demarrius Crossley, hereby declare and affirm that I am a Sovereign human being, endowed with inherent rights and freedoms.

I, Demarrius Crossley, being dully sworn, depose and say:

Article 1: Introduction

I am making this affidavit to affirm my commitment to reaching self-actualization.

Article 2: Declaration of Self-Actualization

I declare that I am committed to personal growth, self-awareness, and realizing my full potential.

Article 3: Goals and Aspirations

My goals include [LIST SPECIFIC GOALS, e.g., developing emotional intelligence, pursuing lifelong learning].

Article 4: Commitment to Personal Growth

I commit to ongoing self-reflection, self-improvement, and personal growth.

Article 5: Verification

I declare that the foregoing statements are true.

IN WITNESS WHEREOF, I have hereunto set my hand and seal, this [Date] Day of [Month], [Year].

Demarrius Crossley, Minister ______________________________

Illinois State }

}ss

Cook County }

Acknowledgement

As a Notary for (County and State), I do hereby certify that on the ____day of __________ 20______ the above-mentioned Affiant, Demarrius Crossley, Minister appeared before me and executed the foregoing document.

Witness my Hand and Seal:

____

Notary Public (SEAL)

Memorandum

To: Recipient Name
From: Minister Crossley of the UNMN Church
Date: (Insert Date)
Subject: **Affidavit To Reach Self-Actualization**

Purpose: This memorandum provides guidance on the creation and utilization of an Affidavit of To Reach Self-Actualization. This affidavit is a sworn written statement that affirms an individual's commitment to personal growth, self-awareness, and realizing their full potential.

Key Components:

1. **Declaration of Intent:** A statement declaring the individual's commitment to self-actualization and personal growth.
2. **Goals and Aspirations:** A description of specific, measurable, and achievable goals aligned with one's values and aspirations.
3. **Commitment to Personal Growth:** A statement committing to ongoing self-reflection, self-improvement, and personal growth.
4. **Self-Awareness:** A statement of self-awareness and understanding of one's strengths, weaknesses, and aspirations.

Importance: This affidavit serves as a formal declaration of one's commitment to personal growth, development, and self-actualization. It can be used as a tool for personal reflection, goal setting, and accountability. This Affidavit is Lawful Notice that the Affidavit To Reach Self-Actualization is a Religious Right and any interruption of it is a Violation of my Religious Rights.

Utilization:

- **Personal Development:** Use the affidavit as a tool for personal reflection, goal setting, development, and growth.
- **Goal Setting:** Use the affidavit to set and achieve specific, measurable, and achieve goals.
- **Self-Reflection:** Use the affidavit as a framework for self-reflection and self-awareness.

Benefits:

- Increase understanding of one's strengths, weaknesses, and aspirations.
- Personal growth and development through goal-oriented efforts.
- Improved overall well-being and life satisfaction.

By utilizing the Affidavit To Reach Self-Actualization, individuals can protect their rights to reach self-actualization; strive for self-actualization take personal responsibility for one's growth and development, and consider all aspects of life, including physical, emotional, and spiritual well-being.

REFLECTION PAGE

1. What is one key insight you gained from reading the Affidavit and Memorandum?

2. How can you apply this insight to your work, studies, or daily life?

Recommendations

The following recommendations are provided to assist individuals, organizations, and officials in upholding, respecting, and defending the unalienable rights presented within this compilation of affidavits and memorandums. These suggestions are intended to foster understanding, encourage lawful conduct, and preserve the protections guaranteed by natural law and the Constitution.

Numbered list

1. **Education-** Promoting awareness of unalienable rights through workshops, printed materials, and open forums.
2. **Documentation-** Maintain accurate and accessible records of all affidavits and memorandum for reference and legal purposes.
3. **Public Awareness-** Encourage respectful public disclosure on the importance of religious and constitutional freedoms.
4. **Legal Standing-** Consult with competent counsel or lawful advocates when asserting or defending these rights.
5. **Preservation-** Store original signed affidavits and memorandums securely in both physical and digital form.

Closing

It is our hope that these recommendations serve as practical guidance for ensuring that the principles contained herein remain protected and respected for generations to come.

Affidavit of Life

Recommendations:

- Use affidavits in conjunction with other resources, protect human life from harm or exploitation.
- Share the affidavit with others, promote dignity and respect for all human life.
- Support initiatives that promote and protect human rights.
- Regularly review and update the affidavit to reflect changes in laws, policies, or practices affecting jurisdiction.

Affidavit of Freedom

Recommendations:

- Use the affidavit in conjunction with other resources, respect and protect individual rights and freedoms.
- Share the affidavit with others, promote and protect freedom of expression and thought.
- Support initiatives that promote and protect human rights.
- Regularly review and update the affidavit to reflect changes in laws, policies, or practices affecting jurisdiction.

Health Affidavit

Recommendations:

- Use the affidavit in conjunction with other resources, prioritize preventive care and healthy living practices.
- Share the affidavit with others, seek medical attention when necessary.
- Support initiatives that promote health equity and access to care.
- Regularly review and update the affidavit to reflect changes in laws, policies, or practices affecting jurisdiction.

Affidavit of The Pursuit of Happiness

Recommendations:

- Use the affidavit in conjunction with other resources, pursue activities and passions that bring joy and fulfillment.
- Share the affidavit with others, cultivate positive relationships and connections.
- Prioritize overall well-being and happiness.
- Regularly review and update the affidavit to reflect changes in laws, policies, or practices affecting jurisdiction.

Affidavit of Contract (Unlimited)

Recommendations:

- Use the affidavit in conjunction with other resources, clearly define the terms and scope of the contract.
- Share the affidavit with others, establish open and effective communication between parties.
- Act in good faith and fulfill contractual obligations.
- Regularly review and update the affidavit to reflect changes in laws, policies, or practices affecting jurisdiction.

Affidavit of Not Contract (Unlimited)

Recommendations:

- Use the affidavit in conjunction with other resources, clearly define the terms and scope of any agreement or understanding.
- Share the affidavit with others, seek clarity and specificity in agreements and contracts.
- Avoid unlimited contractual obligations.
- Regularly review and update the affidavit to reflect changes in laws, policies, or practices affecting jurisdiction.

Affidavit of To Generate Capital

Recommendations:

- Use the affidavit in conjunction with other resources, develop a comprehensive financial plan to achieve goals.
- Share the affidavit with others, explore various funding options, such as investments, loans, or fundraising.
- Manage financial risk and minimize potential losses through careful planning and management.
- Regularly review and update the affidavit to reflect changes in laws, policies, or practices affecting jurisdiction.

Affidavit of To Be Compensated

Recommendations:

- Use the affidavit in conjunction with other resources, understand compensation terms and agreements.
- Share the affidavit with others, seek redress if compensation is unfair or delayed.
- Document work service provided, and compensation received.
- Regularly review and update the affidavit to reflect changes in laws, policies, or practices affecting jurisdiction.

Affidavit of To Travel in the Course of Life

Recommendations:

- Use the affidavit in conjunction with other resources, understand travel laws and regulations.
- Share the affidavit with others, seek assistance from relevant authorities or organizations.
- Plan travel, accordingly, taking into account relevant laws and regulations.
- Regularly review and update the affidavit to reflect changes in laws, policies, or practices affecting jurisdiction.

Affidavit of Privacy

Recommendations:

- Use the affidavit in conjunction with other resources, understand applicable privacy laws and regulations.
- Share the affidavit with others, implement data protection measures to secure personal information.
- Provide transparency regarding the collection, use, and disclosure of personal information.
- Regularly review and update the affidavit to reflect changes in laws, policies, or practices affecting jurisdiction.

Affidavit of Confidentiality from Evasion

Recommendations:

- Use the affidavit in conjunction with other resources, understand confidentiality obligations and non-disclosure agreements.
- Share the affidavit with others, seek legal counsel in cases of breaches or potential breaches.
- Implement security measures to protect confidential information.
- Regularly review and update the affidavit to reflect changes in laws, policies, or practices affecting jurisdiction.

Affidavit of To Hold/Control One's Property

Recommendations:

- Use the affidavit in conjunction with other resources, and understand one's property rights.
- Share the affidavit with others, seek legal counsel in cases of property disputes.
- Document ownership and control over property.
- Regularly review and update the affidavit to reflect changes in laws, policies, or practices affecting jurisdiction.

Affidavit of Self-Defense from Threat

Recommendations:

- Use the affidavit in conjunction with other resources, and understand one's legal rights.
- Share the affidavit with others, seek help when necessary.
- Use reasonable and proportionate force in self-defense.
- Regularly review and update the affidavit to reflect changes in laws, policies, or practices affecting jurisdiction.

Affidavit of To Due Process of Law

Recommendations:

- Use the affidavit in conjunction with other resources, and understand one's legal rights.
- Share the affidavit with others, seek legal counsel in cases where due process is relevant.
- Document all relevant information and evidence to support one's position.
- Regularly review and update the affidavit to reflect changes in laws, policies, or practices affecting jurisdiction.

Affidavit of Opportunity to Defend

Recommendations:

- Use the affidavit in conjunction with other resources, and understand one's legal rights.
- Share the affidavit with others, seek legal counsel in cases where an opportunity to defend oneself is relevant.
- Prepare a defense and gather evidence to support one's position.
- Regularly review and update the affidavit to reflect changes in laws, policies, or practices affecting jurisdiction.

Affidavit of To Be Presumed Innocent

Recommendations:

- Use the affidavit in conjunction with other resources, and understand one's legal rights.
- Share the affidavit with others, seek legal counsel in cases where the presumption of innocence is relevant.
- Ensure due process and fair treatment under the law.
- Regularly review and update the affidavit to reflect changes in laws, policies, or practices affecting jurisdiction.

Affidavit of To Not Be Detained

Recommendations:

- Use the affidavit in conjunction with other resources, and understand one's legal rights.
- Share the affidavit with others, seek legal counsel in cases of detention.
- Know the law and procedures governing detention.
- Regularly review and update the affidavit to reflect changes in laws, policies, or practices affecting jurisdiction.

Affidavit of To Not Be Arrested

Recommendations:

- Use the affidavit in conjunction with other resources, and understand one's legal rights.
- Share the affidavit with others, seek legal counsel in cases of search or seizure.
- Know the law and procedures governing arrest and detention.
- Regularly review and update the affidavit to reflect changes in laws, policies, or practices affecting jurisdiction.

Affidavit of To Not Be Searched

Recommendations:

- Use the affidavit in conjunction with other resources, and understand one's legal rights.
- Share the affidavit with others, seek legal counsel in cases of search or seizure.
- Document all relevant information and evidence.
- Regularly review and update the affidavit to reflect changes in laws, policies, or practices affecting jurisdiction.

Affidavit of To Not Be Seized Without Cause

Recommendations:

- Use the affidavit in conjunction with other resources, and understand one's legal rights.
- Share the affidavit with others, seek legal counsel in cases of seizures or confiscation.
- Document all relevant information and evidence.
- Regularly review and update the affidavit to reflect changes in laws, policies, or practices affecting jurisdiction.

Affidavit of To Remain Silent if Accused

Recommendations:

- Use the affidavit in conjunction with other resources, and understand one's legal rights.
- Share the affidavit with others, seek legal counsel before making statements/decisions.
- Invoke the right to remain silent when necessary to protect one's interests and rights
- Regularly review and update the affidavit to reflect changes in laws, policies, or practices affecting jurisdiction.

Affidavit of Equality in/of the Law

Recommendations:

- Use the affidavit in conjunction with other resources, ensuring equal protection under the law.
- Share the affidavit with others, promote education and awareness about equality.
- Eliminate discrimination and bias in the application of the law.
- Regularly review and update the affidavit to reflect changes in laws, policies, or practices affecting jurisdiction.

Affidavit of Trial by Impartial Jury

Recommendations:

- Use the affidavit in conjunction with other resources, to protect against bias and prejudice.
- Share the affidavit with others, promote transparency and fairness in the trial process.
- Ensure jury impartiality through a thorough selection process.
- Regularly review and update the affidavit to reflect changes in laws, policies, or practices affecting jurisdiction.

Affidavit of To Appeal in Law Against Sentence

Recommendations:

- Use the affidavit in conjunction with other resources, seek legal counsel and representation.
- Share the affidavit with others, gather evidence and documentation to support the appeal.
- File the appeal in a timely manner to ensure consideration.
- Regularly review and update the affidavit to reflect changes in laws, policies, or practices affecting jurisdiction.

Affidavit of To Appeal in Law Against Conviction

Recommendations:

- Use the affidavit in conjunction with other resources, seek legal counsel and representation.
- Share the affidavit with others, gather evidence and documentation to support appeal.
- File the appeal in a timely manner to ensure consideration.
- Regularly review and update the affidavit to reflect changes in laws, policies, or practices affecting jurisdiction.

Affidavit of Exposing Knowledge Necessary to One's Rights and Freedom Recommendations:

- Use the affidavit in conjunction with other resources, seek out knowledge and information about one's rights and freedoms.
- Share the affidavit with others, share knowledge and information with others.
- Promote education and awareness about rights and freedoms.
- Regularly review and update the affidavit to reflect changes in laws, policies, or practices affecting jurisdiction.

Affidavit of Peaceful Association

Recommendations:

- Use the affidavit in conjunction with other resources, establish clear goals and objectives.
- Share the affidavit with others, foster open and respectful communication.
- Promote conflict resolution through peaceful and respectful means.
- Regularly review and update the affidavit to reflect changes in laws, policies, or practices affecting jurisdiction.

Affidavit of Peaceful Assembly

Recommendations:

- Use the affidavit in conjunction with other resources, engage in dialogue and negotiation to resolve conflicts.
- Share the affidavit with others, plan assemblies and demonstrations in a peaceful and orderly manner.
- Respect the law and the rights of others.
- Regularly review and update the affidavit to reflect changes in laws, policies, or practices affecting jurisdiction.

Affidavit of Peaceful Expression

Recommendations:

- Use the affidavit in conjunction with other resources, practice active listening and empathy.
- Share the affidavit with others and express yourself clearly and respectfully.
- Seek Common Ground and peaceful resolution.
- Regularly review and update the affidavit to reflect changes in laws, policies, or practices affecting jurisdiction.

Affidavit of Peaceful Protest

Recommendations:

- Use the affidavit in conjunction with other resources, plan protests and demonstrations in a peaceful and orderly manner
- Share the affidavit with others and engage in dialogue and negotiation to resolve conflicts peacefully.
- Respect the law and the rights of others.
- Regularly review and update the affidavit to reflect changes in laws, policies, or practices affecting jurisdiction.

Affidavit of Chosen Beliefs

Recommendations:

- Use the affidavit in conjunction with other resources; seek diverse perspectives and ideas.
- Share the affidavit with others and reflect on and re-evaluate personal beliefs
- Evaluate evidence and arguments critically.
- Regularly review and update the affidavit to reflect changes in laws, policies, or practices affecting jurisdiction.

Affidavit of To Practice a Religion Past Infinity

Recommendations:

- Use the affidavit in conjunction with other resources; seek spiritual guidance from mentor or teacher.
- Share the affidavit with others and explore diverse spiritual perspectives and practices.
- Practice mindfulness and meditation to deepen spiritual connection.
- Regularly review and update the affidavit to reflect changes in laws, policies, or practices affecting jurisdiction.

Affidavit of Love

Recommendations:

- Use the affidavit in conjunction with other resources, practice empathy and understanding.
- Share the affidavit with others and show appreciation and gratitude towards loved one.
- Nurture the relationship through quality time and meaningful interactions.
- Regularly review and update the affidavit to reflect changes in laws, policies, or practices affecting jurisdiction.

Affidavit of Marriage

Recommendations:

- Use the affidavit in conjunction with other resources, prioritize open and honest communication.
- Share the affidavit with others and show appreciation and gratitude to each other.
- Work together to build a strong and resilient marital relationship.
- Regularly review and update the affidavit to reflect changes in laws, policies, or practices affecting jurisdiction.

Affidavit of Children

Recommendations:

- Use the affidavit in conjunction with other resources, prioritize children's needs and well-being in all decision-making.
- Share the affidavit with others to provide a supportive and nurturing environment for children.
- Advocate for policies and practices that promote children's rights and well-being.
- Regularly review and update the affidavit to reflect changes in laws, policies, or practices affecting jurisdiction.

Affidavit of Family

Recommendations:

- Use the affidavit in conjunction with other resources, prioritize quality time with family members.
- Share the affidavit with others to practice active listening and effective communication.
- Show appreciation and gratitude to family members.
- Regularly review and update the affidavit to reflect changes in laws, policies, or practices affecting jurisdiction

Affidavit Of Security from Abuse

Recommendations:

- Use the affidavit in conjunction with other resources, seek support from authorities and organizations and professionals.
- Share the affidavit with others to promote dialogue and incidents of abuse and keep records.
- Develop safety plans to protect oneself and others from further abuse.
- Regularly review and update the affidavit to reflect changes in laws, policies, or practices affecting jurisdiction.

Affidavit Of Security from Persecution

Recommendations:

- Use the affidavit in conjunction with other resources, seek support from authorities and organizations that protect human rights.
- Share the affidavit with others to promote dialogue and document threats and incidents of persecution.
- Advocate for policy changes that promote human rights and prevent persecution.
- Regularly review and update the affidavit to reflect changes in laws, policies, or practices affecting jurisdiction.

Affidavit Of Security from Tyranny

Recommendations:

- Use the affidavit in conjunction with other resources, support constitutional governance and the rule of law.
- Share the affidavit with others to promote transparency and accountability in governance.
- Advocate for human rights and individual freedoms.
- Regularly review and update the affidavit to reflect changes in laws, policies, or practices affecting jurisdiction

Affidavit Of Security from War

Recommendations:

- Use the affidavit in conjunction with other resources, seek support from international organizations and governments.
- Share the affidavit with others to promote dialogue and negotiation to resolve conflicts peacefully.
- Support humanitarian efforts to protect civilians and prevent harm.
- Regularly review and update the affidavit to reflect changes in laws, policies, or practices affecting jurisdiction.

Affidavits of To Refuse to Kill By Command

Recommendations:

- Use the affidavit to seek legal counsel to understand the implications and protections available.
- Share the affidavit with others and clearly document the objections and the basis for them.
- Communicate objections and concerns with superiors or relevant authorities. Regularly review and update the affidavit to reflect changes in laws, policies, or practices.
- Regularly review and update the affidavit to reflect changes in laws, policies, or practices affecting jurisdiction.

Affidavits of To Live in Peace

Recommendations:

- Use the affidavit to practice empathy and understanding towards others.
- Share the affidavit with others and communicate effectively and respectfully with others.

- Seek peaceful solutions to conflict and disputes. Regularly review and update the affidavit to reflect changes in laws, policies, or practices.
- Regularly review and update the affidavit to reflect changes in laws, policies, or practices affecting jurisdiction

Affidavits To Be Left Alone When Law-Abiding

Recommendations:

- Use the affidavit to regularly reflect and understand the laws and regulations that apply to your situation.
- Share the affidavit with others and document compliance with all applicable laws and regulations.
- Seek legal counsel if you believe your rights are being infringed upon. Regularly review and update the affidavit to reflect changes in laws, policies, or practices.
- Regularly review and update the affidavit to reflect changes in laws, policies, or practices affecting jurisdiction

Affidavits To Be Led By Conscience

Recommendations:

- Use the affidavit to regularly reflect on personal values and moral principles.
- Share the affidavit with others and seek guidance from trusted mentors or advisors.
- Practice mindfulness and self-reflection to stay connected to one's conscience.
- Regularly review and update the affidavit to reflect changes in laws, policies, or practices.

Affidavits To Eat Healthy Foods

Recommendations:

- Use the affidavit to consult a healthcare professional or registered dietitian to develop a personalized plan.
- Share the affidavit with others and plan meals in advance to ensure healthy choices.
- Regularly review and update the affidavit to reflect changes in laws, policies, or practices. Continuously educate yourself on healthy eating habits and nutrition.

Affidavits To Be Free From Unwarranted Invasion

Recommendations:

- Use the affidavit to clearly communicate boundaries and expectations.
- Share the affidavit with others to ensure document boundaries and expectations.
- Regularly review and update the affidavit to reflect changes in laws, policies, or practices. Implement quality control measures to ensure accuracy and efficiency.

Affidavits To Process Affidavits

Recommendations:

- Use the affidavit to establish clear guidelines for affidavit processing.
- Share the affidavit with others to ensure personnel processing affidavits are trained and knowledgeable.
- Regularly review and update the affidavit to reflect changes in laws, policies, or practices. Implement quality control measures to ensure accuracy and efficiency.

Affidavit To Avoid Self-Incrimination

Recommendations:

- Use the affidavit in conjunction with other resources, such as legal counsel, advocacy groups, or community organizations.
- Share the affidavit with others to promote awareness and education about jurisdictional authority and autonomy and invoke the right to avoid self-incrimination.
- Regularly review and update the affidavit to reflect changes in laws, policies, or practices affecting the rights and interests.

Affidavit To Equally Represent our Religious Organization

Recommendations:

- Use the affidavit in conjunction with legal counsel, advocacy groups, or community organizations.
- Share the affidavit with others to promote awareness and education about religious rights and freedoms.
- Regularly review and update the affidavit to reflect changes in one's religious organization and long-term goals.

Affidavit To Empower our own Jurisdiction

Recommendations:

- Use the affidavit in conjunction with other resources, such as legal counsel, advocacy groups, or community organizations.
- Share the affidavit with others to promote awareness and education about jurisdictional authority and autonomy.
- Regularly review and update the affidavit to reflect changes in laws, policies, or practices affecting jurisdiction.

Affidavit To Enforce Each and Every One of Our Religious Rights

Recommendations:

- Use the affidavit in conjunction with other legal counsel, advocacy groups, or community organizations.
- Share the affidavit with others to promote awareness and education about religious rights and freedoms.
- Regularly review and update the affidavit to reflect changes in laws, policies, or practices affecting religious freedom.

Affidavit of Self-Determination

Recommendations:

- Use the affidavit in conjunction with other personal development resources, such as coaching, mentoring, or self-help materials.
- Share the affidavit with a trusted friend or mentor to promote accountability and support.
- Regularly review and update the affidavit to reflect changes in one's goals and aspirations.

Affidavit of Self-Respect

Recommendations:

- Use the affidavit in conjunction with other self-care resources, such as therapy, mediation, or support groups.
- Share the affidavit with a trusted friend or mentor to promote accountability and support.
- Regularly review and update the affidavit to reflect changes in one's self-perception and growth.

Affidavit To Determine Political Status

Recommendations:

- Use the affidavit in conjunction with other resources, such as news sources, policy briefs, and civic education materials.
- Share the affidavit with others to promote respectful dialogue and civic engagement.
- Regularly review and update the affidavit to reflect changes in one's economic situation and financial goals.

Affidavit To Determine Economical Status

Recommendations:

- Use the affidavit in conjunction with other financial resources, such as financial advisors, budgeting tools, and financial education materials.
- Share the affidavit with a financial advisor or accountability partner to promote financial responsibility and progress.
- Regularly review and update the affidavit to reflect changes in one's economic situation and financial goals.

Affidavit To Determine Social Status

Recommendations:

- Use the affidavit in conjunction with other resources, such as educational materials and community programs, to promote social awareness and understanding.
- Share the affidavit with others to promote discussion and reflection about social status and its implications.
- Regularly review and update the affidavit to reflect changes in one's economic situation and financial goals.

Affidavit To Determine Culture

Recommendations:

- Use the affidavit in conjunction with other cultural resources, such as cultural texts, events, and community programs.
- Share the affidavit with others to promote cultural awareness and understanding
- Regularly review and update the affidavit to reflect changes in one's cultural understanding and growth

Affidavit To Determine Spiritual Path

Recommendations:

- Use the affidavit in conjunction with other spiritual tools and resources, such as meditation, prayer, or spiritual texts.
- Share the affidavit with a spiritual advisor or mentor for guidance and support.
- Regularly review and update the affidavit to reflect changes in one's spiritual understanding and growth.

Affidavit To Be Free from Discrimination

Recommendations:

- Use the affidavit in conjunction with other tools and resources promoting equality and inclusivity.
- Share the affidavit with others to promote education and awareness about the importance of equality.
- Regularly review and update the affidavit to ensure it remains relevant and effective.

Affidavit To Be Free from Violence

Recommendations:

- Use the affidavit in conjunction with other tools and resources promoting nonviolence and peace.
- Share the affidavit with others to promote education and awareness about the importance of nonviolence. .
- Regularly review and update the affidavit to ensure it remains relevant and effective.

Affidavit To Be Free from Intolerance

Recommendations:

- Use the affidavit in conjunction with other tools and resources promoting tolerance and inclusivity.
- Share the affidavit with others to promote education and awareness about the importance of tolerance.
- Regularly review and update the affidavit to ensure it remains relevant and effective.

Affidavit of To Reject Assimilation

Recommendations:

- Use the affidavit in conjunction with other cultural empowerment tools and resources.
- Share the affidavit with others to promote cultural awareness and education.
- Regularly review and update the affidavit to ensure it remains relevant and effective.

Affidavit of To Protect the Environment

Recommendation:

- Use the affidavit in conjunction with environmental tools and resources.
- Share the affidavit with others to promote environmental awareness and education.
- Regularly review and update the affidavit to ensure it remains relevant and effective.

Affidavit of Displaying Integrity

Recommendation:

- Use the affidavit in conjunction with other tools and resources for promoting integrity and ethical behavior.
- Share the affidavit with others to promote a culture of integrity and accountability.
- Regularly review and update the affidavit to ensure it remains relevant and effective.

AFFIDAVIT TO FULLY ENJOY ALL HUMAN RIGHTS

Recommendation:

- Use the affidavit in conjunction with other human rights tools and resources.
- Share the affidavit with others to promote awareness and education on human rights issues.
- Regularly review and update the affidavit to ensure it remains relevant and effective.

AFFIDAVIT TO REACH SELF-ACTUALIZATION

Recommendations:

- Use the affidavit in conjunction with other personal development tools, such as journals or meditation practices. Regularly reflect on progress and adjust goals as needed.
- Share the affidavit with others to inspire and motivate them. Seek support (mentors, coaches) to facilitate growth and development.
- Celebrate successes and accomplishments along the journey to self-actualization.
- Regularly review and update the affidavit to ensure it remains relevant and effective.

DAILY AFFIRMATIONS

These affirmations are created to strengthen the spirit, renew the mind, and align one's being with divine truth and inner authority. Speak to them each morning and night with conviction, breath, and faith.

I am Powerful.

I am Great.

I am Successful.

I am Spiritual and I am working in Spiritual Authority.

I am Intelligent.

I am Healthy.

I am Full of Love.

I am Grateful.

I am Humble.

I am Wealthy.

I am a Magnet I Attract; I do not Chase.

I am a Magnet I attract money that comes to me in Abundance

I am Confident.

I am Strong.

I am Joyful.

I am Happy.

I am Peaceful.

I am Worthy.

I am Deserving.

I am Thankful.

I am Full of The Joy of The Living.

I am Full of The Joy of The Lord.

I am in Love with Myself.

My Mind is Still, My Body is Strong, My Spirit is Free.

My Thoughts are Clear, My Heart is Pure, and My Actions are Aligned.

I am Whole. I am Protected. I am Free.

Demarrius Crossley

"Speak what you desire to live; live what you speak."

AFFIRMATION

I, Demarrius Crossley, being of sound mind, conscience, and divine awareness, do hereby affirm that the contents of this book consisting of Affidavits, Memorandums and related writings are compiled, written, and presented in truth, with full faith and under my own divine authority and free will.

This work stands as a living testimony to the unalienable rights of spirit, conscious thought, and lawful expression bestowed upon every being.

In truth, honor, and peace, I affirm that all herein is expressed without deception or malice, but with clarity, love, and conviction.

Affirmed this 23 day of October 2025

Signature: *Minister Demarrius Crossley*

"Truth is the highest form of justice; Truth is the highest form of Godly."

-Demarrius Crossley

Name: Minister Demarrius Crossley

This work is sealed in truth, and stands complete in word, spirit, and So it is,

So mote it be.

www.ingramcontent.com/pod-product-compliance
Lightning Source LLC
LaVergne TN
LVHW080530210926
848481LV00019B/88
* 9 7 9 8 9 5 1 6 6 9 0 1 8 *